To Catch a Cop

To Catch a Cop

The Paul O'Sullivan Story

Marianne Thamm

First published by Jacana Media (Pty) Ltd in 2014

10 Orange Street
Sunnyside
Auckland Park 2092
South Africa
+2711 628 3200
www.jacana.co.za

ISBN 978-1-4314-0170-3

Cover design by publicide
Set in Stempel Garamond 10/15pt
Printed by Ultra Litho (Pty) Ltd Johannesburg
Job no. 002140

See a complete list of Jacana titles at www.jacana.co.za

Contents

Preface

THE CONVICTION OF SOUTH AFRICA's former national commissioner of police Jackie Selebi on charges of corruption in 2010 is without doubt one of the most shameful and tragic chapters in the short history of our young democracy.

That a man, a former struggle hero, who had been entrusted with the task of maintaining the safety and security of his country should have chosen instead to join the ranks of thieves, drug-traffickers, embezzlers and murderers to enrich himself is indefensible. The only conclusion we can reach is that the country's first black police chief had been overcome by greed and self-interest.

Selebi was appointed to head a police force that for over a quarter of a century had acted as the political wing of the Nationalist government rather than a crime-fighting force serving the citizens of South Africa. The intersection between organised crime and the police in this country began long before Jackie Selebi was appointed commissioner.

Prior to 1994, the South African police had cultivated and co-opted wide networks of organised criminals in an attempt to keep track of and eliminate political opponents, particularly in the ANC. In turn, the ANC too had made use of criminal elements involved in drug, diamond and other smuggling rings to counter this offensive. One such player was the underworld boss Cyril Beeka, who cunningly played both sides. Beeka continued to play a role until his murder in 2011. The fallout from this entrenched relationship between law enforcement and criminal bosses continues today.

What is disappointing is that the police service of a newly democratic South Africa in many ways has continued the tradition of the discredited former regime, using police to settle political scores instead of protecting citizens from an entrenched and destructive criminal underclass. We deserve better.

It was not only Jackie Selebi who betrayed the people of South Africa and endangered our lives. Those who should equally share the blame are the powerfully placed individuals who, in the face of irrefutable evidence that the police chief was corrupt, continued to support and protect him. Some of these supporters were Selebi's handpicked recruits, but others should just have known better.

Hundreds of thousands of ordinary South Africans were raped, thousands more violently murdered or robbed of their possessions as the country's police chief averted his gaze and fraternised with some of the most powerful figures in the country's criminal underworld. While drugs flooded communities, wreaking havoc on family life, Jackie Selebi sipped coffee with international drug-trafficker Glenn Agliotti and many other underworld figures. Perhaps we should be grateful – in a perverse sort of fashion – for this friendship, as it was Agliotti who, in the end, would serve as Selebi's undoing. The irony, of course, is that today Glenn Agliotti is a free man who shamelessly continues to place himself in the public spotlight as a minor celebrity of sorts.

Jackie Selebi was also the first African to be elected president of Interpol and turned what should have been a proud milestone for the continent into an embarrassment and a setback. Inexplicably, Interpol too attempted to protect Selebi in the face of clear evidence that he was not fit for office and posed a threat to international law enforcement. Selebi stood on Interpol platforms mouthing platitudes about fighting transnational crime and corruption, wearing a suit bought for him by the South African mafia.

Apart from all this, the damage Selebi caused to the reputation, morale and discipline of South Africa's troubled police service continues to play itself out and will likely do so for many years to come.

Selebi's criminal defence team cost South African taxpayers an estimated R17.4 million and at the time of writing the amount, owed to the South African Police Service, had still not been recovered.

In July 2010, Judge Meyer Joffe sentenced Selebi to a 15-year jail term, a verdict Selebi and his legal team appealed and lost. Selebi reportedly 'collapsed' at home after learning he would have to serve his sentence. A few months later, the minister of correctional services, Sibusiso Ndebele, announced that Jackie Selebi, who was 60 at the time, would be released on parole as he was suffering from alleged kidney failure and the department had 'limited capacity to pay for palliative care'. The disgraced former national commissioner continues to receive his state pension, equivalent to the full salary, index-linked, as well as other benefits, including medical aid.

In 2011 the nephrologist Dr Trevor Gerntholtz, who had volunteered his services at the Chris Hani-Baragwanath Hospital's Renal Unit three days a week for six years, was dismissed when he complained that Selebi had been unfairly bumped up a list of patients who qualified for dialysis. Gerntholtz had pointed out in an interview with Radio 702 that 30,000 patients in South Africa should be on dialysis but that only 5000 were being treated due to cost and capacity constraints. The hospital, said Gerntholtz, applied strict national criteria for patients who required dialysis and these were simply ignored when it came to Selebi. After the interview Gerntholtz, who was also running a money-generating research project at the hospital, was asked to leave immediately.

The former commissioner's preferential treatment in this instance is testimony to the triumph of political solidarity over the needs of ordinary citizens. But there are a few heroes in the long and sordid story of Jackie Selebi's downfall.

There are some of the finest editors and journalists in the country, including the *Mail & Guardian*'s former chiefs Ferial Haffajee and Nic Dawes, investigative journalists Sam Sole and Adriaan Basson (recently appointed editor of *Beeld*) and *Noseweek*'s Martin Welz, to name just a few, as well as several others who fearlessly ferreted out and published a growing body of evidence of deep-rooted official criminality and corruption.

There are the dedicated prosecutors, lawyers and investigators, including former National Prosecuting Authority (NPA) head Vusi Pikoli, former Scorpions Gauteng head Gerrie Nel, and Scorpions investigators Robyn Plitt, Andrew Leask and others. There are the whistle-blowers, undercover moles and some good, hard-working cops who brought what they knew to light. And then there was Paul O'Sullivan.

O'Sullivan has never been publicly acknowledged for the significant role he played in bringing down Jackie Selebi. The Irish-born investigator spent eight years tirelessly putting together a massive dossier detailing Selebi's nefarious deeds. He survived three attempts on his life and spent years, at his own expense, trying to persuade apathetic authorities, including the minister of police at the time, Charles Nqakula, that Jackie Selebi was bad news and should be investigated.

Almost everyone in a position of authority or who could have intervened, from the Independent Complaints Directorate to the public protector, stalled, fudged, hedged and failed to act. Political and party loyalties and interests were placed ahead of responsibility to the people of South Africa, the criminal justice system and the Constitution itself. And in an attempt to deflect attention, some of those fingered not only tried to (literally) shoot the messenger but also embarked on a counter-offensive campaign of disinformation and vilification.

The turning point in the long, sorry story arrived on the night of 27 September 2005, when seven bullets were pumped into 'mining tycoon' Brett Kebble, killing him instantly. Several insightful books have been written not only on Selebi's trial but also the Kebble murder. These include Adriaan Basson's detailed *Finish and Klaar: Selebi's Fall from Interpol to the Underworld*, Barry Sergeant's *Brett Kebble: Inside Story* and *The Kebble Collusion: 10 Fateful Days in a*

R26 Billion Fraud, two comprehensive accounts of how Kebble and John Stratton looted their companies, and Mandy Wiener's racy and unputdownable bestseller *Killing Kebble* as well as her most recent book with Vusi Pikoli, *My Second Initiation: The Memoir of Vusi Pikoli*. All of these publications offer different entry points into the sprawling and convoluted Kebble and Selebi narratives.

This book is my account of Paul O'Sullivan's role in helping to nail not only South Africa's most powerful policeman, but also the world's top cop. It is based on thousands of pages of emails, statements, affidavits, letters, press reports, court records and transcripts as well as interviews with O'Sullivan himself.

This version provides a perspective from his point of view as a key player in the saga. While O'Sullivan's name consistently appears in almost every breaking story around the Selebi matter, his role, for whatever reason, has been played down.

The Jackie Selebi story, and the satellite narratives that orbited around it, make up a truly remarkable chronicle that requires commitment and stamina to grasp fully. There is so much detail, so much subterfuge, lying, dishonesty and cover-up, by Selebi and his cronies that it is extremely challenging to pick out one comprehensive, linear thread. The drama played itself out in different layers and strata of South African society, sometimes simultaneously and often in an apparently unrelated fashion.

The characters that populate the saga, apart from Jackie Selebi, include the then president of the country, his political rival, myriad crooked businessmen, a gallery of rotten, very senior rogue cops, a phalanx of undercover intelligence operatives, two-bit hired guns, scrap-metal dealers, drug and human traffickers, international criminal syndicates and a cast of thousands of common-or-garden-variety petty thugs and criminals.

'Sounds like a movie,' say most of those who have asked about this project. Yes, but what is startling and disturbing is that this is no fairytale. Those of us who have become accustomed to the commodification of crime as 'entertainment' in popular television series have a need to make sense of it by blurring fiction with chilling reality.

Paul O'Sullivan is no suave James Bond in a tuxedo, equipped with special equipment, downing his martini surrounded by a bevy of women. When dealing with criminals he can be abrasive, brusque and uncompromising. But who wouldn't be in a world that is populated with real thugs and dangerous killers, people who kill, maim and disrupt law and order? These are sociopaths and psychopaths who do not care how much harm they cause as they go about their 'business'.

So, what drives O'Sullivan? Revenge? A thirst for justice?

It's simple really. Paul O'Sullivan hates criminals and low-lifes like dogs hate flies. His long career in international law enforcement has equipped him with the intellectual and physical tools to deal with the most canny and violent of criminals. He enjoys hunting them down and, like the radioactive bite that imbues Spiderman with special powers, criminals provide O'Sullivan with an energy and stamina that seem to grow in proportion to the challenges they present him.

Apart from his role in bringing Jackie Selebi to justice, O'Sullivan was also a key player in cracking a rhino-poaching syndicate and putting one of its ringleaders, Chumlong Lemtongthai, behind bars. His work, he says, is far from done. He is presently attempting to ensure that Czech-born fugitive Radovan Krejcir is extradited to his home country to face numerous charges. Apart from this, O'Sullivan has been instrumental in exposing several corrupt individuals, officials and cops, including the Competition Commission's Shan Ramburuth who resigned from his position after clocking up massive bills at the taxpayers' expense watching Internet porn. In 2013, he put two brigadiers, three colonels and many other cops out of work for being corrupt.

In February 2013, Brigadier Steven Choshi, the acting commander at the Roodepoort police station, resigned after O'Sullivan opened a case of corruption against Choshi in which O'Sullivan alleged that, while working at the central firearms registry, Choshi had issued temporary gun licences to criminals in exchange for cash. The brigadier who replaced him, 'Mama' Mangwani, was also suspended when O'Sullivan linked her to payments from Dave Sheer Guns in

Bramley to expedite firearm licences and issue fake export permits.

In the aftermath of the Selebi conviction, O'Sullivan has lodged charges of defeating the ends of justice and breaching the NPA Act against various players in the saga including Lawrence Mrwebi (the controversial current head of the Specialised Crime Unit), Nomgcobo Jiba (former acting head of the NPA), Richard Mdluli (former head of Crime Intelligence), Prince Mokotedi (NPA investigator), Mulangi Mphego (former Crime Intelligence boss), Arthur Fraser (National Intelligence Agency (NIA) deputy head), Manala Manzini (former director general of the NIA), Bulelani Ngcuka (former director of public prosecutions), Brigitte Mabandla (former minister of justice) and Thabo Mbeki (former president). Silverton Case 369-10-12 is still pending but O'Sullivan is determined that those who abused their positions and interfered with the criminal investigation in order to protect Selebi must be held to account.

What is remarkable about O'Sullivan is that he remains convinced that 'the system' is capable of weeding out 'rotten apples', be they powerful policemen, politicians or international crime bosses. For a man who spends much of his time immersed in probing the deadly, unsavoury and cut-throat underworld, he is unsettlingly optimistic about the intrinsic integrity of human nature and the ultimate triumph of good over evil.

In many countries in the world where corrupt politicians and criminals work hand in hand to undermine democracy, there are brave and committed ordinary citizens, individuals in the judiciary, law enforcement and non-governmental organisations, lobby groups, whistle-blowers and political parties who are prepared to take an ethical stand. Sometimes it is at great cost.

We all need good women and men to go out and bat on our behalf. To my mind, Paul O'Sullivan is one of these. Love him, or loathe him – it depends on who you are. But ignore him we simply cannot.

Marianne Thamm

Visit Paul's website at www.poaa.za.com

PART ONE

Chapter 1

The End

ON A CRISP WINTER'S MORNING in July 2010, the South Gauteng High Court, an Edwardian sandstone edifice with a distinctive bronze dome, became a public theatre as one of the most sensational criminal trials in democratic South Africa was about to reach its denouement.

On Thursday, 1 July, the 60-year-old Jacob Sello Selebi, an ANC political heavyweight, former president of Interpol and South Africa's erstwhile commissioner of police, sat in the dock of courtroom 4B awaiting judgment after a humiliating eight-month trial on charges of corruption and defeating the ends of justice.

During the court case, South Africans learned that the country's top cop, the man tasked with combating crime and corruption and ensuring their safety, was himself a criminal. They heard startling evidence of how the chief of the South African Police Service had fraternised with shady underworld bosses, shared classified information with known criminals and received bribes in return for turning a blind eye to drug-trafficking and other serious crimes.

While the judgment in court 4B focused specifically on the corrupt dealings of the politically connected chief of police, the dramatic run-up to the proceedings exposed sinister and far more troubling political undercurrents. Jackie Selebi's criminal activities helped inadvertently to reveal a nexus of intersecting circles of vested interests that included some of the country's top politicians, business tycoons and organised crime bosses. The connections ultimately rippled inwards, all the way to the centre of power, the Office of the President of South Africa. Selebi's criminal dealings became a sideshow to a much more significant main event: the dangerous and bitter struggle for power between two 'factions' inside the country's ruling party, the ANC.

In the years and months preceding the trial, the dirty 'palace politics' of the ANC were laid bare as supporters of former President Thabo Mbeki and those of his deputy and political rival, Jacob Zuma, abused state resources (including ordering illegal wire-taps on law enforcement agencies and private individuals) in an attempt to manipulate the criminal justice system and influence the ANC's internal struggle for leadership.

The heart of the bitter battle pivoted around various counts of racketeering, money-laundering and corruption levelled at Jacob Zuma and related to the multibillion-rand 'arms deal' concluded by the South African government in 1999.

Several individuals were caught in the political crossfire, including Bulelani Ngcuka and Vusi Pikoli, two heads of the NPA. But the most significant casualty of the decade was the NPA's Directorate of Special Operations (DSO), an independent, elite, multi-disciplinary crime-fighting unit known popularly as the Scorpions. The unit was established in 2001 specifically to investigate organised crime and corruption, and its successes, particularly in relation to high-profile ANC members, including Tony Yengeni and Winnie Madikizela-Mandela, indicated that it apparently functioned 'without fear, favour or prejudice'.

But many in the ANC felt the unit was a law unto itself, 'deliberately targeting' its members, and called for its disbandment. At its highly controversial 2007 national conference in Polokwane, where Jacob Zuma was elected president of the party, delegates resolved to get rid of the Scorpions. The Selebi case was to be the

Scorpions' swansong before the unit was defanged, renamed the Hawks and later placed under the auspices of the minister of police.

But that July morning, in court 4B, the focus was on Selebi. Journalists from across the world (many who were in the country for the 2010 FIFA World Cup), Selebi's family members and supporters as well as curious members of the public packed the courtroom.

There was one man in the gallery who was particularly invested in the court's findings. Paul O'Sullivan, dressed in his usual dark suit, white shirt and animal print tie, was instrumental in driving the case against the country's, and the world's, top cop. For the 54-year-old forensic investigator, the conviction of Jackie Selebi marked the end of an almost nine-year crusade to expose the commissioner as a crook. Years of persistent sleuthing – at great personal and financial cost – resulted in what became known as the 'O'Sullivan Dossier'.

The dossier was a carefully compiled folder of sworn statements, emails and photographs from a variety of witnesses linking Selebi with a network of organised criminals and top businessmen. Over the years, O'Sullivan had spent countless hours taking complicated and lengthy statements and affidavits from undercover 'moles' and witnesses, following difficult leads (some of them abroad) and hanging out in public spaces tailing Selebi himself.

Before leaking some of its contents to the media and later handing it over to the Scorpions in 2005, O'Sullivan had tried, in vain, to get various institutions – including the public protector and the Independent Complaints Directorate (ICD) – to investigate claims that Selebi was dirty. In 2004, he made legal history, securing a court order compelling the ICD and the then minister of safety and security, Charles Nqakula, to investigate his commissioner of police. Nothing came of it.

It was only after the murder of the politically connected mining tycoon Brett Kebble in September 2005 that the Scorpions began working with O'Sullivan after learning that names they had been investigating also cropped up in O'Sullivan's dossier.

O'Sullivan obtained several key affidavits which set off 'the domino effect' – netting criminal bottom-feeders and small fry who all rolled over and gave up a slightly bigger fish in the criminal hierarchy. Finally reeling in the biggest fish, Jackie Selebi, marked a highlight in the Irish-born O'Sullivan's 35-year career in international law enforcement.

Judge Meyer Joffe took two days to read out his damning 291-page judgment, which would ultimately vindicate O'Sullivan's relentless campaign to expose Selebi as corrupt and in thrall to the country's criminal mafia. The court rejected Selebi's assertion that his prosecution was part of a conspiracy by the NPA and its various directors. Judge Joffe found that Selebi had lied during his evidence and had shown 'complete contempt for the truth'.

At the end of the second day, Selebi had been found guilty of corruption – accepting bribes of around R166,000 from drug dealer Glenn Agliotti in exchange for showing Agliotti confidential police reports. He was acquitted on charges of defeating the ends of justice. Selebi had originally been charged with three counts of corruption and one of defeating the ends of justice. Sentencing would take place four weeks later and Selebi was released on his own recognisance.

While the evidence presented in the trial represented only the tip of the iceberg in relation to the police chief's corrupt activities, for O'Sullivan it was good enough for the moment that Selebi had been exposed for the crook he was and removed from his position of influence. 'Shame on you, Selebi, shame on you,' he shouted as Selebi and his family shuffled out of the courtroom.

In a prepared statement read out to the media in the courtroom O'Sullivan declared, 'The final score is South Africa 1, Selebi 0. Our country wins. Selebi loses. The 150,000 people murdered, 500,000 women raped, and the two million people who were robbed or seriously injured by criminals while Selebi was chief of police must be breathing a sigh of relief. Selebi and the gangsters you have put into office: I despise you and will see that justice be done which you so richly deserve.'

On 3 August 2010, Jackie Selebi was sentenced to a 15-year jail sentence. Judge Joffe's ruling was searing. He pronounced Selebi 'an embarrassment to the office you occupied' and 'an embarrassment to those who appointed you'. He likened corruption to a 'cancer' that 'operates insidiously, destroying the moral fibre of the nation'. Judge Joffe's words were music to O'Sullivan's ears. For years he had been telling anyone who would listen more or less exactly the same thing.

O'Sullivan regularly attended the court case. One cannot help wondering whether Selebi rued the day he decided to cross swords with the indefatigable Irish South African.

But how did this all come to be? How did the commissioner of police find himself in the cross-hairs of a private individual so determined to expose him that he sold off all his assets – a home and a plane – and spent the next seven years working alone to bring him down?

This is Paul O'Sullivan's story.

Chapter 2

Who is Paul O'Sullivan?

DEPENDS ON WHO YOU ASK, of course.

'A vigilante', 'a self-styled saviour of Gotham', 'a foreign agent' and 'a spy' are just a few of the general descriptions that have been tossed in O'Sullivan's direction by his 'enemies' or by the 'lawyers of his enemies'.

O'Sullivan, quips Martin Welz, veteran editor of the award-winning investigative magazine *Noseweek*, is 'an anarchist'. But Welz quickly adds that it is exactly his type of unorthodox *modus operandi* that is required when dealing with unprincipled and ruthless criminal thugs, whether they're at the top of the food chain or lowly bottom-feeders.

Adriaan Basson, author of *Finish and Klaar*, suggests 'a lot of people have said a lot of things about this bald, brash Irish expatriate; that he's brilliant, evil, conniving, unpredictable, clever, rude, a hero. Have I said mad? Why would any level-headed person spend more than five years investigating the chief of police without financial backing or support?'

When the heat was on, Selebi and his various loyal supporters, including the now retired Lieutenant-General André Pruis, in an attempt to deflect attention, suggested that O'Sullivan was a 'foreign agent' and 'an operative' who was determined to 'destabilise the law enforcement agencies in this country and the criminals that benefit'.

But Selebi's allegation that O'Sullivan was a spy working for MI6 was a wild and desperate shot in the dark. It was a well-worn tactic aimed at deflecting attention from the simple fact that the police chief had befriended, aided and abetted self-confessed criminals.

As author Rian Malan pointed out in a 2008 profile for the *Maverick*: 'A deep undercover agent doesn't file lawsuits, shout his mouth off on talk radio or share his gleanings with investigative reporters. He definitely does not call a press conference where he stands up in a firestorm of camera flashes and calls on Selebi to "resign, finish and klaar".'

Sam Sole, part of the crack *Mail & Guardian* 'amaBhungane' investigative unit, which was also instrumental in exposing Selebi's corrupt dealings and his links to the killers of the share raider and 'tycoon' Brett Kebble, says he has 'a lot of respect' for O'Sullivan. 'Given one man's resources he did a lot of work. He's not constrained by ethical standards or afraid to push people around. The statements that he takes are very good and they're often done on the fly.'

O'Sullivan, a trained engineer, would describe himself as having 'more than 35 years' experience in the investigation of serious crime, including such offences as terrorism, human, drugs and arms trafficking, money-laundering and other transnational organised crimes including murder and robbery and fraud. My experience includes time spent in law enforcement agencies in the United Kingdom, the United States, Cyprus and South Africa.'

He has publicly stated that for six years he worked for the British government in the field of counter-terrorism and espionage and that he is bound by contract with the UK government 'never to mention the work I did for them'.

So, what do we know about Paul O'Sullivan or, rather, what is he prepared to tell us?

O'Sullivan does not part easily with personal information. He is a man accustomed to guarding secrets. 'It's very simple, it's not for public consumption. Why give someone intelligence they don't already have? There are criminals out there who would pay to get that type of information.'

What we do know is that O'Sullivan was born in Ireland ten years after World War II, the son of a strict colonial policeman who served in Palestine and Malaya. It was his father, he says, who taught him to pull his weight. 'My father always said if a country was worth living in, it was worth fighting for,' says Paul.

The O'Sullivan family coat of arms offers fair warning to those who would cross the clan. It features two red lions, a boar, a deer, a snake and a hand clutching a sword. The O'Sullivan motto is '*Lamh Foistenach Abu*', Gaelic for 'The Steady Hand to Victory'. The lions on the shield denote 'dauntless courage', the boar stands for 'perseverance or one who will fight to death', the snake symbolises wisdom, while the deer is said to represent 'one who will not fight unless provoked'. The hand with the sword denotes 'bravery and fighting for a just cause'. Perhaps if Jackie Selebi had been able to interpret these weighty ancestral symbols, he might have had second thoughts about picking a fight with this particular O'Sullivan.

O'Sullivan is married and has seven children, five daughters and two sons. Discussing his children, O'Sullivan reveals a seldom-seen tenderness not generally associated with his sometimes abrupt and forthright public persona. One of the reasons O'Sullivan allows his story to be told, he says, 'is so that one day my children will read it and be proud of what their father did and understand why I was sometimes not there for them'.

Of his rural youth in Ireland, Paul is only prepared to say, 'it was hard. I was brought up on a farm in a very poor environment. We used to take water from a well. We had an outside toilet and we didn't have any electricity. I remember when we did eventually get electricity we played with the switches and the globes popped, so we got into trouble.' At 14, Paul ran away from home and headed to London, where he later joined the army.

Asked about his faith he replies curtly, 'This is a Roman Catholic household.'

Is he spiritual? 'I do believe what you do will come back to you. I call it the Big Scheme of Things. And in that Big Scheme of Things, I can't lose. I can't lose because I never compromise myself.'

The fundamental rule, says Paul, is knowing the difference between right and wrong. 'It's the Ten Commandments. It's the verse from Luke 6:31 – Do unto others as you would have them do unto you.'

So, if we're attempting to create a portrait of the man, we're going to have to rely on outside sources or let his track record speak for itself.

There is a letter Paul has on file dated 3 October 1978 and signed by the deputy assistant commissioner for crime of New Scotland Yard. Its contents offer some insight into O'Sullivan's way of moving through the world, even as a young man of 23.

The letter is written to Mr P.R. O'Sullivan at an address in London and is referenced GN96/78/77 (C2/E).

> Dear Mr O'Sullivan
>
> My attention has been drawn to a case at the Bow Street Magistrate's Court where a man was convicted on 26th of July 1978 of assault occasioning actually bodily harm and possessing an offensive weapon, a knife.
>
> I see from a police report that on 25th July 1978 you were travelling on the Northern Line when you noticed a man, who had boarded the train at Archway Station, take a knife from his back left hand pocket and threaten a young girl who was sitting opposite him.

The man then stood up and challenged everybody on the train to take the knife from him, and when the train arrived at Tottenham Court Road Station you decided to detain him.

I note that when you took him from the train and disarmed him he assaulted you, causing a cut on your right thumb but you managed to subdue him until police arrived.

I was pleased to see that at the conclusion of the case, which had been remanded until 16th August 1978, the Magistrate, Mr E C Russell, made the following statement in open court:

'I would like police to take steps to ensure that Mr Paul O Sullivan is commended for his action in this case.'

I am pleased to have this opportunity to associate myself with the Magistrate's remarks and I would like you to know that your courageous action at the time of this incident is very much admired by the police.

Thank you for your assistance in this case.

Paul is touchingly proud of the detailed letter. 'How many people can say they have a letter from Scotland Yard thanking them?' He is also proud of his other awards: Policeman of the Year 1994 and the 2011 Paul Harris Fellow award, which he shared with former director of public prosecutions Vusi Pikoli, for their pivotal roles in the Selebi trial. 'It's the only award I've been given for it locally,' he mentions in passing.

Apart from this, Paul has written commendations from the

Australian and Canadian governments for his 'work in the field of human trafficking'.

Pat Corbin, past president of the Johannesburg Chamber of Commerce, called Paul in to investigate a suspected fraud involving a R3-million investment by the Johannesburg Chamber of Commerce Medical Aid fund with NBS, known then as the Natal Building Society. Between 1994 and 1996, around R345 million of investors' funds, in what was described as one of the biggest fraud cases ever to have been cracked in South Africa, had been diverted by the Kempton Park branch manager, Vito Assante, and his lawyer, Nicolaas Nel, into private accounts.

Corbin had originally met O'Sullivan when he was the chairman of the Johannesburg Community Police Forum, where Paul 'was getting the police into shape'. Corbin says that it was O'Sullivan who had been able to determine that money invested by the Chamber's medical aid had been stolen by Assante and Nel. 'Paul sorted it out in 24 hours. He proved to NBS that there was no collusion on the part of the medical aid's administrators and we got all our money back.'

Corbin rates O'Sullivan as one of the most 'committed, dogged and energetic' individuals he has ever met. 'He went through tremendous financial difficulties nailing the police chief. Paul follows through regardless of the personal consequences. And this often while coping with ill health.' Corbin is referring here to the ongoing back pain O'Sullivan lives with after having been shot several times. 'Sometimes you will see him grimace but he will never talk about it.'

There is a story Paul tells about his life in England after he left the government service and the employ of IBM UK, where he worked for a period. It's a story about a young spendthrift who almost gets fleeced because he wants to make a quick buck. A moment in his life, he claims, that taught him a lasting lesson about staying on the right side of the law. It is also a story that, in the telling, sounds like an episode of *Inspector Morse*, with everyone calling each other 'Guv'.

Someone who pops up later in the account, but who coincidentally happened also to be working at IBM at the time, is one Jack Kenneth Slipper, a former detective chief superintendent in the London Metropolitan Police and a friend of Paul's father. Known as 'The Slipper of the Yard', Slipper owes his fame to the role he played in the investigation into the Great Train Robbery of 1963 and for tracking down the fugitive Ronnie Biggs to Brazil in 1965. After retiring in 1979, Slipper worked as a security consultant and was employed by IBM in the 1980s and 1990s.

Paul recalls how his late father had made many good friends during his career as a policeman. 'All the old colonial officers went back to the UK and became chiefs of police. Most of them are all dead now, but while they were around it meant that my father knew pretty much anyone who was anybody in the police, which was quite useful.'

Paul left IBM, he says, with a considerable amount of money he had managed to save. 'I was always a spendthrift. This was the mid-'80s and I decided to speculate in property.' His timing could not have been more opportune. The 1980s saw an unprecedented boom in the housing market in the UK as the new prime minister Margaret Thatcher's Conservative government vigorously encouraged private home ownership.

Financial deregulation made it easier for potential homeowners to obtain mortgages and various incentives saw the property market skyrocket. Paul says he made half a million pounds' profit on his first venture. 'It was great! So, I made all this money and I now had even more money than I had ever dreamed of,' he recalls.

Then what appeared to be an 'interesting deal' came to his attention. 'What happened was I managed to buy this property for £176,000 and got permission to build a block of flats on it, which naturally massively enhanced the value. Now it was worth £700,000 and by the time I would take off my architects' and planning fees,

I'd have made clear half a million pounds.' So far, so good.

But things got interesting when someone offered him advice on how he might avoid capital gains tax. 'This guy, who thought he was doing me a favour, says, "You're going to pay capital gains tax on that, which is 25 per cent." So, I think I'm going to lose £125,000 on this.' The man, says Paul, suggested that he could help to find a buyer for the property who would be willing to pay in cash. 'Now I'm thinking this sounds OK. It's not legal but at the time I was young and money is money. So I went along with it.'

The broker found a buyer whom Paul says we should call Joe. The deal was that Paul would meet with Joe, who would explain exactly how this 'tax free' profit could be made.

'So, I meet with Joe and he tells me, "You sell the property to me for £300,000 on the contract, but I meet you in Switzerland and give you a briefcase with £400,000 cash in it. You can pay it into a Swiss bank account and tell the lawyers when you exchange the property that I bought it for £300,000."

Paul says he 'warmed to the idea quite nicely'. 'I would only be paying tax on £100,000 instead of £500,000, so I would only lose £25,000 instead of £125,000. I was saving myself £100,000!'

Before the deal had even been finalised Paul decided to line up other potential properties he could snap up on his return from Switzerland with his 'tax free' profit.

'Then this agent I was talking to one day says he's got just the property for me. Tells me I can pick it up for £450,000 and probably sell it for £600,000 or £700,000 without much ado. I think it looks good and asked to see it.'

The agent drove Paul to the property. 'And I think, bloody hell! This is my own property! This is the property I am in the process of selling! How the devil does he get this right? And guess who is selling it? The agent tells me and it's the same guy I've just said I'd sell it to! Joe!'

Paul 'asked around' and soon discovered he was about to be scammed. The plan worked something like this: the seller, Paul, would meet Joe in Switzerland, where Joe would hand over a bag containing worthless bundles of paper. 'And there's nothing the victim can do about it. You can't go to the cops because you've been trying to commit tax fraud!'

Panicked, the young Paul realised he needed to get out of the deal. He called Joe in an attempt to tell him it was off. 'I said, "Listen, mate, you were not planning to consummate that deal with me. We have not got anything signed. You were planning to screw me. The deal's off."'

Only problem was that Joe wasn't the settling kind of guy. 'He told me that nobody breaks off deals with him and that we were going through with it and that if we didn't he'd pay me a visit.'

Not sure what to do or how to get out of the mess, Paul contacted his father's old friend, Jack the Slipper. 'I explained to Jack that I needed a cup of tea with him. I told him the story and he said, "Don't worry, we'll quickly sort this one out."'

The Slipper, says Paul, 'arranged' to have Joe 'picked up' and taken to the old Scotland Yard building. 'Yeah,' Paul says laughing, 'they scared the shit out of him. And they told him, "The only way we can make this go away is if you can convince Paul O'Sullivan not to pursue charges."' Joe, unsurprisingly, agreed to the terms.

'Jack called me and I went over there and asked this Joe how I could be sure he wasn't going to mess me around.' And then, Paul says, the Slipper reassured him with a 'Don't worry, Guv, if anything happens to you he's going to be the first guy we arrest.' Sorted.

Paul expels a deep and satisfying laugh retelling the story about his youthful self. But after that incident, he says he 'made a rule' he has lived by ever since. 'I vowed I would never try to fiddle my taxes or break the law. I would not have been able to do anything about it. And if there is one thing I have learned in my life, it's that a lot of people prey on greed. You can become a victim of crime simply by being greedy. And if you're not greedy in the first place, you won't get into trouble. I would have been ripped off if I didn't wake up and smell the coffee.'

Today, he says his philosophy with regard to making 'difficult decisions' is simple: 'I ask myself, Can I tell my children about what I am doing? If the answer is no, I don't do it.'

❊

Paul first visited South Africa in 1978, on a break from a 'secret mission' doing intelligence work for the United Nations police service in what was then Rhodesia. And while he says he liked South Africa as a country, he didn't like the politics. 'I liked the place, came back in 1984, liked it some more, came back again in '86 and liked it a bit more. In 1987 I bought a property here to use as a holiday home.'

In the late 1980s the property bubble in the UK had burst and Paul cashed in his assets. 'I thought, I had all these assets here and there, and I just decided to move it all, with my family, to South Africa. And when Mandela was released from jail, I applied for a residence permit.'

Paul had travelled widely on the continent, including Sierra Leone, Libya, Côte d'Ivoire, Zambia, Zimbabwe, Ghana, Kenya, Egypt and Morocco; and South Africa combined for him 'all the benefits of Africa and a developed country'.

He found Johannesburg particularly appealing as a city: it was fast, had a temperate climate, was close to wildlife reserves and is the country's economic powerhouse. 'I didn't emigrate to South Africa. I emigrated to Johannesburg.'

In 1989 he bought a house in Bedfordview, an affluent suburb on the East Rand, and began working the residential development property market locally. What followed was a succession of well-paid senior positions with several companies, including Highmoon and Sage Properties. And, as Rian Malan wrote in his *Maverick* profile, 'O'Sullivan was a driven man and by the end of the decade … his salary had risen tenfold.'

One of his ventures was a 'small investment' at the Randburg Waterfront, a nautically themed entertainment and shopping complex built in 1996 around an artificial lake. The development was an attempt by Johannesburg to follow the success of Cape Town's Victoria & Alfred Waterfront as a popular tourist attraction. Much later, in 1997, Paul was appointed MD of the Randburg Waterfront and earned the moniker Major Dad, after the investigative TV programme. *Carte Blanche* featured a 12-minute insert on his management style and enforcement of strict rules related to underage drinking and general 'anti-social' behaviour.

But back in 1991, a secretary who worked for Paul was the first to suggest that with his experience in law enforcement he consider signing up as a police reservist. The woman's husband was a major in the South African Police at Halfway House (now Midrand) and, after an encounter at a social gathering, Paul duly enlisted. 'My car had been broken into several times and we were having a discussion about crime prevention. He suggested I become a reservist. I felt as a community member I should do something to make it better. It was also partly self-interest, as I wanted to serve my new country.'

His first placement was at the under-resourced Booysens police precinct, which served about 72 suburbs in the region and, he says, he 'became involved from day one'. 'I signed on as a duty detective and was investigating crime rather than doing crime prevention. I was cracking some big cases. I was arresting people for murder, robbery, all sorts of stuff, and then I started doing fraud cases, I found I had a bit of a knack for that.'

Most police reservists are required to perform around 16 hours a month, but O'Sullivan, who clearly thrives in this heightened and potentially dangerous environment, started putting in 10 hours a week, clocking in after work and even at weekends.

Paul also began training recruits at the Police Reserve College, lecturing in crime investigation and South African criminal law, among other subjects, as well as setting exams. About 1,500 reservists, including the current ANC deputy president, Cyril Ramaphosa, were trained by Paul, who by then had become the chief lecturer. It was a position he held until 2000.

The early to late 1990s was an exciting, albeit troubling, transitional period for South Africa, as a negotiated political settlement between the ruling National Party and the recently unbanned African National Congress was taking place.

When Nelson Mandela was released in 1990, as the independent consultant Janine Rauch[1] found, police in South Africa had 'acquired a reputation for brutality, corruption and ineptitude'. The SAP was ill equipped, said Rauch, to deal with 'ordinary crime', which began to spiral out of control during the transitional period. In the lacuna of political uncertainty, it began to feel as if criminals had gained the upper hand.

The era also marked the beginning of a difficult restructuring of the SAP and by 1991 a strategic plan had been drawn up, which included the depoliticisation of the police force, increased community accountability, more visible policing, the reformation of training systems and the total restructuring of the police force.

'I tried to focus my activities on drugs and fraud and apolitical crimes. I locked up drug dealers. I took on cases that other people wouldn't or couldn't take on,' Paul recalls.

An example he offers is the spate of attacks on gay men in the early 1990s at Wemmer Pan, a well-known 'cruising spot' near the suburb of La Rochelle. The Pan was also later to become the hunting ground for serial killer Maoupa Cedric Maake, who murdered 27 people between 1996 and 1997.

The assault and robbery of gay men wasn't a case anyone was going to bust a gut to solve, but Paul resolved to take it on. 'I took it on in my spare time. I set traps for the suspects. I had reserve cops dress like gay men and I had them floating around there with the hope they would get propositioned.'

The *modus operandi* was that the robbers would pose as undercover policemen, 'arrest' gay men, drag them to an ATM and extort money from them. 'Now remember, this was before the adoption of the new Constitution and equal rights for everyone. Being gay was an offence in those days. But I caught the suspects.'

Two of Paul's biggest fraud cases in the 1990s were the Assante

---

1 'Police Reform and South Africa's Transition' by Janine Rauch, presented at the South African Institute for International Affairs conference, 2000.

case and another, a massive scam by the retirement village developer André Bouwer. Assante ripped off around R300 million from investors (including the Johannesburg Chamber of Commerce Medical Aid Fund) and Judge Meyer Joffe, who was incidentally to deliver Selebi's judgment years later, sentenced Assante to 24 years in jail. André Bouwer swindled pensioners out of their life savings and was sentenced to 1620 years, effectively a 15-year jail term.

'But what I learned from the Bouwer case, as I was having lunch with the prosecutor afterwards, is that I should have charged him with ten charges instead of the 1800, of which we got a conviction on 988. The next case I went for, I streamlined, because the law and justice in South Africa can be a long drawn-out process.'

White-collar criminals, as far as Paul is concerned, are 'just gangsters like everyone else'. 'I took them out of circulation. I am proud of that.'

Apart from taking on the fraud cases, Paul also worked the ordinary beat, which of course often placed his life in danger. One night he took three bullets during a shootout on the East Rand. It wasn't the first time he had been shot at, and the bullets, which slammed into his shoulder and back, left him with a lasting slight limp and chronic pain that he seems to ignore.

'That night we stopped this car that had been reported hijacked and these guys jumped out and started running in different directions. I ran after one and my partner chased the other.'

Paul found himself in a clump of bushes and then suddenly heard the gunfire. Two shots slammed into him. 'I fell and then this guy came over and I was on the floor and he shot again, hit me again. My gun was in my hand, so I shot him. I survived.'

Three or four days later, after his discharge from hospital, Paul says he returned to the scene. 'No one had done any investigating! There I was with all my bandages on and there was still blood on the sand. We dug around and found the projectiles buried in the ground.'

Paul believes the law makes provision for police to use 'deadly force'. 'It's there in section 49 of the Criminal Procedure Act. The police have a right to kill if you reasonably believe you are going to get shot. There are a lot more people being murdered by criminals than criminals being shot by trigger-happy police,' he reckons. He does not deny that there are officers who are trigger-happy, 'but quite a few of them have been moved, I can tell you'.

He relives a moment he spent in a small chapel attached to the New South Wales police training headquarters in Goulburn, Australia. Paul had travelled there in the late 1990s to investigate the role of policing and tourism.

'You know I sat in that chapel and they had these memorial stones, dating back to 1820, listing all the police who had died on duty in New South Wales in 170 years. There were 83 of them! We had more cops than that who died in just one year!'

Between his work in the property industry and his part-time policing, Paul began to take an interest in tourism. By then he had transferred to what was the notorious John Vorster Square, the biggest police station in Africa. The station, overlooking a motorway in the heart of Johannesburg, was opened in August 1968 by Prime Minister B.J. Vorster and was the scene of several deaths in detention of anti-apartheid activists, including Ahmed Timol in the early 1970s. Detainees were often tortured on the ninth and tenth floors of the building, which was occupied by the ruthless and feared Security Police.

Paul was instrumental in getting the station to change its name to Johannesburg Central in 1997. 'I brought a Gauteng government application as a private individual to change the name. I didn't think it was appropriate in post-apartheid South Africa. I didn't like having to deal with police in a building called John Vorster Square. It took me two years.'

In his motivation to the then MEC for safety and security, Jesse Duarte, Paul suggested an apolitical name for the station. 'If you go to Jo'burg Central today you will see a plaque I had made. We did it on Heritage Day. We got a band playing, cops marching. I was the master of ceremonies and the mayor, Isaac Mogase, unveiled the new sign.'

Paul was also responsible for removing the old bronze bust of Vorster, which used to glower from a black marble perch in the station's foyer. 'Some of the blokes wanted to deface it, but I said no matter how bad he was, he was part of history. But there wasn't a vehicle to remove it to the police museum, so I locked it in one of the cells for the night. I put B.J. Vorster in jail!' he recalls with a hearty laugh.

One of the key difficulties in the restructuring of the police was the integration of members of former liberation forces and old SAP police members, many of whom were disgruntled. As Rauch observed,[22] 'while the liberation movements did have trained soldiers and intelligence operatives, few were trained in police work.'

At the time, there was also a concern that right-wing groupings, some with links to former police officers, might scupper the political transformation. Over and above this, police needed to regain credibility among the country's majority, who had been for decades at the receiving end of relentless harassment and abuse from the police.

It was inevitable then that some of the older established policemen might have trouble adjusting, while newer recruits, some of them from civilian organisations, needed to create a new space inside a very established militaristic police culture.

'The relatively low salaries offered by the SAPS, and the unpleasant image of the police, meant the ANC government was unable to recruit high-calibre civilians into influential managerial positions in its new police service until quite long after 1994,' wrote Rauch.

---

2 Janine Rauch, 'Police Reform and South Africa's Transition'.

Johannesburg, too, was undergoing a massive transformation and as crime levels peaked in the inner city there was a huge exodus of white business to safer suburbs to the north. Jo'burg became a sort of twilight zone where blocks of flats were 'occupied' and where drug dealers and scammers from across the globe flocked, seemingly finding a safe haven in which to operate.

'In '96–'97 police morale was really low. You'd have cops moonlighting as bouncers, or cops clocking in and then just going to the movies. In some areas there was good work, but that all depended on the station commander.'

Apart from his job as MD of the Waterfront and his police reserve work, Paul was also the founder and chairman of the Johannesburg Central Community Police Forum. Community police forums were introduced to facilitate a more connected police force and to encourage local police commissioners to liaise with and account to local communities.

'We weren't very happy with police effectiveness in Jo'burg. One day, myself and some forum members decided to track cops and see what they did after booking on duty.' Bearing in mind, says Paul, that in those days police did not have cell phones or pagers and some had no access to vehicles. Policemen would patrol the mean streets on foot and in vulnerable twos.

'We just picked two random officers and followed them as they came out of Jo'burg Central. They left, on foot, with their weapons and went to Market Street.' Once there, the two cops caught a taxi to the Jeppe police station in Jeppestown. They alighted, went in, and emerged a short while later dressed in civilian clothing. 'Then they got into another taxi and went down to Jules Street and spent the whole day there cleaning cars! They were double dipping.'

Paul picked up on the demotivation of some of the officers and introduced a series of 'awards' that would single out and reward those who were working hard. 'I wanted to set an example. Get a picture in the paper. Have an award ceremony. Then we'd bring other cops and colleagues to see this and we'd try and inculcate a sense of service.'

The forum was relatively cash-strapped, but Paul and other members managed to convince local businesses, including the well-known law firm Webber Wentzel, to sponsor essential items. 'We got 300 radios and reflective jackets. We went to Public Works and said, "Let's refurbish part of the station." We put in new elevators. We did what it took to stand behind the guys, and that changed how they started to work.'

Paul often draws on sporting or wildlife analogies to unpack his view of crime and dealing with criminals. 'For me to understand something, I need to build pictures in my head. And when it comes to crime I sometimes liken it to playing darts. Catching criminals is like playing darts. Now, I don't play darts, but if I had a go at it, it would go something like this: if you have enough darts, eventually you'll hit a bull's eye. Even the worst cops are capable of hitting the bull's eye if they have enough darts.'

Criminals, says Paul, will always look for a gap or vulnerability in law enforcement. 'If he knows that the cops are not efficient, he knows he can pull a crime off in that area.'

In time, the new anti-crime initiative in inner-city Jo'burg began slowly to pay off. The co-operation between Johannesburg City Watch (which installed CCTV cameras at crime hotspots) and the police saw a relative safety gradually restored to parts of the city. It comes as no surprise that Paul was one of the founding directors of Johannesburg City Watch, having initiated the plan to put cameras up and having raised a large chunk of the cash for the project.

One of Paul's objectives, also as MD of the Randburg Waterfront, was to encourage tourism to South Africa and in the late 1990s he was elected to the board of Tourism Johannesburg. He wanted to create, he says, a new series of 'big five' tourist destinations. These included Jo'burg Zoo, Randburg Waterfront, Gold Reef City Casino, the Rhino and Lion Nature Reserve, and Soweto.

'I got involved in tourism when I saw that it was a big part of the growing economy. I had personal investments as well. At the time I felt that Soweto was or should be an integral part of the tourism drive, and I started pushing to get tourists out there.'

Soweto, the home of many struggle icons, drew a handful of tourists at the time. Many would go on a two-hour tour and then leave again. 'I felt that people should stay longer, spend money in Soweto. I got Kessel Feinstein, now Grant Thornton, to do an audit and the numbers were good. There had been a 48 per cent increase in tourists and the numbers were up from around 100,000 to 150,000.'

By 2013 the numbers had jumped to the millions and today no visit to South Africa is complete without a turn to view historic struggle sites in Soweto. These include the famous Vilakazi Street, once home to Nelson Mandela and Desmond Tutu, and the Hector Pieterson Memorial, commemorating the young student who was shot and killed by police in the June 1976 uprisings.

Paul helped to set up the Soweto Tourism Development Association (SATODA) and initiated a skills training programme. An example of the kind of work, Paul says, was a young waiter at the famous Wandies restaurant who managed to study for a diploma in tourism and marketing and who is now employed in tourism management.

'Visitors and tourists were very worried about crime back then. But if you looked at what was really going on, you'd have seen that Soweto was safer for white people than anywhere else. When people talked about Soweto, they imagined police with bullets and burning tyres and that sort of thing. We tried to dispel that. We looked at the historic sites, Regina Mundi church, Mandela's house, and we raised money for the Hector Pieterson Memorial Square.'

And so it was that Paul found himself at Johannesburg International Airport one summer morning in March 2000, returning from a tourism exhibition in Berlin, where he had showcased Johannesburg as a viable and exciting destination.

Exiting, he lugged a heavy suitcase of leftover brochures that he placed on the pavement outside the terminal while waiting for his driver to collect him. Little did he know that what was about to happen would result in his path inexorably arching towards that of the country's newly appointed first black commissioner of police, Jackie Selebi.

Chapter 3

Jackie Selebi

JACKIE SELEBI DIDN'T GET OFF to a good start.

On New Year's Eve, 31 December 1999, two days before he was due to take up his appointment as national commissioner of the South African Police Service, Selebi arrived unannounced at the Brooklyn charge office in Pretoria. Brooklyn, to the east of Pretoria's city centre, is a catchment area for the city's affluent residents and comprises mostly high-end residential and commercial developments.

December 1999 sparked a low-level global anxiety about the approach of the new millennium (or Y2K, as it became popularly known). Major cities across the world had organised massive 'millennium celebrations' and South Africa was not going to be left out.

In June 1999, Thabo Mbeki had been elected the country's second president after Nelson Mandela ended his term of office. Mbeki and Selebi had enjoyed a long and close personal friendship during their years in exile. Selebi's appointment by Mbeki in 1999 was seen as a political rather than a professional one, as Selebi had no knowledge of or experience in policing or law enforcement.

During his later testimony in court, Selebi recalled the occasion when President Mbeki had originally offered him the job as commissioner. 'I had gone to see the president ... We were preparing for the negotiations in the Democratic Republic of Congo. We were working out the document that would set up the negotiations. At the end of this, when I was leaving the official State House, he got me by the hand, which means there is trouble. He pushed me to a side away from the rest of the people that were there, says, "Jackie, you know we have a problem." "So what is your problem?" "The problem is George Fivaz [the former police commissioner] going. We do not have a commissioner of police."'

Mbeki, said Selebi, told him that he had requested a list of 100 names of potential candidates and the president remarked: 'I looked at this list and the only name that I found that I can think of is you.'

Selebi told the court his initial response had been one of surprise. 'Hah, me? I get back from Geneva to become DG of the Department of Foreign Affairs. Whilst I am doing this now you are telling me I must go to the police? Me in the police! You know where I come from. Me and the police?'

Selebi said that while others in the party might have thought he would make a good commissioner, he had wanted to know what Mbeki himself thought of the suggestion. 'I say you must go,' Selebi reported Mbeki as stating. And that, Selebi said, 'was the end of the discussion. So I then prepared myself to go to the police and that is how it happened.'

But back to 31 December 1999 when Sergeant Raesetsa Jeanette Mothiba had been on duty behind the desk at the Brooklyn police station.

She didn't recognise the newly appointed commander. Why should she? He was wearing civilian clothes. So, when the stranger in front of her had demanded a vehicle to inspect the city's preparations for the millennial celebrations, she immediately questioned the request. Selebi, known for his short temper, must have felt deeply affronted and had shouted at the female officer to 'shut up' and said she was a 'bloody, fucking chimpanzee'.

Sergeant Mothiba filed a complaint with the police's Independent

Complaints Directorate (ICD), which in turn suggested that the matter be 'dealt with' by the then minister of safety and security, Steve Tshwete. Tshwete recommended the ICD should 'guide' the new commissioner with regard to the behaviour expected of him.

Later, the national director of public prosecutions, Bulelani Ngcuka, also found that Selebi's outburst 'does not warrant a prosecution on charge of *crimen injuria*' and that 'it was not in the public interest to prosecute in the matter'. Prosecuting Selebi, reckoned Ngcuka, 'is likely to have a negative and unwarranted effect on public order and morale within the police force' and was also 'likely to cause serious divisions within, across and among the ranks of the police force'.

On the same day Sergeant Mothiba lodged her complaint, it emerged that Selebi had managed to offend and intimidate another officer, Sergeant Julian Mabelane. Mabelane was stationed in Brits in the North West Province and Selebi had summoned him to Pretoria over a family dispute with Selebi's uncle involving a load of cattle feed. The police officer had alleged that Selebi's uncle had stolen the feed. Incensed, Selebi called the officer to his head office in Pretoria and instructed him to apologise personally to his uncle or risk losing his job.

In that case, the ICD found that Selebi had intimidated Mabelane and had caused him 'fear for the security of his livelihood'. But Ngcuka also ultimately declined to prosecute this case.

Jackie Selebi had travelled a long and arduous journey en route to becoming the country's top cop.

He was born in 1950 and grew up in Johannesburg. Selebi matriculated at Orlando High School in Soweto, one of the flashpoint schools during the later 16 June 1976 uprisings.

Having completed a BA degree at the University of the North, Selebi became a history teacher and taught at a number of schools in the 1970s including Musi High School and Orlando West. Adriaan

Bassson, in his book *Finish and Klaar*, quotes Selebi's former student Kaiser Ngwenya, who recalled his teacher as 'a maverick, troublemaker … who was known for his love of Mafia novels'.

Ngwenya also recounted how the younger Selebi had been an overweight young man with a penchant for tight-fitting clothes and Florsheim boots, a popular fashion accessory of the exaggerated Mapantsula style of the 1970s. Mapantsula style expressed an urban, streetwise attitude and way of being that harked back to the street gangs of Sophiatown in the 1950s.

Selebi, like many of the politically active South Africans around him, had become involved with the ANC-aligned South African Students' Organisation (SASO) and had been elected secretary of the organisation. Testifying in 2010, Selebi told the court that he had been arrested several times, once under section 10 of the Terrorism Act, which allowed for detention without trial. He had been held in Benoni for ten months. The year was 1978, the first occasion when Paul O'Sullivan visited South Africa.

In 1979 Selebi and his wife, Anne, fled the country and went into exile in Tanzania where Selebi taught at the ANC's Solomon Mahlangu Freedom College.

In Tanzania Selebi received word that he was 'wanted' in Lusaka. What this meant was that the exiled ANC president, Oliver Tambo, who was based in Lusaka at the time, had sought a meeting. Tambo informed Selebi that he was to make his way to Moscow for further military training. Years later Selebi told the court: 'Here I was wearing sandals and light clothes and being told by the president that on Monday you are getting into an Aeroflot flight, you are going to Moscow. You cannot tell anybody where you are going. So I could not tell anybody. I could not ask anybody for warmer clothes. So I left to go to Moscow with sandals and a shirt and it was strange that I arrived in Moscow and the people at the airport thought I was – something was wrong with me, and I was given warm clothes by them there. So I went there, got the training, never being able to tell my students that I am leaving for another mission. They never got to know until I came back, but even then I could not tell them where I was. That is the nature of the situation that we lived in.'

On his return to Tanzania, Selebi was named head of the 'ANC Youth' and later became the youngest member elected to the National Executive Committee (NEC), the party's 'highest organ'.

In 1991, after Mandela's release the previous year, Selebi returned with his wife to South Africa. 'I was part of a team that worked with the current president of South Africa [Mbeki] and the former president of South Africa [Mandela] in order to initiate the discussions that brought about what was later then called, what is this place in Kempton Park, where the negotiations took place. I was part of that,' Selebi told the court.

With thousands of exiled South Africans ready to return home, Selebi was appointed to head up the ANC's Repatriation Programme. It was, he said, 'the most difficult task'. People who had been exiled for over 30 years needed to find somewhere to stay, to reconnect with family members, to look for work. Selebi recalled: 'The majority of those people did not know where they came from. They came back, they were looking for Sophiatown and I say to them, "Guys, it does not exist. It is now called Triomf. So you cannot find Goodwood Street in Sophiatown." So I had to see how to accommodate, to arrange accommodation for most of these people, some of whom, the way they looked, the baggage that they carried, were rejected by their families at the doorstep.'

It was also in 1991 that Jackie Selebi first crossed paths with the man whom he came to consider a 'friend' but who would later 'pimp' him in order to escape prosecution himself: Glenn Agliotti.

Chapter 4

Where There's Smoke – There's Mirrors

NORBERT GLENN AGLIOTTI, KNOWN as Glenn: self-confessed 'hustler', a 'pathological liar', tax dodger, convicted drug-trafficker and 'sewer rat', according to his estranged, illegal second wife, Charlene Voget.

While by no means an idiot, the smooth-talking Agliotti is a man of little-known professional qualification and dubious character and principle. A man who has the proverbial penchant for women, fast cars, expensive food and drink, sharp suits and 'hooking up' the rich, the criminal and the politically powerful.

Born in Germiston in 1956 to parents of Italian extraction, Agliotti went to boarding school in Middelburg and then later finished high school at St Andrew's boarding school in Bloemfontein. His father, Frank, a racehorse owner who enjoyed socialising in wealthy circles, often took the young Glenn with him.

Overweight, moustachioed and generally obsequious to those whom he perceived as possessing power or influence, Agliotti has had several brushes with the law but has always managed to wriggle his way out of its coils.

While it is almost impossible to separate the fact from the fiction that is Agliotti's life story, some of his personal history emerged in his bail application after his arrest for the murder of Brett Kebble in November 2006 and also later during the Selebi trial.

In the 1980s Agliotti jumped from lowly job-to-job hopping to sudden riches when he was employed by a Japanese trading company selling chemicals across the globe. He soon acquired considerable wealth, which he enjoyed flaunting. He was particularly well known for his largesse, dishing out cash to beggars and paying for other people's meals.

Agliotti claims it was while working for the Japanese that he learned the 'secrets of trading'. He was the man about town, swanning around in hugely expensive cars. He even reportedly owned a yacht in the Mediterranean.

While still married to his wife Vivien, Agliotti proposed to another woman, Charlene Voget, in 1987 and even arranged a 'mock' wedding ceremony. Agliotti thoroughly cuckolded Voget, as the legal part of the ceremony had never been concluded. Still, she remained under the impression that she was the only Mrs Agliotti, living in a home in Hyde Park with her often-absent 'husband', until it was exposed that he already had a wife, Vivien, who lived in another household in Kempton Park.

In 1998, Agliotti and three Democratic Republic of Congo nationals appeared in court on fraud charges, totalling around R18 million, that were related to a 72-ton cobalt shipment destined for the United States and Europe. When buyers of the shipment received their goods, the containers turned out to be filled with sand instead. One of Agliotti's fellow accused died, two fled the country and Agliotti was eventually acquitted. But he was held liable for the loss in a subsequent arbitration hearing into Trans-Atlantic, the company for which he had been acting.

Around this time Agliotti's world began to fall apart after a business venture in printing and trading with his half-brother Sydney had folded. Sydney was later arrested in New York for illicit arms dealing and Agliotti apparently put up US$1 million in legal fees to bail him out.

The next setback occurred when Frank Agliotti died – but not before cutting Glenn entirely out of his will, leaving instead a fortune made in the scrap metal business and property to Glenn's brother Julio. When Agliotti met Dianne Muller, an events co-ordinator, a while later, her father, Martin Flint, would recall that his daughter's suitor drove a battered Japanese sedan and wore off-the-peg clothes from chain stores.

Here's where things get murky. Agliotti made some sort of comeback as a 'commodity trader' and also as a 'fixer' between moneyed and well-connected people.

In 1990 Agliotti made an appointment with Jackie Selebi, who had just been appointed to head up the ANC's repatriation programme. Agliotti was one of several 'businessmen' who popped in at the party's headquarters in Shell House (later renamed Luthuli House), located in downtown Johannesburg, to see if he could render any 'assistance'.

Their first encounter, Agliotti would later testify, ended with a handout when Selebi mentioned an outstanding R1200 medical bill for one of his children, a bill Agliotti volunteered to take care of.

At their first meeting, Agliotti later told the court, Selebi had mentioned how difficult he was finding the resettlement programme and that many of the returning exiles had been penniless and homeless. 'I sympathised with him at the time and felt saddened by what task lay ahead of him. I suggested to Mr Selebi at the time that I would look at the possibility of importing second-hand clothing and selling it and a certain portion going towards the ANC to relocate these people,' Agliotti told the court. O'Sullivan is of the opinion that this venture was a cover for importing counterfeit goods.

Selebi recalled his meeting with Agliotti slightly differently. 'One such person I came to know was Glenn Agliotti, who came to me and said, "We can help. We know. I am involved." He said, "I am involved in export, import" – what is it called, export, import? – whatever – business. So he says to me, "No, man, I can help, shame these people."'

Selebi said the proposal sounded 'fantastic' but he thought Agliotti had suggested that the returning exiles would be given the clothing, as they would not have been able to afford it. The scheme took about nine months to arrange but eventually fell apart when everyone realised that South Africans were rather larger than the average Japanese consumer.

Agliotti and Selebi parted ways but were to reconnect fatefully several years later in 2000, in the company of Nelson Mandela's tailor, Yusuf Surtee, a man Selebi had known for years from their earlier involvement with the South African Students' Organisation. Surtee owned the rights to import several exclusive clothing brands into South Africa and had set up this particular meeting to introduce a burly bodyguard, the former bouncer and karate expert Paulus Johannes Stemmet, to the new police commissioner.

Agliotti had originally introduced Stemmet, owner of a shady security company called Palto, to Surtee when Surtee wanted to 'deal' with a man in Cape Town who had been 'harassing' him. Stemmet, Agliotti claimed, had in turn been introduced to him by a neighbour, Louis Viljoen, who was Stemmet's partner at the time. When Stemmet informed Agliotti that Surtee wanted to introduce him and a colleague, Freddie Burger, to the new police commissioner, Agliotti, always looking for a gap, decided to tag along.

Later, during his testimony and under cross-examination at the Selebi trial, Agliotti alleged that he had been aware that Stemmet had done some unorthodox earlier 'work' for Surtee, planting drugs on the man in Cape Town who had been 'harassing' the importer. But the full extent of Agliotti's relationship with Stemmet, and others connected to him, would only emerge much, much later.

The day Selebi met Paul Stemmet, Freddie Burger, Yusuf Surtee and Glenn Agliotti, he was dressed in his full commissioner's uniform with gold braiding. The end result of this fateful encounter was that Selebi signed Stemmet and other Palto members on as police informants. Selebi, Stemmet later testified, had wanted inside information on Chinese syndicates operating in South Africa, information he most certainly could provide.

Selebi introduced his informants to several of the senior staff that surrounded him including the head of operations, André Pruis; the head of Crime Intelligence, Rayman Lalla; and the head of detectives, Johan de Beer. On the recommendation of these senior policemen, Palto operatives were later issued with police identity cards and many of them promoted to the rank of captain, without the required training or security clearances.

In the not too distant future, Agliotti, Stemmet and their criminal associates would soon drift into Paul O'Sullivan's sights. But in 2001 O'Sullivan was about to be appointed to the job of a lifetime – a newly created position as the Airports Company South Africa's new group executive for aviation security.

Chapter 5

The Suitcase

AND SO IT WAS THAT ON A summer's day in March 2000 Paul
O'Sullivan, dressed in his usual black suit, found himself outside
the terminal at Johannesburg International waiting for his lift. The
suitcase stuffed with leftover brochures from his Berlin trip was
propped up on the walkway next to him.

Johannesburg International Airport (JIA), as it was known
at the time, had been plagued by ongoing criminality and, daily,
tourists and locals arriving at this gateway to South Africa faced a
gauntlet of hustlers, petty thieves, illegal taxi-drivers, pickpockets
and bag-snatchers.

In a 2006 study titled *Security at South African Airports and
State Responsibility*, Advocate R. van der Walt, of the University
of Pretoria, found that in the late 1990s 'a thriving trafficking route
was established from Nigeria to South Africa to Rio de Janeiro'.
'Active organised crime syndicates operating within South Africa
are estimated at about 200 to 240 with at least 150 syndicates engaged
in transnational crime beyond sub-Saharan Africa, particularly
southern Africa.'

Van der Walt identified several international crime networks
operating in South Africa, including Nigerian, Russian, Pakistani

and Chinese syndicates. Many of these networks, she found, easily co-opted South African locals.

That morning, as Paul stood waiting, a man suddenly appeared and made off with his suitcase. The thief must have been watching O'Sullivan and reckoned that the balding, middle-aged man in a suit wouldn't stand a chance. He was wrong!

The thief had sprinted only a few metres when he found himself wrestled to the ground by the furious owner of the piece of luggage. 'Another guy appeared and tried to get me off him,' Paul recalls, adding, 'but I managed to fight him off as my driver pulled up.'

The accomplice must have realised they had underestimated the situation and fled. O'Sullivan, in the meantime, accustomed to arresting fleeing suspects, twisted the suitcase-snatcher's arm behind his back and frog-marched him about 150 metres to the nearest charge office. 'I told the sergeant at the desk that I had just arrested this guy for trying to steal my bag and he just nodded at the man and told me to leave him there and that they would "sort him out",' Paul recounts.

Acutely aware of police procedure, O'Sullivan waited for the duty officer to take a statement and open a docket. But nothing happened. 'I got really angry and told him, "This is how it works. I want a cell register number, I want a booking number in the occurrence book, I want to see a case number in the system."' The duty officer's lacklustre retort was the usual 'the computer isn't working'. Leaving the charge office, O'Sullivan handed the duty officer his business card and informed him that he wanted a case number by the end of the day or he would report him to the station commander.

Surprisingly, the case later made it to court. Paul was called to testify and the thief was given a three-year sentence. O'Sullivan asked the magistrate to impose a harsh sentence as a deterrent to other criminals, who seemed to be operating with impunity at JIA. He told that court that in targeting tourists these criminals, and others of their ilk, tarnished the country's reputation internationally. The uninterested policeman, in the meantime, found himself charged with corruption and out of a job.

O'Sullivan was determined not to let matters rest with the conviction of the thief and requested a reservist transfer to the SAPS office at the airport. 'I decided I was going to make a difference and do something. I met the station commander and he was happy to have me there and to bring more reservists. After all, it was going to make his figures look good. So, we recruited 50 reservists, anyone who could speak a foreign language: Russian, Chinese, German. They were all particularly useful. I decided it was time to get stuck in.'

The police reserve unit at the airport made over a thousand arrests during its first year on the beat. 'In the first year I was a detective sergeant. But as a reservist your rank is immaterial. It's what you do that is important. I started working landside [the area of the airport with public access] getting rid of the taxi-drivers. I started working with ACSA because they had no legal power themselves and then I began to realise there were other issues too.'

JIA is viewed as an international border, which presents specific security concerns. International air traffic to JIA had increased considerably since 1994. The total numbers of departing passengers rose by 3.1 million to 9.5 million and aircraft landings increased by 59,112 to 187,423.[3] About 37 kilometres of fencing surround the airport and it requires around 1200 people per shift to keep operations flowing smoothly, for bags to be offloaded, for cargo to be inspected, for customs officers to check passports.

In his first few months as a reservist at the airport, Paul and his team made a string of arrests, drawing in corrupt cops, customs and immigration officials, cleaners and other airline staff. Incidents that occurred are too numerous to list but some of those O'Sullivan remembers are startling in their audacity.

'I remember spotting a cleaner who looked a bit sheepish. Cleaners would wheel these wheelie bins airside to landside, to dispose of the rubbish. I was wearing a jacket that said "border police" and I went over and asked him to open the bin.' Inside,

---

3 ACSA Annual Report 2001.

Paul discovered an illegal Pakistani immigrant crouching under a black bin bag. 'He just looked up and grinned at me. There was a tremendous flow of illegal immigrants at the time: Chinese, Indians, Pakistanis. They used to end up in sweat and spaza shops. They'd keep them there for two or three years and then send them back through legal channels. The illegals would go to the embassy and report that their travel documents had been stolen. They were given an emergency travel document and off they went, with their real passport hidden in their luggage.'

Another noticeable irregularity was the daily queue of customs and immigration officials outside the airport's foreign exchange outlets. The Forex staff had clearly become so accustomed to the routine that they thought nothing of it. 'I thought, Why the hell are they queuing here selling foreign exchange for local currency?'

Paul set up concealed cameras at customs booths and trapped several officials receiving illegal cash slipped between the pages of passports of arriving 'visitors'. 'These customs officials were simply taking the cash and stamping the passports and letting them through.'

On another occasion, a furious altercation in the international departures lounge drew Paul's attention. There he encountered three men involved in a punch-up. Beside them lay an apparently discarded tote bag. 'I tried to stop them from fighting and then I asked them whose bag it was on the floor. They all looked at each other, shook their heads and denied that they had anything to do with it. They told me they were from Pakistan.'

Examining the bag, Paul found about US$3 million in cash stuffed inside. He escorted the three men to a holding area with the intention of interviewing them later. 'While we're there, this police sergeant wandered over and starting taking an interest in the case. He asked me what was in the bag.'

Moments later the phone in the holding area rang and a man who identified himself as a lawyer claiming to represent the three detained Pakistani nationals informed Paul he was on his way to meet with his clients.

'I said, "Fine, no problem, what are your clients' names?" He couldn't tell me. Then I told him, "By the way, they have a bag with a lot of US dollars and I will be taking possession of that. You are not coming through. If you don't know their names, how can you be representing them?"'

In the meantime Paul managed to get the suspects' names and had taken down statements, using a reservist who served as an interpreter. A while later, the same police sergeant who had enquired after the contents of the bag, returned and casually flipped through the incident book. 'Moments later the bloody phone rings again and now the lawyer says he has the suspects' names. It didn't take much to work out the cop was in cahoots with the lawyer.'

More importantly at this point, Paul needed to find a safe place to store the millions in dollar bills. 'I realised if I booked it into the SAP 13, which is a custody store, it would be gone. So I phoned the station commander, who suggested we call the Reserve Bank.'

But it was after-hours and the Reserve Bank was closed. The only way the cash was going to be safe, reckoned Paul, was to stash it somewhere in the building, and the safest space he could think of was the roof space above his office. He removed a few ceiling tiles, placed the bag in the hollow and waited.

Around 2 a.m. the phone in the holding area rang once more. 'This time it was a superintendent from another police station who said he had received instructions to come and collect this money. He wanted my location and threatened me with arrest if I didn't tell him.'

Paul was certainly not going to part with the money, and the following morning at 8 a.m. contacted the Reserve Bank and waited for an official to collect the cash.

Within five months of transferring to JIA, O'Sullivan had drawn up a crime-prevention plan for the airports, which he sent to the ACSA executive committee in May 2001. The plan highlighted numerous security weak points: too many access doors between the landside and the border, the lax issuing of permits to staff who had access to sensitive areas, absent guards, doors left open, staff who had no idea what they were meant to be doing. The list seemed endless.

In June 2000, a private security company, Khuselani Security and Risk Management, with Professor Noel Ngwenya as its apparent CEO, had tendered for and won the highly lucrative R99-million-a-year contract to provide security at the country's main airports. Over a period of three years Khuselani stood to make around R280 million, with an option to renew for a further three years.

Rian Malan, in his *Maverick* profile on O'Sullivan, describes Ngwenya as 'a comet who blazed brightly for a year or two and then vanished into the obscurity from whence he came'. In the 1990s Ngwenya had been employed with the state arms company, Denel, and realised that new opportunities were evolving in the security industry. Ngwenya, coincidentally, also happened to be friends with Commissioner Jackie Selebi, who had been the guest of honour at the party Ngwenya threw to celebrate his company's winning of the airports tender. This fact would only emerge much later, though.

At the time, O'Sullivan had been unaware of the backroom machinations that surrounded the awarding of the Khuselani contract and that were about to escape the Pandora's box he would crack open.

ACSA's then chairman, Mashudu Ramano, a former financier and businessman who took up the position in 2000, had been so impressed with O'Sullivan's report that he phoned him a week later and asked him to present his strategy to the ACSA board. At the presentation Paul suggested security at ACSA, which controls the country's ten largest airports, be elevated to an executive level and that a single individual be tasked with the critical responsibility.

Before 1993, the country's nine major airports were wholly owned and operated by the state. ACSA had been established in 1996, majority-owned by the South African government through the Department of Transport. In 1998 it was partially privatised when a 25.4 per cent shareholding was offered to private sector shareholders, including Aeroporti di Roma and five empowerment consortia. The company was completely restructured and tendering concessions for non-aeronautical services were opened up.

Ramano and the board took O'Sullivan's advice and requested that he write up a job description for the position, which would then be advertised. 'Ramano said to me, "We'll be placing an ad and if you are prepared, we'd like you to apply,"' recalls Paul.

So, apply he did, making it through three rounds of interviews along with three or four other candidates. The final interview panel consisted of three ACSA directors and the then minister of transport, Dullah Omar.

'Afterwards I waited outside. And then they called me in and said, "By the way, can you start tomorrow?"' It was 24 July 2001 and Paul O'Sullivan had landed a job that was going to offer huge challenges and rewards. 'My salary package with bonus was about R1 million a year. It was quite another job.'

Chapter 6

Getting Stuck In

FOR MOST TRAVELLERS, AIRPORTS are transient, 'non'-spaces where time is suspended, compartmentalised and removed from everyday routine. Airports or train stations are buffer zones between 'home' and 'elsewhere'. Waiting to board or depart, passengers tap away at electronic devices, or read magazines or newspapers in departure lounges or coffee shops, trapped in a schedule not of their making.

For some, airports are pregnant with emotion – the melancholy of separation or the joy of a promised reunion. Most people who enter this 'non'-space are blissfully unaware of the existing parallel universe – the formal structures that enable its existence and functioning.

Criminals across the globe are drawn to these 'non'-spaces where there is a sense of impermanence and where belongings and goods worth millions are shuffled through at an unstoppable pace. Gaining control of a port of entry to a country opens up endless lucrative opportunities for criminals seeking easy access to the invisible tributaries of transnational organised crime that criss-cross the globe.

South Africa is a signatory to several international treaties and protocols aimed at eliminating crime, terrorism and corruption at the country's airports. The country has committed itself to a number of United Nations, Non-Aligned Movement and African Union frameworks guaranteeing effective control and safety at these international points of entry and departure.

Advocate Van der Walt's 2006 study, however, highlights major breaches in South African security standards.[4] 'It has been pointed out that permissive environments make ideal home bases for criminal organisations and that cartels increasingly make use of aircraft and had become ingenious in using commercial cargo to traffic drugs. South Africa's international obligations call for effective port control, anti-corruption, -criminal and -terrorist measures,' she writes.

Van der Walt suggests that organised criminals are provided with 'the most favourable conditions for infiltrating South Africa with weak airport security measures, air links into Africa and the rest of the world, rife corruption, porous borders (including ports of entry such as international airports), poverty and high levels of unemployment, lucrative local markets, well organised local criminals and gangs used as partners to carry out dirty work.' She warned that unless effective preventive policies were competently implemented, 'such criminal activities will continue to increase significantly in volume and frequency'.

So, while passengers arriving at and departing from Johannesburg International may have been lulled into a specific mental state required to navigate the 'non'-space, Paul O'Sullivan was, by now, more than aware of the nests of criminal opportunists, many of them actually employed at the airport, who seemed to lurk in every corner, from the parking lots to the toilets, from the baggage carousels to the security desks.

4 Adv. R. van der Walt, 'Security at South African Airports and State Responsibility' (September 2005, updated April 2006).

On 25 July 2001, O'Sullivan arrived at JIA as ACSA's newly appointed group executive for aviation security, and hit the ground running. That evening, gun-toting robbers disarmed guards at one of the airport's perimeter gates and made off with their cell phones and firearms. It was the gate closest to the Guard Force depot, where precious goods were safeguarded prior to or after transit. O'Sullivan, who hadn't yet been assigned an office, immediately investigated and advised the acting security manager of the airport of steps that needed urgently to be taken.

But nothing seemed to come of his suggestions, and six days later an even more daring robbery took place when armed men simply drove through the same, now unguarded, perimeter gate and into the 'secure' area next to the Guard Force depot of the airport. There the robbers casually relieved cargo of around US$16 million in cash and diamonds from a Swiss Air aircraft, when it arrived outside the depot, loaded the booty into their vehicle and drove out.

It was time for radical action, thought Paul. He immediately investigated where security breaches could be occurring and found that card readers (for security staff) had been inoperative and unused for months, that audits highlighting shortcomings had been completely ignored, that gates had been broken and out of use for months, or else were often left unlocked and unattended, that contract security were in effect completely feral, with no management of any description, and that absolutely no procedures were being followed. Open season, in other words.

Soon, an entire shift of security guards was arrested for stealing 300 cell phones contained in cargo. Meanwhile, taxi-drivers parked at the airport were purchasing 'huge volumes' of soap and toilet paper from cleaners. Paul also discovered that police on duty were smuggling drugs. 'Off-duty police officers, cleaners and security would be found in their droves strolling around as if they owned the place,' said Paul.

Without an office, a secretary or a workstation, O'Sullivan began issuing orders verbally. 'For the most part, my suggestions fell on deaf ears and the security exposure at JIA continued.'

Complaints poured in from passengers whose baggage had gone missing or had been rifled through, airlines who felt security was lax, hotel guests who had been robbed, drivers who had been threatened in airport parking lots, and passengers who had been followed home from JIA and robbed and hijacked.

Paul's verbal warnings escalated into a series of memos and emails to various executives, including the airport manager at the time, Bongani Maseko, as well as Thele Moema, the new manager of security at JIA. While customs officials and the police stationed at JIA did not fall under ACSA's jurisdiction, the company could issue direct orders to the private security providers, Khuselani, which O'Sullivan proceeded to do.

With the knowledge and full support of Ramano, O'Sullivan began keeping detailed reports of endless incidents of compromised security that were occurring at the airport. And each time he logged a transgression by Khuselani, he shot off a letter to the company's management.

By August 2001, matters had grown so alarming that Paul met with the Khuselani CEO, Noel Ngwenya, at the airport to warn him that the service his company was rendering 'was completely unacceptable' and that if matters did not improve, ACSA would be forced to cancel the contract. Ngwenya, Paul recalls, appeared remarkably cavalier at the meeting. 'He didn't seem to care about the threat to cancel the contract.'

Weeks went by and still O'Sullivan, doing spot checks in the dead of night, found serious breaches of security. He photographed open doors, deserted stations, guards on duty sleeping, cleaners squirrelling away toilet paper in air ducts. The list grew long and worrying. Each time he dashed off polite and courteous emails to Maseko, listing breaches and requesting him to come up with a plan to deal with these.

In September 2001, O'Sullivan flew to New York on an audit with the US Port Authority and was in the city when the attacks on the World Trade Center occurred on 11 September. 'I saw it live and I had first-hand experience of what could go wrong. I flew out on the first plane back to Jo'burg and I decided to take very strong and immediate measures to step up security.'

On 24 September 2001, a Lufthansa freight manager, Johan van der Merwe, was shot dead by robbers in the cargo area, just after the delivery of gold bullion valued at R50 million. The robbers left empty-handed, as the keys to the armoured truck were with the driver, who had left for the toilet and, upon hearing the shots, had fled the scene.

By October 2001, O'Sullivan had sent over twenty letters to Khuselani, with absolutely no response or reaction. It was time to act. O'Sullivan informed Ngwenya that he would be forced to alter Khuselani's contract – which was a one-term agreement with a further three-year option – to one month's notice.

Ngwenya and Khuselani, Paul warned, were on thin ice, considering the now global security alert in the wake of the Twin Tower attacks in New York. 'I had hoped they would see this as a wake-up call and told them that if they fixed things I would reverse the situation, but if they did not fix things, they would be gone.'

Later that month O'Sullivan was paid a surprise visit by two men. They were Vuyo Ndzeku and Lungi Sisulu, son of the struggle stalwart Walter Sisulu. Both men claimed to have been the founders of Khuselani and alleged that Noel Ngwenya had simply removed them as shareholders; Sisulu while he was overseas, and Ndzeku while he had been serving a jail sentence, as he alleged, on trumped-up charges of drug dealing.

Noel Ngwenya's brother, the judge Jerome Ngwenya, had also been a shareholder in Khuselani Security and Risk Management and had had a prior business relationship with Ndzeku. Judge Jerome Ngwenya and Ndzeku had been partners in three companies: Khuselani, Swissport South Africa (a baggage and cargo handling company) and Zwelibanzi.

Like the witches in *Macbeth*, Sisulu and Ndzeku forewarned

O'Sullivan of a series of events that were about to occur. Firstly, they alerted O'Sullivan to the relationship between Ngwenya and Selebi and informed him that the police commissioner was most certainly going to pressure O'Sullivan not to cancel the Khuselani contract. Secondly, Selebi was planning to have him replaced with a certain 'Director Shabalala'.

Their parting shot was that they had gained information that Selebi was in the process of arranging for Paul to be dismissed as a detective sergeant in the police reserve. Their words to O'Sullivan were, 'Selebi will cancel your ticket.'

Sisulu and Ndzeku also warned O'Sullivan that if none of these steps threw him off course, Ngwenya would most certainly mount a campaign of vilification and, if that didn't work, Paul might even find his life endangered. 'I didn't pay much attention to these warnings and allegations at the time because I believed that the commissioner of police wouldn't possibly get involved in a dispute between a security contractor and ACSA!'

Sisulu and Ndzeku's first prediction materialised a few days later, on 17 October, when O'Sullivan received a call from André Pruis, Jackie Selebi's assistant, summoning him to a meeting with the commissioner.

Selebi, dressed in full uniform, met O'Sullivan in the JIA VIP lounge and relayed his concerns about ACSA's potential cancellation of Khuselani's contract. At the meeting Selebi mentioned his intention to lobby for the SAPS to take control of all security at the country's airports.

The following day Pruis called O'Sullivan and issued an instruction that no contracts be cancelled and that none of the security contractors at JIA should be 'changed'. O'Sullivan asked for the instruction in writing, but, unsurprisingly, this did not materialise.

The same week, a Superintendent Harry Glazer contacted

Paul to ask him to resign immediately from the police reserve on instruction from the provincial commissioner. Glazer told Paul that the instruction had come from Selebi himself. 'I said no way and told him that I had no intention of resigning and that the commissioner should state his reasons in writing,' said O'Sullivan.

On 29 October, as the dire security situation at JIA continued and Khuselani simply appeared to ignore complaints from ACSA management, O'Sullivan, backed by the chairman, Ramano, cancelled Khuselani's contract, effective from 30 November.

The cancellation would deprive Khuselani of around R130 million as well as a further R280 million over the next three years. On 30 October, Khuselani's legal affairs manager, Thabo Msibi, dashed off a letter to O'Sullivan, copying in 'Commissioner J. Selebi, National Commissioner, South African Police Service'. The letter not only inadvertently revealed Selebi's hand in the matter but also exposed his relationship with Khuselani's CEO, Noel Ngwenya.

'In writing your letter … you acted in contravention and violation of the directives and direct instructions from the office of the National Commissioner of the South African Police Service. Your letter is in direct violation of government policy read with the provisions of the National Key Points Act. Your [sic] were specifically instructed not to remove operating security companies and personnel from the national airports as the national airports are governed by the National Key Points Act,' wrote Msibi.

Msibi then ironically pointed out: 'your letter compromises state security,' and then played the proverbial race card, suggesting O'Sullivan's action 'is in direct conflict with the government policy of black economic empowerment'.

Msibi's letter was ill informed legally and its threatening tone also indicated that Khuselani, and no doubt Ngwenya, clearly felt emboldened and in no way perturbed by allegations of gross incompetence.

The first misinterpretation of the law can be found in Msibi's suggestion that the SAPS were responsible for security at National

Key Points. At the time these Key Points fell under the South African National Defence Force.

Second, Selebi had not issued (or in fact had any authority to issue) any directives or written instructions to anyone at ACSA. ACSA's legal team had in fact requested that these 'instructions', as well as references to relevant government policy that enabled them, be forwarded to the company. The request was ignored.

The third question ACSA's lawyer wanted answered was why the country's police commissioner had been copied into a letter that was, in essence, 'a straightforward contractual dispute'.

An eerie silence followed.

On 1 November 2001, ACSA appointed a new CEO, Monhla Hlahla. The Limpopo-born Hlahla had previously worked for the Development Bank of Southern Africa, managing several large municipal infrastructure projects.

Hlahla hardly had time to settle in when she found herself immediately drawn into the dispute between ACSA and Khuselani. Ngwenya, clearly sensing a new opportunity or possible ally, immediately contacted the CEO and threatened that he would take action if his company were not immediately reinstated.

Hlahla turned to ACSA's group legal manager, Rishi Thakurdin, to determine whether proper procedures had been followed in the cancellation of the highly lucrative Khuselani contract. Six days later, on 6 November, Thakurdin supplied Hlahla with a one-page legal opinion that 'We confirm that the cancellation of the contract was done within the powers of the Chairperson and the authority delegated by Mr Ramano to Mr O'Sullivan'. He also advised that in view of the value of the contract, the cancellation still needed to be ratified by the ACSA board at its next meeting.

So confident was Thakurdin of the correctness of the decision that he recommended to Hlahla that ACSA should reply to Khuselani that O'Sullivan had been 'duly authorised to act' and that the company was 'free to proceed with any legal action it may deem fit'.

Meanwhile, Hlahla had made arrangements to meet Selebi, no doubt at that stage wanting to sound him out, as he had been copied into Khuselani's legal letter to ACSA threatening court action. When Paul learned the meeting was to take place at JIA, he advised Hlahla against it as he had begun to suspect that Selebi 'had other agendas'. Besides, Paul told Hlahla, security was his portfolio and, if such a meeting were to take place, he should surely be present. But the three-hour meeting went ahead without him. When he questioned her about it afterwards, Hlahla, says Paul, reassured him that they had 'just talked about general things, nothing about security'.

More or less coincidentally, Sisulu and Ndzeku's earlier prediction that O'Sullivan would be suspended as a police reservist materialised in a letter on an SAPS letterhead, signed by Senior Superintendent E.G. Trollip, station commander of the SAPS Johannesburg International charge office. Trollip wrote: 'this office hereby informs you that as a result of your management position held at Airports Company SA and the fact that you are an active member in the Police Reserve Service at SAPS JHB INT Airport, your services as a reservist sergeant at SAPS JHB INT Airport are to be terminated.' A livid Paul immediately filed an appeal, which was subsequently rejected.

'You are requested to hand in your appointment certificate, all SAPS uniform pieces, ACSA permit, SAPS equipment to Inspector N. Venter at SAPS JHB INT Airport with immediate effect.' The gloves were coming off.

In the meantime, Hlahla had clearly emerged from the meeting with Selebi doubting or questioning her own legal team's advice. She contacted Thakurdin, requesting him to provide 'fresh advice'. This Thakurdin duly supplied and, surprisingly, backtracked entirely, now advising that the cancellation of the contract be revoked and that Khuselani be reinstated.

Sensing a conspiracy, Paul suggested that an independent legal opinion be sought. When this was provided, it matched Thakurdin's original advice – the cancellation of the Khuselani contract had been perfectly legal.

❉

On 21 November, a week before Noel Ngwenya lodged court papers against ACSA, Mashudu Ramano did something extraordinary. He recorded a message that he left in the safekeeping of his secretary, Roelien van der Walt, in the event that 'something should happen to me.' The transcription makes for chilling reading:

Mr Mashudu Ramano on November 21, 2001 in the presence of his Personal Assistant, Ms Roelien van der Walt:

… Ramano: My name is Mashudu Romano. Over the past four months, since the beginning of August, I have been, my security has been, I've had security problems.

A former employee of the Airports Company of South Africa, Kevin Cockroft, had told Carmine Bassetti (Executive Director) that he knew people that would put bullets through my head and that he was aware that the ANC was doing an investigation on Mashudu and that within the next few weeks Mashudu will be finished.

Subsequent to this, to the termination of this contract with ACSA, I had people visit my home under different guises, people phoning my home and informing people at home that they are working with a cosmetic company and they are trying to find out how many children we have, what their ages are and so on.

And we had incidents where people came and jumped into the yard and fired shots at the security that was there at home. I had to employ the services of bodyguards and there are records that have been kept by Stallion [security company] and Paul O'Sullivan at ACSA of the various incidents that have taken place at my house.

This past week, I don't know the date, oh or … well, this past month, sometime in October we changed the contract of Khuselani Security.

And Khuselani is headed by a gentleman called Noel Ngwenya.

And Noel Ngwenya apparently has certain relationships with certain politicians and when we cancelled the contract Noel then appealed for help to the Commissioner of Police, and the Commissioner of Police then arranged a meeting at ACSA, that meeting was supposed to discuss an incident that took place in Cape Town where he was, he felt that he was not treated well, but during the course of that meeting with Paul O'Sullivan and Bongani Maseko, he mentioned that there were certain changes that Cabinet was contemplating and that, you know, they wanted to place all the security of the different airports in the hands of the Police and that we shouldn't make any changes to any contracts to any security companies at the airports.

And subsequent to that meeting, he then wanted to have a meeting with the new CEO of ACSA and he went to that meeting to tell the CEO of ACSA, firstly that we shouldn't change the contract of Khuselani and that certain Ministers, and Minister Radebe was having discussions with Minister Dullah Omar to inform him that ACSA should not cancel the contract of Khuselani, even though Khuselani was not performing. Monhla Hlahla, the CEO of ACSA, then told the Commissioner that the Airports Company reports to the Minister of Transport and that if there were any instructions relating to how and what the Airports should do, they should come through the Minister and through the Chairman of ACSA, which is myself.

He then said, that he doesn't ... he would never meet me, because he has instituted an investigation into my affairs, into Mashudu and that within two weeks, he would have a report, which they are going to expose whatever it is that their findings are going to be. And the statements of the Commissioner are almost identical to the statements that Kevin Cockroft made when he was discussing with Carmine Bassetti.

It seems to me that there is a link between what Kevin Cockroft said and what the Commissioner is now saying. And perhaps there is a link between the problems, the security problems that I am experiencing and having with the events that are now beginning to unfold.

... The date today is the 21st November 2001, and the name is Mashudu Ramano.

Six days later, on 27 November, Khuselani, sensing that the winds might be changing, launched an urgent application in the High Court, requesting an order to stay the cancellation of the contract pending the outcome of arbitration. The judge, Max Labe, dismissed the complaint, with costs, in favour of ACSA and described the complaints against Khuselani as 'legion'.

Game over? Not quite. Things, as everyone, including Paul, was soon to find out, were about to escalate to the next level.

Three days after Khuselani's High Court application was dismissed, police swooped at dawn on a hotel in Johannesburg and arrested Ramano on trumped-up charges of being an illegal immigrant. Rumours were that Selebi had given instructions for the arrest. Ramano was temporarily hiding out in the hotel after the mysterious shootings referred to in his recorded statement had taken place at his home.

Of course the chairman's arrest made headlines and the *Mail & Guardian* carried a two-page spread. When he read the piece, it was obvious to Paul that someone (he suspected a secretary he had shared with Hlahla) had leaked false information to the media. 'Evidence wa ka Ngobeni, the journalist who wrote the story, had clearly been provided with information from personal bank statements that had been stolen from my old office which Hlahla now occupied.'

Ngobeni had suggested that an amount of R500,000 deposited into Paul's account might have been a bribe from a rival company hoping to secure the JIA security contract. Paul explained that he had recently sold some shares, intending to buy another property, and encouraged the journalist to check his side of the story.

Paul's 'job of a lifetime' was turning into a bad dream that would soon reach nightmarish proportions.

On Thursday, 6 December 2001, just after 1 p.m., Paul pulled his Audi TT Roadster out of the ACSA head office complex in Johnson Road, Bedfordview, en route to Johannesburg International for a meeting. It was a glorious Highveld summer's day and Paul opened the roof of the convertible. Ever attentive, he immediately noticed a red VW Golf with tinted windows parked about 150 metres away on a grass verge on the opposite side of the road.

Heading towards the highway, Paul kept sight of the red car in his rearview mirror. The vehicle had pulled off shortly after Paul and was obviously following him. A short distance later, the red car suddenly sped up, crossed into the right lane and drew level with Paul's roadster. The two cars cruised momentarily side by side.

'I looked to the right and observed that the occupants of the car were two males, both wearing balaclavas on their heads. The passenger window was open and, as I looked at the passenger, I saw that he was taking aim at me with a gunmetal-coloured firearm. It appeared to be a 9mm.'

Paul, who is accustomed to defensive, pre-emptive driving, made a split-second decision, slammed on the roadster's brakes and pulled over. The Golf kept moving but screeched to a halt about 100 metres ahead before the driver frantically attempted to make a three-point-turn. 'I made a quick U-turn and drove away at high speed,' Paul recalls.

Paul, who was divorced at the time, was grateful for once that his family and children were securely outside the country.

Five days later, O'Sullivan laid charges of intimidation and attempted murder against Selebi and Ngwenya. He made a statement under oath, setting out his suspicions that the botched attempt on his life had something to do with what was going on at ACSA.

'My company has recently cancelled a high-value security contract by a company called Khuselani Security. Prior to such cancellation being confirmed, the purported owner of the company, a certain Noel Ngwenya, conducted a personal vendetta against myself to try and intimidate me from proceeding with the cancellation.'

In the affidavit Paul highlighted the warnings Sisulu and Ndzeku had offered, Commissioner Selebi's attempts to reinstate Khuselani, and the fact that he had recently been suspended as a police reservist.

Meanwhile, back at Johannesburg International, it appeared as if, for the criminals at least, it was 'business as usual'.

At the end of December 2001, Paul flew to London on business and managed to fit in time to see his children abroad. Back in the hotel room he turned on the TV and was horrified to learn that yet another heist involving millions had occurred at JIA. 'No one called and told me. I sent my kids back to Ireland and flew back to South Africa and got stuck in. The whole job, the whole thing had been facilitated by cops, security guards and ACSA employees.'

A later detailed analysis of the robbery revealed that criminals had received advance warning of a shipment of US$93,000 in diamonds and US$9.5 million in cash that was being sent by a diamond company in Israel on a KLM flight to Johannesburg. US$7.5 million was destined for a bank in Luanda, and US$2.0 million had been en route to a bank in Kinshasa.

The anticipated arrival of the booty in Johannesburg was 26 December, but because the 25th was a holiday, the shipment only left Amsterdam the following day and arrived in Johannesburg on 27 December.

Shortly before the plane landed, a bakkie, driven by a man who flashed a permit that had been reported missing in April 1999, drove onto the airside area of the airport. Two minutes later, another vehicle, driven by a security company guard, pulled up.

The KLM flight docked at Alpha 5 just after 8 a.m. on 27 December and the cargo was unloaded. Two guards accompanied the load, one from Khulani Fidelity and the other from Protea. The Khulani Fidelity guard then diverted the cargo to the Cargo Service Centre instead of the Guard Force depot in the opposite direction.

While arrangements had been made for an SAPS escort for the valuable cargo, no one had summoned them. This omission was significant. And so the cash and diamonds made their way to the

KLM cargo section of the Cargo Service Centre, where the bakkie screeched up and four armed men offloaded the spoils onto the getaway vehicle.

Video footage of the robbery showed the Khulani Fidelity guard insisting that the robbers take his cell phone in an attempt to cover up his complicity in the crime. The police would most certainly have examined records from the guard's phone, as without it there would be nothing to implicate him, or so he thought.

In the meantime, the syndicate had positioned two men as lookouts at the Jet Centre and the Charlie gates. As the bakkie with the haul sped through the Jet Centre gate, the lookouts opened fire on a security vehicle now pursuing the robbers, wounding a female security guard in the process. The thieves then made off along the Northern Perimeter Road into Bonaero Park.

It was a devastating end to what had been an *annus horribilis* personally for O'Sullivan. As 2001 drew to a close, he sincerely hoped that the attempt on his life would alert anyone with common sense to the fact that something deeply troubling was amiss and that dark and dangerous forces were at work.

Chapter 7

Selebi on the Beat

AT HIS INAUGURATION 'RECEIVING command of the South African Police Service' from former commissioner George Fivaz in 2000, the new top cop, Jackie Selebi, amused those gathered with the quip that he was 'still practising how to wear a uniform'. In closing, the new commissioner announced that he was convinced that 'policing, despite all our good intentions and initiatives, will not succeed unless all the people of South Africa become actively involved'.

Ironically, Paul O'Sullivan was, at the time, arguably a rather sterling example of just such a citizen activist – along with thousands of others – who sat on community police forums, or who joined safer neighbourhood projects and watches or the police reserve.

Selebi's parting shot at his inauguration was a triumphant 'This is our country – we will not allow any criminal to take control of it'. But by then the commissioner had already begun to fraternise, whether he was aware of it or not, with shady underworld characters, including Agliotti and Paul Stemmet and his private security company, Palto.

One of Selebi's first controversial decisions as commissioner was to embark on a mass recruitment drive for police officers. The SAPS had received a massive budget increase and around 70,000 new recruits, many of them unskilled and untrained, had been absorbed into the service.

In a 2013 paper titled 'Roots of the Crisis Facing the South African Police', Gareth Newham, head of the governance, crime and justice division of the Institute of Security Studies, suggested that 'Selebi was less interested in the quality and integrity of these recruits, and his unwillingness to learn from extensive policing experience around him or from international studies meant that he had little appreciation of the dangers that mass recruitment drives could pose'.

Selebi also appointed unqualified individuals to senior positions 'regardless of their expertise or abilities', according to Newham, and truncated police training from two years to one. Station commanders soon found themselves supervising 'large numbers of inadequately trained recruits without additional support'. The effects of Selebi's early decisions were to continue to reverberate negatively for years to come.

By 2001 Selebi and Glenn Agliotti were regularly meeting and shopping together at the upmarket Sandton shopping centre in Johannesburg. It is prudent to remember that in 1999 police had already become involved in Paul Stemmet's company Palto. Bear in mind also that Stemmet had been introduced to Selebi through Mandela's tailor, Yusuf Surtee – a meeting Agliotti attended.

Palto, staffed with former police Special Task Force members, had operated as a private VIP protection service and had been involved in several illegal acts of extortion. In June 2000 Palto members lobbed an explosive device at the US software giant Microsoft's headquarters in Sunninghill, Johannesburg, in an attempt to get the corporation to use their security services. Palto was also behind an attack arranged by a prominent Johannesburg businessman on a debtor. In that case Palto operatives detonated a device in the target's Koi fishpond.

Palto members, who had all been issued with police appointment cards and promoted to the rank of captain in the police reserve, were clearly having a field day, possibly secure in the notion that the country's senior officers and chief of police had given them their blessing, so to speak. At the time, Palto members were deeply involved in the smuggling of contraband cigarettes and other imported counterfeit goods, which the unit would illegally seize (pretending to be under instruction from the SAPS), only to resell elsewhere.

In 2001 Agliotti's girlfriend at the time, Dianne Muller, was the managing director of an events company, Maverick Experience Exhilarator. Dianne's father, Martin Flint, was a six per cent shareholder and the company's BEE partner was African Renaissance Holdings. Maverick had been approached by the US-based organisers of the Special Olympics to host a two-week event in South Africa to raise funds for intellectually challenged athletes.

Muller had met Agliotti in the early 1990s and the two became romantically involved in 1995 after both had lost partners to freak accidents – Agliotti's girlfriend Brigitte had been declared brain dead after a horsing accident and Muller's fiancé had died in a plane crash. Muller would later become a key witness in Selebi's trial, and her detailed accounts of events were pivotal in the commissioner's later conviction on charges of corruption.

And so it was that in 2001 Muller's company became involved in the organisation of the Special Olympics 'Flame of Hope' leg of the project during which a torch would be carried from Sun City via Robben Island to the steps of Parliament in Cape Town.

Eunice Shriver Kennedy, sister of the assassinated president John F. Kennedy, had founded the Special Olympics in 1968. Her daughter Maria Owings Shriver was married at the time to Arnold Schwarzenegger, a former Mr Universe, film actor and controversial governor of California. Schwarzenegger, it was agreed, would visit South Africa to generate interest and create awareness around the event.

While Agliotti did not work with or for Muller, she provided him with an office at her Maverick suite in Gallagher Estate, a business park and convention centre situated between Johannesburg and Pretoria. Agliotti had used his connection with Selebi to introduce Muller to the police commissioner.

At that time, Agliotti not only met Selebi to discuss the Special Olympics event, but was also on more casual 'friendly' terms. In his later testimony Agliotti recounted how the two had often just hung out together in shopping malls and coffee shops. 'We frequented Sandton City when he was shopping or I was shopping; on various occasions we would have coffee together at the Brazilian Coffee Shop as it was known then and at Europa on one occasion.'

Stemmet, who was at that time bulkier than the Terminator himself, took care of security and transport arrangements around Schwarzenegger's visit.

In 2002 Palto and another company, Associated Intelligence Network (AIN), owned by Warren Goldblatt, began training police units in Sudan. Selebi had met with Palto and AIN 'operatives', as well as Sudanese officials, and illegally authorised the training. This he had no power to do, as only the National Arms Control Committee, which falls under the Department of Defence, could approve the training of foreign police or troops by South African nationals.

It was more than clear that Selebi was ignorant, didn't care or wasn't paying too much attention to the statutory or legal parameters of his duties and powers as commissioner.

In January 2002, while Paul O'Sullivan found his life in danger and ACSA management was increasingly sidelining him, a major drugs bust occurred at a depot in Kya Sands, an industrial area in Johannesburg. The truth (or rather a close approximation of the truth) about the bust only emerged much later during Selebi's trial, when Agliotti gave his version of the raid and his role in it.

On New Year's Day 2002 Agliotti contacted Paul Stemmet,

informing him that he needed help transporting the contents of two 20-foot containers that had arrived at the City Deep depot in Johannesburg from Durban. The cargo, apparently boxes of tiles, needed to be shifted to Randburg Self Storage in Kya Sands and belonged to a certain Mrs Chen, a clearing agent. The mysterious Mrs Chen, often referred to as Mommy Chen, had offered a 'ridiculous amount of money' for the job and Agliotti agreed to pay Stemmet R70,000, an unusually generous amount Stemmet later recalled, as Agliotti usually paid around R10,000.

Stemmet, wearing his police informer cap, had contacted Captain Wayne Kukard and Morné Nel, tipping them off about the shipment and the fact that the boxes probably contained drugs. Kukard then arranged for a SAPS technical support team, working with Palto, to make the bust.

Names that cropped up at this early stage were to prove highly valuable, especially to Paul O'Sullivan, in his later investigation of Selebi. One of them was Anthony Dormehl, the son of a pastor, who owned Premium Transport, a company that Stemmet and Agliotti often used to transport goods, including contraband tobacco and liquor, consignments of shoes and even Arnold Schwarzenegger's luggage during his visit to South Africa.

At around 4 p.m. on 2 January 2002, the SAPS and Palto units positioned themselves near the Kya Sands depot and observed as the boxes were loaded onto Dormehl's ten-ton truck. An hour later the truck, tailed by the police–Palto surveillance team, pulled out of the depot en route to a house in Bryanston. Once there, the SAPS–Palto team swooped and found a stash of 1.2 million Mandrax tablets worth around R40 million concealed inside the tile boxes. The house itself was a fully equipped drug factory with gas cylinders and baking and heating trays.

It was a huge bust and Commissioner Selebi rushed to the scene to meet with a contingent of excited journalists. He posed for photographs sporting a wide, toothy grin while clutching a giant, transparent plastic bag of Mandrax tablets. The commissioner triumphantly told journalists, 'We are going to get to that person [behind the racket], that's for sure.'

In a later damning statement made to the Scorpions, Stemmet claimed that Agliotti had called him after the bust and asked if he knew about or had anything to do with the sting. Stemmet denied any knowledge, claiming he had left the scene after the drugs had been loaded from the warehouse onto the truck. Agliotti informed Stemmet that Mommy Chen 'was going to be furious' about the bust.

The day after the bust, Stemmet contacted Selebi and alerted him to Agliotti's involvement in the transport of the shipment of drugs. 'Commissioner Selebi became very angry at Glenn's involvement,' Stemmet confessed, adding, 'but after informing Commissioner Selebi about Glenn's involvement he [Glenn] was never arrested.'

Stemmet, apart from being paid R70,000 by Agliotti to arrange the transport of the Mandrax, was also paid R400,000 by the police for tipping them off. Nice work if you can get it.

In the meantime, Agliotti, clearly hedging his bets, called Selebi from Johannesburg International while checking in to board a flight to Italy for his annual family skiing holiday. During the conversation, Agliotti told Selebi that it was in fact *he* who had informed police. 'I asked him if he was happy with the operation and he indicated that he was ecstatic at the work that Paul Stemmet and the boys had done,' Agliotti told the court later.

Paul Stemmet's information to Selebi that Agliotti had had a nefarious involvement in the shipment of Mandrax seemed to entirely slip the commissioner's mind, as he made no mention of it in his departure-lounge conversation with Agliotti. Later, Agliotti again called the commissioner from Italy to enquire if there was any 'reward money', as he, Agliotti, had been the 'source of information'.

Tracking the fine and faded thread of truth in the testimonies of a clutch of drug lords, thieves and crooked cops is challenging enough, but there are a few obvious questions and anomalies surrounding the Kya Sands bust that even an imbecile would have picked up on. One such anomaly was that Agliotti was only signed on by Captain Nel as a police informer on 23 January, almost three weeks after the 3 January bust at Kya Sands. Agliotti had been paid a R10,000 'registration fee' and had chosen the codename Pino Piconne, Italian for pickaxe. He was later paid an additional R100,000 cut of Stemmet's R500,000 fee.

Of course, during Selebi's trial the state prosecutor, Gerrie Nel, would ask some of these questions, the most obvious being whether Agliotti, on his return from his Italian sojourn, had been debriefed by police or had any discussions about the huge drug haul or his role in it. 'Nothing, whatsoever,' Agliotti casually replied.

As Adriaan Basson points out in his book *Finish and Klaar*, why would police need to pay Paul Stemmet R400,000 for information that Selebi had already allegedly obtained free from Agliotti? 'If he didn't know, as is Stemmet's version, why did he keep Agliotti as a friend and source after being told by Stemmet that he [Agliotti] was involved in drug trafficking?' asked Basson.

A third question of course is why the truck owner Anthony Dormehl had never been questioned by police about his links to Agliotti.

In the end Selebi's boast that 'We are going to get to that person [behind the racket], that's for sure' proved hollow. The drugs mysteriously vanished, as did all those arrested during the bust. The mysterious Mrs Chen, one can imagine, must have breathed a sigh of relief.

In March 2002, two months after the Kya Sands bust, Agliotti was to make the acquaintance of a man whom he would be charged with murdering three and a half years later: Brett Kebble.

It was Paul Stemmet who had suggested to Kebble that he meet with Agliotti because the latter 'had a close relationship with Selebi'. Stemmet and his company, Palto, had been engaged by Kebble to do 'security work'.

Brett Kebble fancied himself as a sort of 21st-century Barney Barnato, the British 'Randlord' who played a major part in diamond and gold mining in South Africa in the late 1800s and who was coincidentally the founder and previous CEO of the company that Kebble now controlled 115 years later. At the time, Kebble and his father, Roger, had shot to prominence in the mining world for a series of complicated, highly lucrative and, as it turned out for Brett, fraudulent deals.

Kebble had needed someone 'reliable' to do intelligence work on behalf of his companies Johannesburg Consolidated Investments (JCI) and Consolidated Management Mining Services (CMMS), among others. Essentially this meant spying on a rival company, Durban Roodepoort Deep (DRD), and its board member Mark Wellesley-Wood, who had begun to suspect that the Kebbles might be behind irregularities that he and other shareholders had picked up. After his murder in 2005, it emerged that the politically connected, high-flying Kebble had spirited away some R26 billion in stolen shares and other complicated financial deals.[5]

Patrick Bond, director of the UKZN Centre for Civil Society, writing in 2012 for the political magazine Counterpunch.org, described Kebble as 'extremely good at his game, up to the point the inverted pyramid crashed in mid-2005. More brazenly than any other previously-and-still-empowered South African, he utterly scammed the new political elite, investors and the cultural crowd with his patriotic white-friend-of-black-empowerment-and-the-arts hustle.'

And so, in March 2002 Agliotti was introduced to Brett and Roger Kebble, John Stratton, the CEO of JCI and Kebble's influential confidant (whom many viewed as the 'puppet master' behind some of Kebble's deals), as well as Hennie Buitendag, JCI's CFO. The meeting had been arranged, said Agliotti, because the Kebbles had 'certain problems with a company called AIN [Warren Goldblatt's security outfit, Associated Intelligence Network] who had been appointed by DRD Gold' to investigate the Kebble empire.

---

5 For the full complexity of Kebble's corporate fraud, read Barry Sergeant's two comprehensive tomes on the scandal, *Brett Kebble: Inside Story* (2006) and *The Kebble Collusion: 10 Fateful Days in a R26 Billion Fraud* (2012).

The Kebbles hoped that Agliotti, with his access to Selebi, would take their 'problem' to the police chief to make sure it was 'dealt with in the correct manner'. The 'problem' was that Roger Kebble, Brett's father, had been arrested earlier at Johannesburg International Airport on charges of fraud. The Kebbles alleged that AIN, financed by DRD, had bribed police to arrest Kebble Snr in order to 'humiliate and embarrass' him.

DRD claimed that Roger, while on the board of that company, had channelled money through a close corporation he owned, Skilled Labour Brokers, to the labour consultancy Global Economic Research and that he had diverted some of this money to his private account. The Kebbles tasked Agliotti with taking their grievance to the very top of the police hierarchy.

Agliotti later testified that he had approached Selebi and that Selebi had in turn arranged a meeting with top police officials – Mulangi Mphego, the deputy commissioner, and Ray Lalla, the head of police intelligence – and with Kebble's representatives, John Stratton and the former judge Willem Heath, who had been contracted by the Kebbles to represent JCI. 'I cemented a relationship with them [the Kebbles], and because of my relationship with Selebi they wanted him on board. I said to them it would cost one million US dollars, which was my consulting fee, and they agreed to that,' Agliotti later testified.

The 'axis of evil', as Paul O'Sullivan was to dub the relationship between Selebi, Stratton and Agliotti, was slowly taking shape.

Chapter 8

Things Fall Apart

2002 KICKED OFF AS DRAMATICALLY as the previous year had ended.

On 3 January, a week after the largest heist ever to take place in South Africa, an arms cache of over 200 guns worth R1 million was discovered unattended in the cargo section of JIA. The 226 Yugoslavian-made hunting rifles had been transported by the Greek national carrier, Olympic Airlines, and, remarkably, had not been detected by either Olympic staff or local customs officials. The guns had apparently simply been abandoned in the cargo department.

ACSA's CEO, Monhla Hlahla, was quick to claim a victory for the South African Police Service at an impromptu press conference to which she invited Commissioner Selebi. Hlahla told gathered journalists: 'I am happy that the presence of the SAPS at Johannesburg International Airport is bearing fruit.'

The same day the arms cache had been discovered at the airport, Hlahla and the Gauteng commissioner, Perumal Naidoo, pulled Paul aside and spent two hours urging him to withdraw the charges he had lodged in 2001 against Ngwenya, Selebi and others. 'Naidoo threatened that I would not win this "war" with Selebi. At the time I was hoping to just get back to my job and to return to my life as I knew it, so I withdrew the charges,' O'Sullivan recalled.

A few days after the exchange with Naidoo, Paul was driving from Johannesburg International to the ACSA offices in Bedfordview when the same red VW Golf involved in the December gun-toting incident sped up behind him. Paul braced himself as the vehicle pulled up alongside in the slow lane. He had anticipated that the occupants were armed, but when the passenger window of his Mazda 6 exploded, O'Sullivan initially assumed that the Golf had rammed him. 'When I heard the bang I slammed on my brakes and the Golf sped off ahead of me.'

Up ahead, the passenger in the Golf turned to face Paul and took aim with a firearm. Paul lunged for the weapon he carried in a holster on his right hip, slid open his window and opened fire across his windshield. 'I fired three or four shots at the car up ahead. I saw the man's head snap back before the car veered off to the side of the freeway. Then I just sped off past it.'

Later, Paul discovered that apart from the shattered window, a bullet had penetrated the car door and had also taken a small nick off his tie. Justifiably livid, he immediately reinstated his complaint against Selebi and Ngwenya. Now he added Commissioner Naidoo to the growing list of 'conspirators', as he described them.

Soon afterwards, as O'Sullivan once again pulled out of the ACSA head office and onto the freeway, he found himself being tailed by a black BMW. Was he being paranoid? O'Sullivan needed to be certain before taking any evasive action. When he slowed down, the car stuck to his tail; when he sped up, it kept up with him.

Paul contemplated his next move. Up ahead he spotted an embankment and reckoned if he sped off down it, he could loop back onto the adjacent freeway.

It was time to act. Paul suddenly slammed on the car's brakes and hurtled off down the embankment. He watched as the BMW swerved, went into a tailspin and came to a standstill facing oncoming traffic.

'I was acutely aware that people were out to kill me. I started conducting my life in a different manner. I was cautious of where I went and how. At that stage I wasn't married and didn't have a family in South Africa to worry about. I was comfortable that I could look after myself, and I did.'

But as much as he felt he could look after himself, circumstances were clearly taking their toll. Apart from having to move regularly to secure locations, he also lost over 10 kilograms. The stress also began to affect his eating and sleeping habits. What exacerbated all of this was that he felt sidelined and persecuted by the very people he believed should have had his back.

Years of experience in law enforcement led to Paul's suspicion that someone inside ACSA was watching him closely, monitoring his every move. He wasn't sure who the culprit might be, but he had an idea. Besides, shots had been fired and a war had clearly been declared. He could not sit back and twiddle his thumbs. While he realised he needed to keep his wits about him to stay alive, he was also determined not to allow these threats to derail his professional life.

In mid-January, Hlahla met with Paul in her office and suggested he take a six-week 'sabbatical', ostensibly to recover from recent traumatic events and, she said, until 'things settle down'.

Paul no longer trusted anyone. Why would Hlahla want him out of the way? And if she really was concerned for his safety and his life, why not determine why he had been targeted in the first place? After all, he was her head of security.

Hlahla was due to make a submission to Parliament's Transport Portfolio Committee about the rampant crime at JIA and Paul suspected this might have been the real reason she wanted him out of the way.

When she did present to the committee, Hlahla claimed the high levels of crime were due to a shortage of SAPS members, a statement Paul felt amounted to a cover-up of the true picture. Hlahla made no mention of Khuselani Security and its role in the sorry bigger picture, or the fact that most of ACSA's own staff, who were meant to be supervising the contractors, were either corrupt or incompetent. O'Sullivan felt that Hlahla had given 'exactly the message that she knew Selebi wanted to hear, which was why she needed me out of the way and suspended me on trumped-up allegations'.

Meanwhile, O'Sullivan had initiated his own investigation into Noel Ngwenya. His interest had been piqued when a source close to the Khuselani CEO informed Paul that the businessman enjoyed a lavish lifestyle.

'Look, I have no problem with people spending hard-earned money on things they like. But sometimes you have to look at someone, the job they do, and the lifestyle they lead and ask the question "Where is all this money coming from?" Often you will find that these are the spoils of ill-gotten gains. I wanted to find out more about Ngwenya and the source of his good fortune.'

O'Sullivan had been fed information that the day before Lungi Sisulu and Vuyo Ndzeku paid him a visit, Jackie Selebi had been chauffeured from his office in Pretoria to Noel Ngwenya's offices in Kempton Park. The meeting had lasted approximately an hour before Selebi was deposited back in Pretoria.

'Something wasn't right, so I decided to do a tax audit on Khuselani. I am a certified fraud examiner and I know that wherever you find corruption you find other activities, usually tax evasion. People do this because they need money to offer bribes.'

At this point the dire security situation at JIA was regularly making news. Negative headlines such as 'MPs to Probe Airport Safety' and 'Airport Security – Conspiracies in the Air' were featured in a range of media, from authoritative magazines to the tabloids. The series of daring heists, Khuselani's suspension, the arrest of the ACSA chairman, Mashudu Ramano, the attempts on Paul's life, his lodging of a complaint with the ICD against the national commissioner, Selebi, and the Gauteng commissioner,

Perumal Naidoo, and the ongoing tensions in management, all served to sketch an unsavoury and deeply troubling scenario at the country's busiest international airport.

Several international carriers also announced an embargo on flying valuable cargo to the country. In January, Dutch carrier KLM, Germany's Lufthansa and Air France all opted to avoid dealing with JIA, a move that could have resulted, in the long term, in serious economic consequences not only for the airport but also for the South African economy.

The same month, in a desperate attempt to counter the negative publicity, Hlahla announced the launch of Operation Octopus, a multi-pronged initiative drawing in SARS, the Civil Aviation Authority, Home Affairs and 'the intelligence community' under a joint command. 'We need a paradigm shift. We have to know just what needs to be provided at an airport the size of Johannesburg; whether the people who check the cards and man the gates and so on are the best available and how they should act. I will personally co-ordinate that plan,' Hlahla told the media.

O'Sullivan, as ACSA's executive head of security, was conspicuously absent at the media launch. As far as he was concerned, the entire exercise was doomed to failure, as it would be handled 'by the same incompetent or corrupt JIA team that had brought about the lapses of security in the first place'.

The truth, said Paul, was that the ACSA manager André Olivier and Hlahla 'did not want to cope', as he had already provided them with copious reports setting out exactly what should be done; reports that he felt had all been deliberately ignored, as they were both following Selebi's personal agenda.

Paul thought that a crucial point the ACSA management seemed to be missing was 'the fact that 100 per cent of the private security being supplied to protect airports had been deployed on the basis of corruptly and fraudulently awarded tenders, and those ACSA officials charged with the duty of ensuring compliance were being bribed'.

A few days after the Operation Octopus launch, O'Sullivan

discovered an envelope slipped under the door of his office by Hlahla. It contained a highly disturbing letter in which she informed him that the company was investigating a claim of sexual harassment against him as well as a purchase he had made of a polygraph machine for use at Durban Airport. The letter and the allegations, Paul understood, were two new lines of attack, and he ramped up his defences accordingly.

So far, his investigation into Ngwenya had yielded more than enough evidence for a case to be made on multi-million-rand VAT fraud charges. O'Sullivan arranged for a meeting with a SARS special investigator, Paul Swanepoel, and presented his case. O'Sullivan agreed to hand over all the relevant files, but asked that SARS first send an official letter to him, in terms of the Act, demanding such documents, lest Hlahla accuse him of breaching security. It was convincing enough to secure an official SARS directive ordering an audit of all documents relating to the Khuselani-ACSA contract, including all invoices and receipts. O'Sullivan tasked his temporary secretary with collating the file, which she duly did.

A few days later, says Paul, Hlahla summoned him to her office and issued what she termed a 'direct instruction' for him to call off the investigation into Ngwenya, as Khuselani was no longer operating at ACSA.

'I told her that I couldn't call it off and that I had already sent the documents to SARS. I was lying. The file was in my car and I was planning to take it through later. I quickly called my contact at SARS and told them that if Hlahla phoned, they should confirm that they had already received the documents.'

Hlahla did indeed contact SARS minutes later and was advised that the files had already been delivered. O'Sullivan says he now knew for sure that Hlahla was 'on the wrong side of the fence and was devious in her efforts to stop me and get Khuselani back at the airports. On the other hand I was going all out to get Ngwenya behind bars.'

Later that year, Ngwenya would be found guilty of fraudulently filing VAT returns, resulting in a loss of R30 million to SARS, of paying bribes to SARS officials to help cover up the theft and of paying off ACSA officials to win the ACSA tender for Khuselani. In May that year he was sentenced to three years in jail.

As February 2002 rolled round, O'Sullivan found himself suspended on trumped-up charges, involving an alleged 'unscheduled' flight he had undertaken from Lanseria to test security at JIA. 'I realised that this was turning into a massive campaign of intimidation, vilification and even attempted murder,' O'Sullivan recalls.

Suspended on full pay and with time on his hands, O'Sullivan began to investigate every single avenue that might lead to the culprits behind the 'campaign'. It didn't take long for him to begin to locate the scattered pieces of the puzzle. During his investigation O'Sullivan dug out a copy of a memo written by Petko Ivanov Atanassov, ACSA's aviation services manager, to Dino Colbert, the company's internal auditor, in February. In the memo Atanassov revealed that André Olivier had been deeply involved in the corrupt awarding of the tender to Noel Ngwenya and Khuselani.

Atanassov claimed that there had been persistent 'rumours' about Olivier during the period when the contract was awarded to Khuselani. 'I had these rumours confirmed when I was approached by Olivier, prior to Khuselani starting at the airports, at which time he suggested to me that I should take up employment with Khuselani. In this regard he advised me that he was personally involved with Khuselani,' Atanassov later stated in a sworn affidavit.

He spoke of meeting with Ngwenya, who had offered him a job with his company. Then there was an incident in which André Olivier personally intervened when Ngwenya was arrested by police for stealing the cell phone of a fellow passenger passing through an X-ray machine at JIA. Atanassov revealed that JIA security had summoned the police, who had already opened a case and placed Ngwenya in custody. 'In the normal course of events, and without Olivier's intervention, Ngwenya would have been detained and charged for the offence of theft,' said Atanassov.

Ultimately the memo confirmed Paul's assertion that there

had been an orchestrated drive to get rid of him. Atanassov's furious statement opened with the words 'I state that this case is an orchestrated campaign built on foul accusations fabricated by a corrupt and disloyal employee of ACSA – André Ernest Olivier'. Bingo!

Paul had also been alerted that Olivier and Selebi were conspiring to have him arrested on charges of carrying a firearm in a restricted area. It was a charge that was nonsensical: he had been an executive official in charge of security at ACSA at the time, and in fact the only person authorised to decide who should or should not be allowed to carry arms into the restricted areas of airports.

Pre-empting the strike, O'Sullivan used his considerable experience writing statements, to pen a comprehensive explanation to the chief prosecutor of the Kempton Park Magistrate's Court, where a warrant for his arrest was being sought. O'Sullivan was crunching this elephant, one mouthful at a time.

The later conclusion of an audit by Ebony Forensic Services into the awarding of the Khuselani contract was that André Olivier had indeed acted in an unethical manner from Noel Ngwenya before or after the tender had been awarded.

Pearl Moshebi, a secretary who had worked for Khuselani, provided investigators with an affidavit stating that Olivier and Sam Mokgotsane, ACSA's aviation security manager, had often popped into the company's offices while tender documents were being prepared. 'At that time Prof. Noel Ngwenya was struggling to pay employees' salaries and claimed the company had no money, as they were paying a lot of people to get the ACSA contract.'

Auditors recommended that Olivier be charged with misconduct or dishonesty with regard to the awarding of the Khuselani security contract. By September, Olivier knew he was a gonner and jumped before he could be pushed and charged, announcing his resignation in a short email to his colleagues.

Curiously, Hlahla chose not to prosecute or discipline Olivier, a senior official who had been seriously fingered in the report, and instead gave him a half-million-rand golden handshake. Paul's suspicions were that she might be protecting Olivier, as Paul had informed her that he intended to press charges. His hunch was later confirmed when Hlahla kept Olivier's resignation from him. What made matters worse is that Olivier left ACSA with a 'handsome' bonus and a clean record.

In his general observations, Nceba Gomomo, CEO of Ebony Forensic Services, noted: 'the manner ACSA treated Mr Paul O'Sullivan after the cancellation of the Khuselani contract could be seen as victimisation and could attract liability on the part of the company'. Gomomo added that O'Sullivan was the type of employee 'your company should keep'.

And there one would have thought the matter might have rested. In the fairytale version Paul should have been welcomed back with open arms. But conditions were growing increasingly untenable.

In a letter to Hlahla, Paul did not hold back: 'I have received absolutely NO support from ACSA, other than the offer of a sabbatical ... Were it not for the emotional and moral support given me by the Chairman [Ramano], I doubt I would have made it this far.'

For Paul O'Sullivan, nothing could serve as more provocation than any attempt to tarnish or damage his reputation. For him reputation maketh the man (or woman), and in this case it appears as if he fell victim to the writer and philosopher William Hazlitt's observation: 'a man's reputation is not his own keeping. It lies at the mercy of the profligacy of others.'

'I have been in South Africa for almost 12 years, during which time I have built up an impeccable reputation in the business world. Most importantly I have been portrayed as a man of integrity and with principles that I am able to stand by. I have also been portrayed as a man of determination, who gets the job done. Because of the total failure of ACSA to stand by me in this difficult time, I have been isolated and left out in the cold as a sitting target for the criminals that have almost brought JIA to its knees,' O'Sullivan let rip.

In March Paul was reinstated but found his reception frosty. He also discovered that he had been sidelined, as new instructions had been issued that each manager would take care of the security in their area and Paul was to confine himself to audits. He was also informed that he would be provided with an assistant, appointed by Hlahla, who would act as a mediator in all dealings between her and Paul.

In July, after an intervention, O'Sullivan and Hlahla signed a memo acknowledging their 'history of conflict and mistrust' and both undertook to try to mend the relationship. This included mediated monthly counselling sessions, though these proved difficult to schedule, as Hlahla, he says, did not turn up to any of them. While O'Sullivan sat in her meeting room, waiting, Hlahla was attending to other activities, including running the Johannesburg Water Board or other of her non-executive positions. 'I just carried on. It was very difficult. I kept on highlighting security failure after security failure, theft after theft, left, right and centre.'

In August 2002 JIA made headlines again when two dummy bombs were smuggled past security guards during a Civil Aviation Authority test. Paul kept up the pressure in spite of the trying circumstances. His own investigations suggested ongoing irregularities involving ACSA staff. 'I found out the new CEO [Hlahla] was involved with a company supplying us with all our firefighting foam, they paid her R75,000 in one year, as so-called director's fees, which she did not disclose to ACSA, and for that R75,000 she attended only three meetings. The guy in charge of building projects had his own building company in Durban and used ACSA's engineers and consultants at a knock-down price for his own construction works. I found many other conflicts of interest and I suggested an internal audit. Vernon Naidoo resigned from the board in July 2003, after a forensic investigation recommended 13 charges be laid against him.'

Matters were destined to implode. Finally, on 17 January 2003 they did after a confrontation between Paul and an adviser to the new minister of transport, who had been meeting with Hlahla in the ACSA boardroom.

A few days later Paul O'Sullivan was fired. 'There was no hearing. I was told my contract had a clause that I could be given three months' notice. "Here you go," Hlahla said. I had to be out of my office at 4 p.m.'

Paul spent two hours packing his files. His parting shot was to send a letter to all staff at ACSA, telling them that their CEO was corrupt.

But if those who were out to get him thought they'd seen the last of Paul O'Sullivan, they were wrong. They were about to reap the whirlwind they had sown.

PART TWO

Chapter 9

Storm Clouds Gather

IN 2003 PAUL O'SULLIVAN FOUND himself out on a limb, the parameters of his life increasingly narrowing. Unlawfully dismissed from his dream job and convinced he was target of a concerted and relentless campaign by powerful interests to discredit and vilify him, O'Sullivan began to prepare himself for the confrontation of a lifetime.

Of course there were also the life-threatening encounters with armed, masked assassins who lurked on highways.

Meanwhile, away from the battles that plagued O'Sullivan's professional life, more portentous storm clouds were gathering. These would, over a period of time, soon darken South Africa's national political landscape. By 2006, several casualties were to find themselves drawn into the eye of this political tornado. O'Sullivan, too, would find himself one of several accidental players in a vicious endgame.

In 2003 Bulelani Ngcuka, a lawyer and former anti-apartheid activist, had occupied the position of national director of public prosecutions for five years. The National Prosecuting Authority (NPA), a constitutionally mandated body, was established in August 1998 'to ensure justice for victims of crime by prosecuting without fear, favour and prejudice'.

By 2002/3 NPA conviction rates had increased impressively – in specially created commercial courts in Pretoria and Johannesburg – to 96.2 per cent and 93.54 per cent respectively.[6] Ironically, the first such conviction was O'Sullivan's case against Vito Assante, a case where the investigation file was so comprehensive that Assante pleaded guilty and accepted a 24-year sentence. Apart from these commercial cases, convictions in ordinary courts had also improved dramatically.

The NPA consisted of a national director of public prosecutions (Ngcuka) and several specialised 'business' units, including the Directorate of Special Operations (DSO), known as the Scorpions. This unit was headed by the lawyer Leonard McCarthy. The Scorpions, a multi-disciplinary task force of trained professionals, including prosecutors, forensics experts and detectives, was formally launched in January 2001. Members were better paid than ordinary police and drove a fleet of powerful, black VW Golfs with distinctive decals featuring a red scorpion poised to strike.

From the start, the relationship between the Scorpions – the investigating arm of the NPA – and the SAPS was fraught and antagonistic. Instead of co-operating, the two law-enforcement agencies would find themselves pitted against each other in a bitter political turf war. O'Sullivan says that Selebi deliberately fanned the flames of this small war, turning it into a raging inferno, for no other reason than to create the impression that the Scorpions wanted his blood so badly they would cook up cases against him. The truth, he believed, was that Selebi wanted the Scorpions shut down before they got to him.

Early on, Scorpions investigations and arrests made for excellent press, as suspects were often cuffed and dragged off in 'Hollywood-

---

6 *The Mail & Guardian A-Z of South African Politics*, edited by Paul Stober and Barbara Ludman (Jacana Media, 2004), p. 105.

style' swoops in the full glare of publicity. By 2002/3, the NPA's Asset Forfeiture Unit (AFU) had deposited R18 million into the Criminal Asset Recovery Fund, money ring-fenced for use by the criminal justice system. The Scorpions also launched several high-profile fraud investigations, including one into Winnie Madikizela-Mandela, who was convicted in 2003 on 43 counts of fraud and 25 of theft amounting to R1 million and relating to fraudulently obtained bank loans.

But the investigation that would ultimately see the unit flying too close to the flame was one launched in 2001 to probe allegations of corruption in the awarding of R42 billion worth of arms deal contracts signed by the South African government in 1998.

The first casualty was the ANC's chief whip, Tony Yengeni, who was convicted of accepting a discount on a luxury Mercedes-Benz 4X4 from DaimlerChrysler Aerospace, the company that secured a contract to supply radar for naval corvettes bought by the government as part of the arms deal. Yengeni was a member of the ANC's National Executive Committee and also head of the Joint Standing Committee for Defence, a body that played a key role in the awarding of the contracts.

The arms deal subsequently became the worm that still eats away the heart of post-democratic South Africa. Allegations of widespread corruption and kickbacks to powerful party members continue to be probed and investigated and have in the process been used to settle political scores and bitter in-fighting.[7]

While it was initially feared that the Scorpions, with Ngcuka as its head, might be too close to the ruling party to act with impartiality (Ngcuka had deep roots in the ANC), the authority soon gained a reputation for fearlessness. In October 2002 the NPA announced that its probe into the arms deal would expand to include allegations of bribery and corruption against Jacob Zuma,

---

7 For a full exposé of the pernicious global arms trade and the 1998 arms deal and its impact on South Africa, read Andrew Feinstein's two insightful works, *After the Party: A Personal and Political Journey inside the ANC* (2007) and *The Shadow World: Inside the Global Arms Trade* (2011).

the country's deputy president. This declaration, for some in the ANC, was proof that the NPA was not as independent as it had claimed to be and was being used as a political tool, specifically by Thabo Mbeki, the incumbent president, against Jacob Zuma, his political rival.

On the periphery of this simmering tension within the ANC, the mining tycoon Brett Kebble squatted, like a toxic toad, poised and ready to strike. Kebble had learned in late 2002 that the Scorpions, on instruction from the then minister of justice, Penuell Maduna, were investigating him on various charges of fraud. Keen to throw the NPA off his scent, he tagged himself onto a growing band of disillusioned ANC members who felt that Jacob Zuma was being unfairly persecuted.

Barry Sergeant reckons: 'Kebble was convinced, beyond reason or rhyme, that he was doomed under Thabo Mbeki's presidency' and that Kebble 'plotted far and wide in the political arena, he feared nothing and sought to destabilise the Mbeki government. He focused on forging ties with various individuals in politics, law enforcement and intelligence services.' Sergeant writes that Kebble's support of the political elite, in the ANC Youth League in particular, was essentially aimed at mobilising support for Jacob Zuma as well as aligning himself with fellow 'victims' of the 'manipulated' Scorpions.

In August 2003, Bulelani Ngcuka detonated a political depth charge that would send shockwaves rippling through the country's body politic for years to come. At a press conference he announced that the NPA had elected to prosecute Schabir Shaik, Jacob Zuma's financial adviser, on charges of fraud and corruption.

A month before, Ngcuka had called an 'off-the-record' press briefing for some of the country's top editors at a hotel in Sandton. During the meeting Ngcuka candidly, but rather foolishly, discussed several cases the NPA was working on at the time, including the ongoing corruption charges against Jacob Zuma. Vusi Mona, then editor of the Sunday paper *City Press*, went public after the meeting, claiming Ngcuka had used the opportunity to 'violate citizens' rights, particularly their constitutional right to human dignity, under the guise of an off-the-record meeting'.

Ncguka claimed that the deputy president had been unable to meet his monthly financial commitments and that he found himself in this situation because 'he surrounded himself with Indian people'. Ngcuka also implied that Brett Kebble was paying 'protection money' to the ANCYL.

At the August press conference, however, Ngcuka told those gathered that while there was a *prima facie* case of corruption against Jacob Zuma, 'our prospects of success are not strong enough. That means that we are not sure if we have a winnable case. Accordingly we have decided not to prosecute the deputy president.'

A month later, Ngcuka felt the full sting of a counter-offensive campaign from the Zuma camp when a newspaper published allegations that the NPA head had, in fact, acted as a spy for the apartheid government in the 1980s.

On 19 September, President Mbeki appointed a commission of inquiry, headed by a former judge, Joos Hefer, to probe the allegations. For over a week the hearings, which were televised live, dominated headlines and forced those who had cooked up the rumour into the open. The verdict, after days of dramatic but entertaining testimony by the former transport minister Mac Maharaj and the ANC intelligence operative Moe Shaik (Schabir's brother), was that there was no evidence proving that Ngcuka had been a spy. Still, Ngcuka's proverbial goose had been cooked. However, what the Hefer Commission did serve to highlight was the battle lines that were being drawn inside the ruling party.

A month after the findings of the Hefer Commission, Jacob Zuma filed a complaint with the public protector, Lawrence Mushwana, protesting the manner in which the NPA had conducted its investigation against him. Brett Kebble followed suit.

In November 2003, Bheki Jacobs, an intelligence operative and the man who has now been credited with blowing the lid off the arms deal, was arrested in a dramatic early-morning raid on his home in Cape Town. Moe Shaik sat at the Hefer Commission and proudly announced, 'I met with the commissioner of police only yesterday [which was a Sunday], we have arrested one of the information peddlers and more are to follow.' This dramatic announcement was clearly intended to intimidate any like-minded individuals, or others in the Jacobs camp.

The peripatetic Jacobs, who had originally leaked a document naming high-profile ANC politicians, including Selebi, who received bribes and kickbacks to the Independent Democrats leader, Patricia de Lille, was subsequently charged with plotting to assassinate President Thabo Mbeki and using false passports.

Jacobs was driven from his home to the air force base in Ysterplaat from where he was flown to Pretoria in a Beechjet, privately owned by the SAPS and often used by Commissioner Selebi to attend official functions. Jacobs, who died in 2008, was later acquitted. His computer, seized at the time of his arrest, was never returned.

On its flight to Ysterplaat from Johannesburg, the only passengers on the Beechjet were Deputy Commissioner André Pruis and his wife, who were headed to Cape Town on a break. O'Sullivan suggests that this was not the first or last time that Pruis used the jet for private trips.

2003 was the year key pieces of the South African puzzle were being shifted into place outside public view. Already then, the Serious and Violent Crime Unit had begun to probe the relationship between Glenn Agliotti, Palto and Jackie Selebi, but the allegations, contained in affidavits given by Palto members, didn't seem to ripple any further than the manila dockets that bound them. The Serious and Violent Crime division was one of Selebi's own 'units' and he exercised tight control over it. Captain Venora Henderson, while pointlessly searching for evidence that did not exist against O'Sullivan and interviewing Petko Atanassov, confided to Atanassov that the members of the unit were 'tired of doing Selebi's dirty work'. She referred in particular to the fact that they had been forced to arrest Mashudu Ramano, ACSA's chairman, in November 2001, in a last-ditch attempt by Selebi to keep Noel Ngwenya's company at the airports.

The *Mail & Guardian* published a story quoting from the affidavits, which clearly indicated that 'Agliotti was or is still involved with the Italian, Russian and Chinese mafias' and, as one policeman alleged in his sworn statement, 'it was also put to me that Commissioner Selebi was aware of these operations'.

By then O'Sullivan had already set out, in copious letters and other correspondence to the police's ICD, the public protector and even the minister of police, his reasons why the country's top cop should be probed. To O'Sullivan it was obvious that the actions of a powerful police commissioner who was close friends with a man found guilty of tax fraud and who had bribed his way into securing a multi-million-rand security tender deserved closer scrutiny. Surely the shocking levels of serious crime at the country's best-known international airport, the damage it wreaked on the country's reputation and the threat it posed to society were grave and worrying? And was it really unreasonable to expect someone in authority to consider Paul's charge that there *was* most certainly a link between his endeavours to expose corruption at JIA and the attempts on his life? But all of O'Sullivan's letters and emails were either fobbed off or ignored.

At the end of that year he wrote to Charles Nqakula, then minister of police, asking, in the light of the Hefer Commission and the unlawful arrest of Bheki Jacobs, whether his commissioner of police was immune from investigation and above the law or whether the country was moving back into a 'police state'.

He suggested that while the media had claimed that the feud between the Scorpions and the SAPS was sparked by 'political camps', he was of the opinion that entirely different groupings were pitted against each other; 'those in the Low Ethics Camp and those in the Normal Ethics Camp'. 'Those in the Low Ethics Camp are using dirty tricks, smear campaigns and unlawful searches and arrests, those in the Normal Ethics Camp are simply doing what they are being paid to do, clean up and put a stop to corruption by civil servants and ministers and others in the Low Ethics Camp.'

'I regret the need to write and request this, which is my final step before launching a series of High Court applications to rectify the serious breach of rights I have suffered,' O'Sullivan wrote.

He ended the missive warning the minister that 'this matter will not go away on its own and my stance against criminal conduct and corruption has been wrongly misinterpreted as being a trouble maker for the ANC, a party I much admire and support'.

He signed off, 'A loyal (and proud) South African'.

Chapter 10

Going It Alone

O'SULLIVAN'S LETTER TO THE minister offers some insight into his binary view of the world: there are those who are corrupt and criminal and those who are not. And in this world you are either for the criminals or against them; on the side of good or on the side of evil. No grey.

O'Sullivan's exit from his high-powered job at ACSA and his dramatic claim that the commissioner of police and the ACSA CEO, Monhla Hlahla, were behind his axing had naturally made for sensational press. Soon afterwards he learned that only the most loyal of friends and business connections were prepared to associate with him. Many others simply stopped taking his calls and ignored him when they encountered him in public. In an interview shortly after he left ACSA, O'Sullivan remarked, 'I have only 10 per cent of my friends and associates left' and 'after it became clear I was heads-up against Selebi, my business interests dwindled to almost nothing'.

As he contemplated his future, O'Sullivan understood he had nothing left to lose. This wasn't some low-key criminal matter that could be settled or dealt with in an uncomplicated fashion. He knew that there had to be more to the police commissioner, and now he was determined to go the distance, all the way, no matter the cost.

His much-valued reputation was at stake and he harnessed every ounce of his considerable energy and drive to focus singlemindedly, to the exclusion of everything else.

At this early stage, the two largest targets that loomed in his cross-hairs were Monhla Hlahla and Jackie Selebi. For now, some of the other key players, Glenn Agliotti, Paul Stemmet, Brett Kebble, Clinton Nassif, Anthony Dormehl and a cast of other two-bit walk-ons, were way off the radar. But not for long.

Over at the JCI empire, Brett Kebble and John Stratton were hatching their own counter-offensive. In 2004 Kebble, with the help of Agliotti, established a 'slush fund' of around R10.7 million to finance various 'projects', mostly related to 'security' and spying on rival Mark Wellesley-Wood, Durban Roodepoort Deep's CEO.

Kebble had bought, for R350,000, a shelf company called Spring Lights, from Martin Flint, Agliotti's then fiancée's father. Money flowed into Spring Lights from various sources, including Kebble's company JCI, from Agliotti himself and from the former judge Willem Heath, who consulted for the Kebbles. Because the company had been registered in his name, Flint signed all the cheques but only on instruction from Agliotti. Flint, a chartered accountant, dutifully filled in the counterfoils in the company's chequebook. Some entries were marked 'JSGA' (Jackie Selebi/Glenn Agliotti) or simply 'JS', and these would later prove pivotal in the state's case against Selebi.

In February 2004 Paul still concentrated on trying to force a formal investigation into Selebi. But when his letter to the minister of police in November the previous year appeared to have been ignored, he made good on his threat and turned to the Johannesburg High Court.

On 30 March 2004 Paul filed case 04/2450, asking the court to compel the minister of police to conduct a proper investigation into his national commissioner. In his responding affidavit the minister breezily passed the buck, suggesting that he didn't have the power or authority to appoint a board or institute a judicial review. He also argued that the courts could not force him to do so and that he had, in the meantime, instructed the provincial commissioner Perumal Naidoo to respond to O'Sullivan's allegations 'on my behalf'.

In fact the minister, in forwarding copies of the pleadings to Selebi and his loyal supporters and ordering them to respond, had prejudiced any future 'independent' investigation by the ICD, even if the ICD were inclined to follow their mandate, which they weren't. The ICD later handed the file to Cliff Lyons, a detective sergeant from Scotland Yard, who had been sent on a busman's holiday for six months in South Africa, to help bolster the ICD's investigative capacity. O'Sullivan only met Lyons once, and his immediate perception was that Lyons 'would have been out of his depth investigating shoplifting'. Lyons later wrote that O'Sullivan was a bitter man who had an axe to grind and refused to give over the names of witnesses.

Selebi, in his answering affidavit, predictably denied that he had conducted a 'vendetta' against O'Sullivan, that he had intimidated him or had been involved in any other of the events listed in the court papers. Selebi ended with the veiled threat that he 'reserved my right to sue the Applicant [O'Sullivan] for defamation of character based on the false allegations he has levelled against me'.

André Pruis, Selebi's loyal sidekick, also hastened to his boss's defence and denied any wrongdoing. Perumal Naidoo confidently denied and countered all Paul's allegations but added a little twist, suggesting that only the president of the country, Thabo Mbeki, was authorised to conduct an inquiry into the national commissioner of police, as he had made the appointment.

In his lengthy and detailed reply O'Sullivan punched legal holes through every single argument, not only pointing out where Selebi, Naidoo and Pruis had perjured themselves, but also that the ICD had already investigated the national commissioner on other occasions (when he had called a policewoman a chimpanzee) and that the Police Act did in fact make provision for the ICD to investigate Selebi.

O'Sullivan made legal history that year when the acting High Court judge Nazeer Cassim ruled in his favour, ordering the minister of police to refer the matter to the ICD within 15 days.

In a long follow-up letter to the minister, O'Sullivan resubmitted the details of the original complaint he had sent to the ICD in 2003, setting out exactly why the national commissioner and others should be investigated. He ended the correspondence offering to help with the inquiry. 'I have a number of names of persons that may give insight into what has been going on behind the scenes, which names have to remain confidential at this stage for the protection of the individuals concerned.'

Winning this court battle brought a brief respite. O'Sullivan braced himself for round two, a lengthy dispute with ACSA for his unlawful dismissal.

By the end of 2004 it became evident to O'Sullivan that no one was going to investigate his complaints. The ICD, which had the manpower and resources to interview witnesses and piece together a case, seemed uninterested and out of its depth.

O'Sullivan kept up a steady stream of emails to the ICD for at least two years, providing leads and a list of witnesses who needed to be interviewed. He kept the prime witnesses' names secret, as he wanted to keep his powder dry; he also wanted to see how they would handle the first list provided, before entrusting them with the key witnesses. He was right to be cautious, as the ICD did not even meet with the witnesses, but elected instead to phone them and come right out and ask them if they had agreed to be a witness for O'Sullivan against Selebi. Naturally, this had the desired outcome and shut down the witnesses, while letting O'Sullivan know that the ICD was untrustworthy, if not downright dishonest. He let them have it in a barrage of emails that must have left them squirming.

In 2006, the year he began to unravel the web around Selebi, O'Sullivan regularly communicated with Tlou Kgomo, manager of the ICD's Anti-Corruption Command. In his replies Kgomo provided dozens of lame excuses as to why he was unable to follow leads or initiate any meaningful investigation. 'I read your affidavit and I realised without support from the witnesses, it will not be possible to prove any wrong doing on the part of Commissioner Selebi,' Kgomo wrote.

Almost six years after Paul had lodged his original complaint with the ICD, it was more than clear that the directorate lacked the ability, motivation and political will to investigate the country's top cop. If Selebi was to be brought down, it was up to O'Sullivan and the Scorpions.

By 2004, Bulelani Ngcuka had clearly tired of the highly public personal and political onslaught and tendered his resignation. After the findings of the Hefer Commission, Ngcuka originally came out of his corner fighting, telling journalists that 'despite personal suffering and peril, I am now more determined than ever to carry on with my job'. In July 2004 Ngcuka's spokesperson, Sipho Ngwema, explained that his boss's departure was 'for his personal growth, he has to look elsewhere, for other challenges'.

Jean Redpath, writing in a 2012 monograph on the NPA, *Failing to Prosecute? Assessing the State of the National Prosecuting Authority in South Africa*, for the Institute of Security Studies, noted that 'the number of cases prosecuted with a verdict achieved in 2003, at the peak of Ngcuka's tenure, has yet to be matched subsequently'.

Ngcuka's departure was a temporary setback for O'Sullivan. He believed at that point if there was anyone or anybody that would take his complaints seriously, it was going to be the NPA.

Meanwhile, the country's national commissioner was going places. In October 2004, at the 73rd Interpol General Assembly in Mexico, Jackie Selebi was elected president of the international policing body. Selebi had been the vice-president of Interpol's African region from 2002, and this was the first time in the organisation's history that an African had been elected to the prestigious position. It would also be the first time that an Interpol president would have to step down to face allegations of corruption.

Interpol's secretary general, Ronald Noble, welcomed the new president, saying his election 'represents an historic moment. His experience as Commissioner of Police of South Africa will be a great asset to all of Interpol's member countries.' Of course, in June that year Selebi had already accepted R10,000 from the drug-trafficker Glenn Agliotti. By December 2004, he had also, according to Agliotti's later testimony, accepted two large amounts, one of R200,000 and another of R100,000, both in cash neatly packed into large envelopes.

In an attempt to lobby support for his election to the position, Selebi had earlier wined and dined African police chiefs at a Paris restaurant. His drug-trafficking friend Glen Agliotti footed the bill, which amounted to around R30,000.

Out there in the world, Jackie Selebi seemed to be moving about with ease. And while he was most certainly aware that O'Sullivan was sniffing at his heels, he contemptuously dismissed him and seemed more than confident that he was somehow untouchable.

Meanwhile, over at JIA, it was Groundhog Day. At the end of December, a Nigerian passenger carrying a briefcase containing US dollars was abducted while leaving the airport and later found dumped in Hillbrow. It didn't surprise O'Sullivan when he later learned that an ACSA security official, Kowie Jacobs, and a police inspector, Levy Madisha, had been arrested in connection with the kidnapping. This reconfirmed to O'Sullivan that JIA was 'rotten to the core'.

Chapter 11

Coming at Ya Suckers

By 2005 O'SULLIVAN REALISED he was in deep.

Losing his ACSA job had deprived him of an income. If he was going to hunt and bring down Jackie Selebi, he would have to float the investigation himself. O'Sullivan began selling off some of the property assets he had acquired over the years. There was also the plane he owned and which he sold in late 2006 when cash started getting tight. This was, he understood, going to be the fight of a lifetime, and he was determined to let nothing get in the way.

Step one was transforming a room in his Bedfordview home into an 'operations centre'. It was here that he was to spend months holed up, attempting to join the dots. At this stage he had no idea where the journey would take him.

On one of the walls in the office he traced the outline of an organogram, a map of sorts of the country's criminal underworld, which would soon be crowded with a gallery of rogues. It began with only two names: Jackie Selebi and Monhla Hlahla. 'At that stage all I had was the tape recording on Mashudu Ramano made a week before he was arrested. One of my sources, a cop, had told me that Selebi had issued the order and that he had also been behind my firing.'

The investigator embarked then on what he termed 'low-level intelligence' missions, probing the ACSA MD's various directorships and financial interests. He believed Hlahla's behaviour clearly implicated her in the grand ACSA–Khuselani conspiracy. Apart from her attempts at revoking the legal cancellation of the Khuselani contract, there was what he believed to be her campaign of vilification and defamation aimed at sidelining him completely.

Then there was the obvious question why she had allowed André Olivier, ACSA manager, and Vernon Naidoo, its company secretary, group executive for corporate governance and chairman of the tender board, to resign (and collect golden handshakes in the process) after the forensic audit suggested they had acted unlawfully or unethically. Paul was puzzled as to why Hlahla would let both men escape the consequences of the Public Finance Management Act.

Hlahla, Paul believed, had also deliberately misled Parliament and had been in cahoots with Noel Ngwenya and Jackie Selebi in her attempt to persuade Parliament's Transport Portfolio Committee that the SAPS be made responsible for security at South Africa's airports.

Then there was the smaller matter of a complimentary trip in July 2002 to the Farnborough Air Show, fully paid for by a British aviation security equipment manufacturer. And, lastly, there was the CEO's various apparently undeclared conflicts of interest.

Hlahla soon found herself in the headlines. She tried to brush off the attention by saying that O'Sullivan was fabricating the stories and bribing journalists. When this didn't work, says O'Sullivan, Hlahla used ACSA funds 'to hire a spin doctor to personally visit various media editors to make off-the-record allegations against me in an attempt to get the editors to close their doors to my so-called "false" allegations. Her futile attempts failed.'

In April 2005 the online business publication Moneyweb posted a damning assessment of Hlahla and her management titled 'What's R850-m Between Friends?' The piece, by Julius Cobbett, had O'Sullivan's prints all over it and read:

Monhla Hlahla, managing director of the Airports Company of South Africa (ACSA), appears to be drowning in a sea of potential conflicts of interest.

Last week more than a few eyebrows were raised when Moneyweb reported that Hlahla and non-executive ACSA director Lulu Gwagwa were two of the main participants in Imperial's latest proposed BEE deal. The deal could result in the main stakeholders owning up to R110-m worth of Imperial stock. The proposed deal raised questions of potential conflicts of interest. The vast majority of Imperial's car rental business is conducted at airports. Moreover, Imperial is a major stakeholder in Tourvest, which has the concession for retail outlets in airports around the country.

The choice of cars raffled in a country-wide airports marketing campaign is perhaps also no coincidence. Any recent visitor to Johannesburg, Cape Town or Durban airport will almost certainly have noticed that patrons of the airports' retail outlets can win a Rover (less recently, the raffle car was an MG). The marketing of this campaign is visible even on ACSA parking tickets.

The campaign is conducted by the Merchants Association (MA), the official organisation of all shop owners and franchisees at Cape Town, Durban and Johannesburg International Airports. Both ACSA and Tourvest have seats on MA's 'exco'. There is little doubt that the car brands MA chooses to raffle receive good exposure from the campaign. The sole importer, distributor and retailer of MG and Rover is, yes, Imperial. Incidentally, it seems the choice of manufacturer was unfortunate: MG Rover has subsequently gone bust, leaving the lucky winner with a service dilemma.

But it appears that possible conflicts of interest are nothing new to ACSA's upper echelon. In its 2003 financial year, the state-owned monopoly spent R850-m on operating expenses. At the time, Hlahla sat on the board of at least six high-profile organisations. At least two of these were significant beneficiaries of ACSA's copious budget.

In January 2003 Hlahla was appointed to the board of Chemical

Services Limited (Chemserve) as independent non-executive director. Either directly or indirectly, a significant portion of Chemserve's revenue is sourced from ACSA. Chemserve supplies all of ACSA's aviation fire-fighting chemicals. It is also the major provider of aviation chemicals to SAA and Airport Handling Services, both of which pay rent and other fees to ACSA.

The King II report on corporate governance is unambiguous about the role of an independent non-executive director: he or she should not be 'a significant supplier to, or customer of the company or group'.

Official ex-ACSA sources claim that Hlahla failed to disclose her appointment to Chemserve to ACSA's executive committee. At the end of 2003, Hlahla resigned from the board of Chemserve, apparently on the insistence of disgruntled colleagues.

In the same year, Hlahla served as the chairman of Johannesburg Water (which buys chemicals from Chemserve). Hlahla also held – and still holds – a position as non-executive director of Air Traffic Navigation Services, the company that makes sure planes don't collide into each other.

In the 2003 year, Hlahla also served on the boards of SA Tourism; the International Marketing Council; the Airports Council International (Hlahla was appointed to the board in December 2003; she is currently vice-chairperson); and, according to the Chemserve annual report, the Institute of Retirement Funds.

There are few that would deny that Hlahla had an exhaustive brief in the 2003 year. Assuming she spent just one day a month on five of her non-executive appointments, the positions would detract 60 days from her working year.

The average work year consists of roughly 220 days. Hlahla would be left with just 160 days to run the country's airports.

Again, the King report is clear on taking on too many non-executive positions: 'Executive directors should only be encouraged to hold other non-executive directorships only to the extent that these do not interfere with their immediate management responsibilities.'

Although it is likely that Hlahla's other directorships detracted heavily from her time at ACSA, there is no evidence that she paid the remuneration she received at these positions over to her full-time employer. The remuneration was hardly negligible: Hlahla received

R75,000 for attending three Chemserve board meetings.

The person who chairs ACSA's sub-committee on corporate governance is Lulu Gwagwa, one of the beneficiaries of Imperial's proposed BEE deal.

Another corporate governance kingpin within ACSA, Vernon Naidoo, resigned from the board in July 2003 after a forensic investigation recommended that 13 charges be laid against him. At the time of his resignation, Naidoo was ACSA company secretary, group executive for corporate governance and chairman of the tender board.

Naidoo left the ACSA board with full pay and his bonus. To date, ACSA has neglected to lay any charges against Naidoo, an apparent breach of the Public Finance Management Act (PFMA).

Of course all of the above poses serious questions about the corporate governance within ACSA. As a state-owned enterprise, ACSA is required to comply with King II and the PFMA.

The 2004 annual report contains two full pages of prose dedicated to ACSA's apparent commitment to corporate governance. It is, however, silent on some of the more serious issues that occurred during the year under review, including Naidoo's resignation.

A few months later, another report appeared in the *Mail & Guardian* in which Hlahla responded that it was 'okay' for her to have a stake in two companies that were major service providers to ACSA, because her shareholding was too minuscule for it to constitute a conflict of interest.

ACSA and Hlahla attacked Moneyweb, charging that the publication had 'failed to corroborate the allegations of wrongdoing on Ms Hlahla's part as well as provide evidence as to how the organisations she is involved with have received any financial benefit from ACSA as a result of her position as Managing Director of ACSA. We are waiting, though not with bated breath, as to which friends and companies benefited "significantly" as you claim from ACSA's R850 million budget.'

Whatever the response or reaction, O'Sullivan was satisfied that Hlahla's conflicts of interest had been aired publicly. Whether anyone cared much about this was another issue entirely. There were bigger fish in the frying pan and public attention was now captivated by the in-fighting within the ANC.

On 3 August that year, Hlahla received the Businesswoman of the Year award from the Businesswomen's Association (BWA). As she accepted the accolade at a gala banquet at the Sandton Convention Centre, an armed robbery took place at a retail outlet inside JIA.

O'Sullivan learned that two of the five-person panel that voted to give Hlahla the title had benefited from dealings with ACSA and that the entire panel had ignored the fact that it's easy to make a profit when you have a monopoly, such as ACSA's. 'When profits don't look good, you just raise the landing fees and passenger taxes. Hlahla did this year after year, until the airlines just couldn't be squeezed for any more, then she just quietly slipped out the back door, leaving ACSA's finances in a shambles and heavily indebted,' said O'Sullivan.

✳

With Hlahla's personal and financial affairs now out in the open, Paul turned his attention elsewhere.

It was clear that a number of highly organised syndicates were behind much of the crime (not only at JIA) that plagued the country and that regularly made disturbing headlines. Experience had taught the investigator that where criminal syndicates flourished, it was usually due to official collusion and corruption, often in the highest echelons.

O'Sullivan began concentrating on finding irrefutable evidence of the links between the police commissioner and various crime syndicates and criminals in the country, whether they wore pinstripe suits or biker jackets. He cast out several lines of investigation, starting, as any good detective would, at the bottom of the feeding chain. The city's strip joints, nightclubs, casinos and other entertainment venues provided less imaginative criminals lower down the pecking order with ample and lucrative opportunities to intimidate and extort. These were also the twilight zones where human beings played out their shadow side, the spaces where women were trafficked and sold for sex, where drugs were peddled, where huge amounts of cash were being shuffled around far away from official scrutiny, a world where those who refused 'protection' were dealt with violently. Shoe leather would have to be burnt, O'Sullivan would have to get back out there and ferret out what he needed, without the help, support or backup from any organisation or structure.

One avenue he knew could potentially provide leads was his old network of law enforcement friends and colleagues. And while O'Sullivan was no longer in the police reserve, he still paid his annual membership subscriptions to the International Police Association and joined in their regular meetings and socials, where he felt respected. 'I went to all the social gatherings. There were all these reservists and permanent force members there and I quietly let it be known that if anyone had any information about Selebi they should get in touch with me.' O'Sullivan's networking exercise would pay off in time.

Paul, in the meantime, had equipped himself with whatever was required for this unusual solo mission: bugging devices, an extra weapon and special law enforcement software capable of finding connections that might escape human calculation.

O'Sullivan also set up surveillance of Johannesburg's nightspots, 'policed' by squads of ruthless steroid-taking 'bouncers', some employed by the lawless Elite Security Group. Vicious turf wars regularly resulted in predictable violence and the settling of scores.

For years, Elite, founded by the former boxer Mikey Schultz and six friends in 2000, regularly featured in newspaper reports. Elite had been fingered in drug-trafficking, money-laundering, racketeering and extortion, but on the whole suspects miraculously seemed to escape successful prosecution.

In 2004 and 2005 O'Sullivan spent countless nights inconspicuously hanging around Johannesburg's popular nightspots, watching who came and went and who hung out with whom. 'I took statements from nightclub owners who'd been beaten with baseball bats, I got video footage of Schultz's goons trashing venues and assaulting patrons. It was enough to use later.'

That year Mikey Schultz, wary of the headlines Elite was making after an assault outside a popular nightclub, surrendered his shares to his business partners and cut loose. It was his old carousing buddy, Clinton Nassif, who had encouraged Schultz to leave and join him in his new security venture, Central National Security Group (CNSG). Nassif had recently landed the Kebbles as his largest client and needed to beef up his manpower.

Nassif, of Lebanese extraction, grew up in the once-white, working-class suburb of Mayfair to the west of the city. He owned a vehicle scrapyard in Johannesburg, a graveyard where many hijacked vehicles in the country ended up being dismembered for spares. Sensing a lucrative gap in the 'protection and security' market, Nassif set up his own 'security company'.

Glenn Agliotti met Nassif through a mutual friend during a languid Wednesday round of golf in 2003. Nassif, Agliotti testified later, came highly recommended as 'a person involved in the security industry having very good contacts within various government organisations, including SARS'. Out on the green, Agliotti casually mentioned that he was 'consulting' for the Kebbles and that he also, coincidentally, happened to have a close friendship with the country's national commissioner of police, Jackie Selebi.

The encounter with Agliotti must have set Nassif thinking and a week later he called to set up a meeting. The two chatted over breakfast and agreed that Agliotti would hook Nassif up with the Kebbles. The Kebbles, Nassif learned, were unhappy with the 'service' Paul Stemmet's Palto had been providing.

It was John Stratton who met with Nassif and Agliotti in Cape Town and who subsequently signed on CNSG. It was the start of a highly lucrative association for the former scrap-vehicle dealer. The Kebble contract made up 90 per cent of CNSG's business and Nassif's newfound success soon found expression in a bling lifestyle, which included a fleet of hugely expensive, flashy cars.

O'Sullivan was aware that CNSG was involved in extorting money from club and restaurant owners who refused to use the security group's 'protection services'. He also suspected that CNSG was linked to other criminal networks, but, at that stage, was not quite sure how.

O'Sullivan began cultivating 'moles' and insiders, paid from his own pocket, who were part of the inner circle not only of CNSG but also in the national commissioner's office, Wachthuis, in Pretoria. By late 2005 O'Sullivan had infiltrated both organisations. 'I knew Nassif, Selebi and Pruis's every move. And then the information really started to flow in. I knew I would soon catch my goose.'

While the moles burrowed away, O'Sullivan started chasing another lead: Selebi's apparent connection to a private, multi-million-rand beach development at Uvongo, a resort on KwaZulu-Natal's south coast. The resort had been developed by the Durban-born businessman Gavin Varejes, who was in turn friendly with Andrew Phillips, owner of the 'upscale' Johannesburg brothel the Ranch and its adjoining tantalisingly named strip club, Titty Twister Go-Go Bar.

Phillips had been Varejes's intended co-purchaser of the multi-million-rand resort, but the arrangement had apparently fallen through when Phillips found himself embarrassingly accused of human trafficking, living off the proceeds of prostitution and running a brothel. Phillips would find himself caught up in an epic court battle that would only be finalised 12 years later with his acquittal.

It was Phillips who had originally been involved in arrangements for the country's police commissioner and his family to holiday at Uvongo Falls in 2000. O'Sullivan suspected that if you were the national police commissioner and you were going to holiday with dogs, you were bound to pick up fleas. 'I didn't know exactly where Uvongo Falls fitted into the picture, but I was taking all these photographs anyway,' said O'Sullivan.

A year after Selebi's first holiday jaunt to Uvongo Falls, Varejes became embroiled in a nasty legal battle with Tigon, a financial services group, which had sued Varejes and his then business partner, Tony Strike, for R210 million. Tigon claimed that Varejes and Strike had misrepresented the value of a cellular accessories company, Europoint, which they had sold to Tigon. Later, Varejes and Strike, using their connection to Selebi, convinced SARS that Tigon and its MD, Garry Porritt, had committed tax fraud amounting to around R200 million.

While O'Sullivan's organogram was growing, he was not yet finding clear links between any of the bit players and his key suspect.

Varejes would later deny that he had ever paid for Selebi's holidays and claimed he had merely enjoyed a 'social' relationship with the commissioner and that they had worked together on various 'philanthropic projects'. O'Sullivan, however, managed to secure proof that Verejes had indeed paid for and been refunded by Selebi after both men learned that the investigator was probing their relationship. O'Sullivan managed to get a copy of Selebi's cheque sent to Varejes proving this.

The corrupt links between Selebi and Varejes would be revealed much later during Selebi's trial when Agliotti provided an affidavit setting out how Xantium, a JSE-listed company, had tendered for two contracts with the SAPS. The first contract had been worth around R13 million and Selebi had requested a payment of R200,000 if the tender was awarded.

The second contract, worth R60 million, was a joint venture between Xantium and Gavin Varejes's company. Agliotti said that in this case Xantium's founder and CEO, James Murray, had given him cash 'to hold on behalf of Xantium' in order to pay bribes. 'In regard to this tender, JS did not want payment up front but insisted on a share of the contract, in the amount of 10 per cent,' said Agliotti.

In the end neither of the bidders won the tender, which was ultimately awarded to Mecer. As it turned out, and despite his assurances to the contrary, Selebi had no ability to influence the tender and was simply hoping that his horse, Xantium, would come in first and he would strike it rich.

It was during the course of O'Sullivan's investigations into Varejes that strip-club boss Lolly Jackson first began to feature in the bigger picture. Jackson, O'Sullivan discovered, had corrupted a Jo'burg City Council planning enforcement officer, Alan Wheeler, buying him several motorcycles in exchange for his turning a blind eye to planning violations at his establishments. O'Sullivan conducted a *pro bono* investigation into Wheeler on behalf of the City Council, which later resulted in Wheeler's suspension. Wheeler quickly resigned, hoping to escape criminal prosecution.

O'Sullivan, in turn, lodged a charge of corruption against Jackson and Wheeler, a case that mysteriously disappeared. The 'buying' of dockets by the accused from corrupt policemen is a well-known and seemingly entrenched habit in South Africa.

While Jackson posed no threat to O'Sullivan at the time and was not in any way directly linked to any of his investigations into Selebi, the investigator hoped that uncovering the corrupt relationship between the strip-club boss and Wheeler would render Jackson vulnerable. O'Sullivan sought to use this as leverage to extract valuable information from Jackson about key players in the Jo'burg underworld. O'Sullivan had, of course, made a copy of the corruption docket that he opened with SAPS and that had subsequently 'disappeared', and used this to convince Jackson to co-operate with him.

At the time O'Sullivan was keen to prove the links between Phillips, a fellow strip-club owner, Varejes and Selebi. He thought this would be a good starting point in proving Selebi was corrupt.

While O'Sullivan was, at the time, singlemindedly chasing leads in his Selebi investigation, the meeting with Jackson would lead later to his involvement with two equally nasty characters in the criminal underworld: Kevin Trytsman, a fake undercover NIA agent, and Czech fugitive Radovan Krejcir.

In the meantime, out of public view, various undercover state intelligence operatives were going about their business gathering information that would later be used in a range of unlawful 'campaigns', one of them being to stop Jackie Selebi from being prosecuted.

✻

Back in 2004, O'Sullivan parked the Varejes investigation and went fishing inland, on the streets of Johannesburg, where the second biggest specimen in the shark pool drifted into view.

Apart from his insider moles, O'Sullivan had also employed the services of an investigator to trail Selebi and observe his movements. 'I started to build up a picture of where he went, who he met with. I saw some of the people he met with were best described as shady characters. All the time I was building my little map on the wall,' said O'Sullivan.

Of course it didn't take long for O'Sullivan to single out the extrovert Glenn Agliotti. Overweight no doubt from too many breakfasts, lunches and suppers and dressed like a dandy whilst going about his 'business' trafficking drugs, the careless Agliotti did not suspect he was being followed. By then the commissioner and the drug lord were having regular meetings in Sandton coffee shops and often wandered around like two bros fingering merchandise at exclusive clothing boutiques. 'So now I'm focusing on Agliotti and where he fits into this picture,' said O'Sullivan.

Agliotti, O'Sullivan learned from his source inside CNSG, was somehow connected to Clinton Nassif. But how? The only way of finding out, he reckoned, was to pay the company a personal visit. In April O'Sullivan made an appointment with CNSG, posing as a potential client. A guide offered to show him around various CNSG 'projects' and clients starting with JCI House, the high-rise, downtown headquarters of Brett Kebble's Potemkin mining empire. The setup was professional, sophisticated and hugely impressive but not enough to earn the kind of money Nassif was publicly flaunting. O'Sullivan reckoned the CNSG boss had to be raking in money from other sources as well.

The next stop on the guided tour was CNSG's headquarters,

housed in a building in Selby. 'It was like an industrial car park with a suite of offices inside,' Paul recalls. The gabby guide proudly informed Paul that the company employed several cops, many of them from the notorious Murder and Robbery Unit, who were moonlighting for Nassif's company. CNSG also ran 'ops' from a special control room, and the guide bragged that the company had the capacity to pull whatever information a client might 'need' – police, phone, bank and SARS records. Paul took in the office with staff hunched over state-of-the-art technology, pecking away at keyboards.

On their way out, the guide handed O'Sullivan a glossy CNSG brochure. Paul flipped through, the guide looking over his shoulder. One of the listed directors of the company whose photograph featured in the brochure was Ntombi Matshoba, not someone O'Sullivan recognised or knew. Nodding at the picture of the young woman, the guide quipped, 'Keep it to yourself, but she's Jackie Selebi's mistress.' O'Sullivan perked up immediately. What on earth was Selebi's former secretary and romantic side-dish doing working for Nassif and how did she get there?

Back on the wall at home another face, Ntombi Matshoba, was added to the organogram, which was, by now, getting nicely crowded. There was also Brett Kebble, Clinton Nassif, Jackie Selebi, Paul Stemmet, Gavin Varejes and Glen Agliotti. But still they floated like separate atoms.

At this point O'Sullivan was playing his cards close to his chest, not sharing his information with anyone. 'From early 2005 to 2006 I didn't go near the media. I only gave them stuff on Hlahla and how security had gone belly-up at JIA. Every time there was an incident, I provided journalists with inside information. As far as Selebi was concerned, the media were completely unaware of the fact that I was gathering information.'

The investigator was already pretty sure CNSG was involved in a smorgasbord of criminal activity, including racketeering, drug-running, money-laundering, smuggling counterfeit goods and cigarettes (with police collusion), human trafficking and fiddling its taxes. 'The web was getting bigger and bigger and I realised it was probably the biggest crime syndicate in the country pushing billions of rands, and that police were in on it!' said Paul.

How to prove it all was the challenge at this point.

✳

On 31 August 2005, around 7 p.m., shortly after Stephen Mildenhall, a fund analyst with Allan Gray Associates, pulled into the driveway of his home in Cape Town, three bullets slammed into his body.

Mildenhall, who had been responsible for the Allan Gray investment portfolios, had just returned from a radio interview about a loan agreement between Investec and Brett Kebble's flailing companies JCI and Randgold and Exploration. Allan Gray had set strict conditions on the loan agreement, as it was highly likely that JCI would default. One of the conditions was that the boards of both companies be reconstituted sans Brett Kebble.

As Mildenhall alighted from his car and the electronic gate rumbled shut, he noticed two men wearing beanies emerge from a car parked outside. The men pushed their way through a side gate and cornered the analyst, demanding his wallet and keys.

The gunmen tried to force Mildenhall to leave with them and, as he backed away, fired three shots. The men fled, leaving the analyst, who survived the attack and subsequently relocated overseas, bleeding in his driveway.

In an affidavit Agliotti later claimed that he had been present at a meeting where Kebble and Stratton had instructed Nassif to 'take care' of Mildenhall, as he was creating 'problems' for JCI. Nassif, in turn, had ordered hitmen Mikey Schultz, Faizel 'Kappie' Smith and Nigel McGurk to carry out the instruction. The three men headed off on an accident-prone road trip to Cape Town, where they had hired two local thugs for R50,000.

Kebble and Stratton had been 'very happy' with their work, the shooters later confessed.

*

The same month as the Mildenhall shooting, Paul's earlier networking exercise with police colleagues paid off. A captain in the reserve at the Sandton police station called to say he thought he had something Paul could use. Aubrey Shlugman met with Paul and over coffee recounted how he and fellow officers had responded to a robbery in Morningside. A double hijacking had taken place at an upmarket complex, but the attackers had already fled. Shlugman and his colleagues accompanied the complainant to his home to begin the routine taking of statements.

Later, at Selebi's corruption trial, Shlugman would testify: 'While we were processing, an unknown white male and white female walked into the apartment. The white male, I heard him on his cell phone, obviously he was standing behind me with this white female, and he called, he said to me that "the commissioner would like to speak to you".'

Captain Shlugman had been somewhat taken aback and asked, 'Which commissioner?' to which the man replied, 'The national commissioner.'

Obeying the order, the officer took the phone and immediately recognised Selebi's voice. After the captain briefed his commissioner on the situation at the crime scene, Selebi instructed him to 'look after' his friend.

On his way out, Agliotti, who lived in the same complex where the hijacking had taken place, handed Shlugman his business card. It read 'Glen Agliotti, JCI'. As his parting shot, Agliotti couldn't help bragging, 'The commissioner is a good friend of mine. I had breakfast with him this morning in fact.'

Paul took a detailed statement from Shlugman with a quickening heart. He had found a small but highly valuable missing piece of the puzzle, which was slowing taking shape. 'It was another little nail in Selebi's coffin, and at that stage I was gathering quite a few of those,' says Paul.

Shlugman's final paragraph in the statement he dictated to Paul is revealing of Agliotti's assumption that the commissioner would always be on speed dial or that the SAPS were essentially at his beck and call. 'About two or three weeks later on a Sunday evening at approximately 21h50, I was telephoned by Agliotti and he advised me inter alia that there was a problem at the complex, that he had tried to get hold of Selebi, but that Selebi's phone was on voice mail. I advised him to call Sandton Station, which was just up the road, and he asked for the number, which I gave him.'

Chapter 12

Collateral Damage

OUTSIDE THE CRIMINAL HUNTING ground where Paul O'Sullivan was attempting to smoke out the bad guys, an altogether different kind of culling was taking place on the country's political killing fields. At the end of May 2005, Deputy President Jacob Zuma's friend and 'financial adviser', Schabir Shaik, was convicted in the Durban High Court by Judge Hilary Squires and handed two 15-year prison terms for corruption and a further three years for fraud.

The charges all related to monies 'loaned' to Jacob Zuma (bribes in essence), the writing off of money in Shaik's company's books to hide these payments to Zuma, and the brokering of a bribe for the deputy president with French arms company Thomson-CSF.

The judgment and sentencing set off a chain reaction that would tear the ruling party apart and continue to haunt it for years to come.

About two weeks afterwards, it became increasingly clear that Zuma did not regard the sentencing of his financial benefactor as an obstacle and confidently declared, 'My conscience is clear.' Even an intervention by former president Nelson Mandela urging Zuma to resign yielded no result. Zuma refused to budge.

In a live televised speech delivered to a joint sitting of Parliament, President Thabo Mbeki announced that he was constitutionally obliged to accept Judge Squires's decision and how it might impact on national politics. If he did not act, the president said, it would signal that his government was soft on corruption.

'We have had no precedent to guide us as we consider our response to the judgment by Justice Squires. We have therefore had to make our own original determination on this matter guided by what we believe is in the best interest of the Honourable Deputy President, the government, our young democratic system and our country,' President Mbeki told the nation.

He added that while he was aware that Shaik might lodge an appeal, current circumstances had dictated 'in the interests of the Honourable Deputy President, the government, our young democratic system, and our country, it would be best to release the Honourable Jacob Zuma from his responsibilities as Deputy President of the Republic and member of the Cabinet.'

Mbeki could not have dreamed that late winter's day that he had just turned the first sod of his own political grave. While Jacob Zuma was fired as the country's deputy president, he remained the deputy president of the ANC.

Behind the scenes, Jacob Zuma and his supporters began to gird their loins for the fight of a lifetime. While the wily Zuma might have been temporarily down, he was certainly far from out.

Chapter 13

Kebble Pops His Clogs

ON THE EVENING OF 27 SEPTEMBER 2005, a Tuesday, around 9 p.m., the 41-year-old Brett Kebble was shot dead as he apparently headed off to a dinner engagement with a business associate, Sello Rasethaba. At first it appeared as if several unknown gunmen had 'ambushed' Kebble, pumping seven low-velocity bullets into his ample chest while he was driving his silver Mercedes in Melrose Avenue. The tycoon's car had rolled for about 400 metres before it clipped the pavement and came to a standstill after crashing into a railing on a bridge crossing the M1. Kebble's bloodied corpse lay slumped in the driver's seat for over two hours as police swamped the scene.

It was a sensational murder, one of the country's leading, albeit troubled, businessmen cut down in a hail of bullets on his way to dinner. The motive for the killing was not immediately evident. It appeared as if nothing had been taken. The full lurid details of Brett Kebble's 'assisted suicide' were only to emerge much, much later when Glen Agliotti was arrested for the murder in November 2006.

The crime scene on the night of the murder was chaotic as various interested parties descended on it. Even worse, police left the site entirely unattended a mere five hours after the killing, allowing journalists, curious onlookers and passers-by to contaminate whatever evidence might have been available.

A day after the killing, Kebble's car was towed by a private company from the Norwood premises of the SAPS Serious and Violent Crime Unit to Danmar panel-beaters, owned by Mike Groenewald, brother-in-law of Mikey Schultz. The car was parked in the Danmar yard where various 'interested parties' poked around and cleaned it up. It was booked out eight days later by Captain Johan 'Dick' Diedericks, the new investigating officer who had been assigned to the case. It later emerged that Diedericks was the brother of one of the cops who had been moonlighting with Nassif's company CNSG. The pair were colloquially known as Big Dick and Little Dick.

Roger Kebble, who had been travelling abroad when his son was murdered, appointed his own investigators: Professor Jan Botha, a forensic pathologist, and Dr David Klatzow, a renowned Cape Town forensic specialist. Former judge Willem Heath, who was already on the Kebbles' payroll, was also roped in. Selebi later ordered Kebble Snr to call off his private experts and warned that if he didn't, police would back off from the investigation.

It might not have been a bad option, as the Selebi-led SAPS investigation of the Kebble murder was like an episode of the Keystone Cops, the bumbling policemen in the early-20th-century silent movie comedies. Klatzow, never one to mince words, told a journalist that it was 'one of the most appalling police investigations I have had the misfortune to be involved in'.

It was little wonder then that the SAPS kept a low profile, as wild speculation and rumours of a conspiracy surrounding Kebble's murder circulated in the popular press.

Brett Kebble's murder was to stir up a hornet's nest that would eventually draw in the Scorpions and lead them inadvertently one step closer to investigating and exposing Jackie Selebi.

✳

About a month after the murder, on 23 October 2005, O'Sullivan sat down with one of his moles inside CNSG, an informant called 'CS', or Casual Source. He took notes that were astounding in their detail and revealed the scope and extent of criminal involvement and just how deep its roots were.

The full, unedited statement makes for riveting reading and is reproduced here for your edification and delight.

STRICTLY PRIVATE AND CONFIDENTIAL
Interview notes

Interview with a casual source 'CS', who met with writer on 23-10-05 and provided certain information.

Notes were taken verbatim at the time of interview and typed later the same day by the writer.

SUBJECT Kebble Murder [Clinton Ronald Nassif 'CRN', Central National Security 'CNS' & Jackie Selebi 'JS']

CSCS says CRN is involved with some gangsters and that they plan hits and intimidate club owners to get what they want, names Mikey Schultz, Nigel McGurk. CS says McGurk shot a guy at The Glen shopping centre. CS says they (Nassif, Schultz & McGurk) own brothels, or clubs that front for brothels, named 2, being Prive Club in Bedfordview, Camelot near Hyde Park, also said that they sometimes go on Friday to The Lounge in Sandton, where they run up a big bill and don't pay it, as they have intimidated the owner who is too scared to make them pay.

CS says Glen Agliotti 'GA' is a friend and business partner of CRN and also a friend of JS. CS says that they (all 3) own a place in Midrand called Mavericks and that every two weeks or so, a large amount of cash is picked up from Mavericks and dropped off at Standard Bank Southdale. Says the Bank Mgr, a certain ...., arranges to bypass the FICA rules and banks the cash clean, the cash is said to be proceeds of drug deals and normally is between R1m & R2m. Says the bank manager has left Standard Bank and now works directly for CRN, but still has friends inside the bank and pays them to 'launder' the money and 'ignore' the FICA rules.

CS says every month CRN and GA go to London where they stash money in bank accounts there and money for Selebi is kept there too. Selebi arranges for them to get the money out through the Airport (Jo'Burg), where he has people placed that can arrange for it to happen. Someone called Shabalala.

CS says Henry Beukes, ex Murder & Robbery cop, works for CRN and gets all the information he needs on cases they work, by getting it from serving cops. CS says Beukes was laid off for medical reasons and Selebi knows he is working at CNS and made sure he got the 'boarding' ticket. This is a right to get an early pension.

CS says there is also a Captain ...., who is currently (and for some time) on suspension from the SAPS and works for CNS and is the 'middle man' between CNS and the SAPS, in terms of getting 'stuff' from the SAPS computers and, because of the links with Serious & Violent Crime Unit, 'stuff' that normal cops can't get. Says they (CNS) get work to do and charges clients for it and the cops do all the work and can't even do their own work they have so much to do.

CS says there is an André Burger, ex Serious & Violent Crime Unit, ex Brixton Murder & Robbery Unit, who heads up all CNS investigations, which includes lots of investigations for Brett Kebble & family and Burger gets anything they want and can even arrange, via other cops and Selebi, for people to be arrested.

CS says the main typist to CNS is a certain .... She types everything and each night the hard drive is removed from her computer and locked away. If they suspect that someone might raid the place, such as Scorpions etc, they will take out the hard drive and remove it from site.

Christine Duvenhage is CRN's PA and the same rules apply to her hard drive on the computer. They are paranoid about being raided and often do an exercise to see if they can 'clean up' in less than two minutes.

CS says there is a ...., who has links to the State Prosecutors (together with ....) and is able to 'buy' any case to be 'dropped' so that people get off the hook, for example the guys at 'Elite' who keep getting into trouble and he has to sort things out for them. This guy has an office at .... Road, Isando, where he keeps details of all the cases and what he's done for CNS and CRN. He also has a man at SARS, someone called 'Andrew' last name unknown to CS, who arranges all the PAYE for the guys so that no-one has to pay anything to SARS. This Andrew is on the 'payroll'.

CS says that Selebi has a stake in CNS through a black female by the name of Ntombi, who is really Selebi's 'girlfriend' or 'mistress' and is the 'BEE' component of CNS. CS says he overheard Ntombi on the phone with Selebi many times and also heard her threatening an unknown party with words like 'Listen, the commissioner will be back in South Africa next week and if you don't pay by then, you will have to deal with him'. CS says he assumed this to be Selebi, as he knew the arrangements with her.

The panel beaters, Dan Mar Auto, is owned by Mike Groenwald, who is Mikey Schultz's brother-in-law. Mikey was really the one that arranged for the car (Kebble's car) to go there and it was decided to say it was the police and that CRN took it back, when it was in fact Mikey Schultz that arranged everything and even knew in advance what was going on.

CS says Roger Kebble arranged for his sons (Guy & Brett) to be followed and Guy arranged for Brett to be followed and Brett arranged for Guy to be followed and that none of them trusted the others. They also did telephone taps and got cell-phone records, not just on the Kebbles, but on others as well.

CS says there is a company called .... (Pty) Limited, in Springfield or near or in the old Putco Bus depot and that there is a steel cabinet that was moved there after Kebble was shot and this cabinet contains all the details of all the secret information CNS obtained, such as phone taps etc.

It also contains MTN/Vodacom stuff which will show that Kebble was checking up on various people and that CNS and the SAPS were doing all the Intelligence gathering.

CS says there was an explosion at Harmony mine that was 'arranged' so that Kebble could buy it. Also says Kebble wanted 'Skeet' or 'Skeat' out of the way, also wanted Mark Welsley Wood out of the way and that Clint Nassif 'arranged' through Selebi for Wood to be arrested and that he (CRN and JS) got a big payout for doing that.

CS says there was a company called JCI Resources, and .... used to work for South African Secret Service before he went there. There was also a guy called ...., who is a big friend of CRN and some 30 or 40 Million Rand went missing and Brett Kebble asked CNS together with Gobodo Forensics to do an investigation and the investigation found that Brett Kebble had taken the money and was also involved in serious tax fraud and Brett said he was just trying to find out how good they (CNS) were and that they could forget the investigation.

CS says that everyone who did the investigation got big cash 'payout' for keeping quiet.

Brett Kebble also arranged for under-cover surveillance on all directors of JCI and CNS did the work using cops and others.

CRN wanted to get weapons up to Angola (Namaqua Diamonds). .... was used to help organise it, together with JS. CS says .... used to work inside CNS and he had been put there by JS, to look after his interests. This changed when Ntombi came on the scene, as Nico could not be a BEE person.

CRN allegedly told the CS and others that JS said they (CNS) should put together a large group of well-trained operators and go up to the Sudan and that he (JS) would arrange for all the protocols to be approved up front so they wouldn't have any trouble. This deal was cancelled because JS said he was being watched and it would have to wait.

CS says that large volumes of drugs are being moved at the clubs by the Elite guys, and the cash goes through CNS banks, and via Mavericks.

CS says advocate .... also helped .... to screw ABSA bank by divorcing him from his wife. It is a 'paper' divorce only and that everything is in Beukes' wife's name so the bank can't get it.

CS says that firearm control is a big problem. Says that they use someone to get firearms in someone else's name and they are issued to untrained personnel.

The interview lasted about one hour.

Follow-up interview on 19-11-05

CS says there is a Close Corporation called Universal Technical Enterprises cc, which is 'owned' by Selebi, but he uses other cops to be his front for him. That they receive vast sums of money from the government funds, for providing the SAPS with surveillance technology.

This cc is based in Pretoria and Selebi also uses it to carry out surveillance on political enemies and personal enemies and rents out the services to others he is connected with, for example, Sandy Majali paid Selebi big money to use Universal Technical Enterprises to do some work for him (Majali) in connection with court cases he has with some reporters from either the *Sunday Times* or the *Mail & Guardian*.

CS says that Nassif provides Selebi with personal security at Police Headquarters and at his house, but the State pays for it.

Says there is a link between Agliotti, Nassif and some guy called 'George', a Yugoslavian guy who used to work for Andrew Phillips as a casino manager and now runs the private lounge at Gold Reef City, where he helps launder money for some of the guys in the group. Says Agliotti bought George a luxury car.

CS says that Selebi has taken steps to ensure that all his contacts and business associates change their phones to MTN, as Selebi has friends inside MTN that will 'wipe clean' all incoming and outgoing call records, thereby ensuring that no-one can ever get evidence of the deals they are doing and who they are dealing with. He got Agliotti, Ntombi, Schaefer and many others to change to MTN.

The interview lasted 15 minutes.

✳

Brett Kebble's murder or 'assisted suicide' was a turning point for so many individuals and organisations orbiting this modern-day criminal Svengali. People like Selebi, Agliotti and Nassif, organisations like the ANC Youth League and young politicians like Fikile Mbalula were now cast adrift upon a changing, rocky shore.

It was also the moment that a corner of the scrim concealing the nefarious deeds of the country's rich, powerful and corrupt was momentarily lifted.

Meanwhile, over at Paul's old stomping ground, JIA, nothing had changed. In October 2005, around a thousand passengers found themselves trapped inside the terminal for an hour while a shootout between police and armed robbers raged outside. The robbers eventually fled through a hole they had cut in the perimeter fence, leaving a cop fighting for his life and without the booty that was waiting to be loaded onto a KLM flight.

Chapter 14

And They All
Came Tumbling
Down

SOMETIME IN NOVEMBER 2005 Paul O'Sullivan sent an anonymous, 'top secret' letter to Charin de Beer, who was, at the time, director of public prosecutions for the Witwatersrand Local Division. Deliberate red-herrings were slipped into the note, to suggest that it could not have come from O'Sullivan. However, the crux of the allegations obtained from 'CS' was also included.

De Beer had made headlines that year as the lead prosecutor in the Jacob Zuma rape trial and was known for her uncompromising cross-examination of the accused.

While O'Sullivan had already met with the senior Scorpions investigators Herbie Heap, and Ivor Powell, he wanted to ensure that the explosive revelations in the 'CS' tip-off notes were seen and noted by people higher up in the hierarchy. When O'Sullivan originally met Heap, much of the evidence he had secured was still circumstantial. But the disclosures by 'CS' altered matters significantly.

Prior to Paul's letter, De Beer and her deputy, Gerrit Roberts, had met with Captain Diedericks, who was heading the Kebble murder investigation. Diedericks explained to De Beer and Roberts that cell phone companies were refusing to release records of calls between various suspects and the victim on the night of the shooting.

The national commissioner's number, he told them, had shown up, and investigators were keen to obtain billing records. Diedericks hoped De Beer could help with the matter. Cell phone service providers then generally kept records for a few months, and in relation to the Kebble matter time was running out. Soon, all cell phone activity on the night of his murder would be erased.

Diedericks recounted to De Beer a peculiar meeting between Selebi and other top cops at his head office in November 2005, two months after Kebble's murder. The meeting was supposedly convened to discuss police progress on the case. At that meeting, the SAPS forensic investigator Paula Roeland, along with her supervisor, Sharon Schutte, explained that they had been trying to map cell phone calls made around the time and scene of the murder. Roeland plotted that Kebble and Agliotti had definitely spoken to each other at least seven times on 26 September, the night before the murder, but that Agliotti's phone appeared to have been switched off on the day of the killing.

Roeland, testifying later at Selebi's corruption trial, recalled that there had been speculation that Agliotti might have had more than one cell phone and that they had needed to determine whether this was the case. In the course of the discussion the name of a police reservist who had been at the scene of the murder popped up. The police commissioner suddenly whipped out his cell phone, tapped out a number and then said, 'Hello, Glenn, what is that story you told me about the reservist?'

Taken aback, Roeland asked Selebi whether he had just spoken to Glenn Agliotti, a question he simply ignored. She then asked if the commissioner could give her Agliotti's number, to which he curtly replied, 'I don't know numbers.'

After the meeting De Beer wrote to Gerrie Nel, Gauteng head of the Scorpions, asking for his help in urgently retrieving the cell phone records before they were erased. She also attached Paul O'Sullivan's anonymous letter. The two together made an interesting starting point.

The Scorpions had, of course, been aware for quite some time of allegations that Selebi was crooked. Journalists like Sam Sole and Adriaan Basson of the *Mail & Guardian*'s investigative unit, amaBhungane, as well as Kashiefa Ajam of the *Saturday Star*, had also been probing the criminal underworld and Jackie Selebi's connections and reports appeared regularly in the press.

It was inevitable that all roads would sooner or later lead to Selebi. But in early 2006 the journey was just beginning. It was to be sidetracked, for a while, by the Kebble murder and investigation.

For O'Sullivan, the real risk at that point was that his crucial statements and evidence might end up in Selebi's hands. Witnesses, sources and carefully cultivated moles would be vulnerable. And who knew what might happen, as Nassif's CNSG thugs were certainly not averse to indulging in a bit of kneecap crushing, a shooting or even murder?

De Beer and Roberts arranged for a meeting with the National Prosecuting Authority's new director of public prosecutions, Vusi Pikoli, as well as other senior Scorpions staff. Pikoli, a lawyer and former activist who had received military training in Angola, had been a deputy director general and director general in the Department of Justice before his appointment in February 2005. The chair had been kept warm by the former prosecutor and magistrate Silas Ramaite for a year after Bulelani Ngcuka's resignation.

At the meeting De Beer requested that the Scorpions take over the investigation into Kebble's murder in the light of Commissioner Selebi's unusual behaviour at the meeting about cell phone records and the fact that his number had popped up along with Agliotti's during the SAPS investigation. Captain Diedericks, meanwhile, had suddenly been removed from the investigation soon after he requested De Beer's help. Speculation at the time was that he had begun to ask too many uncomfortable questions about his national commissioner.

*

It was evident that Brett Kebble's murder was part of a much bigger complex picture. Somewhere, the thieving tycoon's life and crimes intersected with a thriving and dangerous criminal underworld, which, in turn, doubled back to Jackie Selebi.

In March 2006 the Scorpions made a major breakthrough.

Nassif, in the meantime, had been tipped off that there was a mole in the organisation who was supplying information to someone called Paul O'Sullivan, who was chasing Selebi. Nassif immediately commenced a hunt for the mole and CS warned O'Sullivan that they were looking for him. O'Sullivan, realising that cell phone communication could be traced, found a phone booth and called Agliotti. Disguising his voice, he warned the drug lord, 'Glenn, it's a friend, but I cannot tell you who I am. I wanted you to know that Paul Stemmet is giving information out about what's going on and he's trying to finger you for all sorts of crimes – take care.' Then O'Sullivan hung up.

It was the only way, says O'Sullivan, to steer the heat away from his inside man. He says he also knew that Agliotti, while possessed of the gift of the gab, 'had very low intelligence and would not cotton on to what was going on'. The plan worked.

By now feeling threatened himself, Paul Stemmet, owner of Palto and once Brett Kebble's and Jackie Selebi's go-to guy, stepped out of the shadows and offered to provide a statement that would blow the lid off a range of illegal activities. Stemmet wasn't coming clean because of a sudden road to Damascus moment. The former body-builder had made a tidy little fortune as a police-informant-cum-criminal but had been angered when Selebi 'deregistered' him and accused him of 'embellishing the truth'.

Paul's ploy had also turned up the heat, especially now with Nassif hunting for the leak. Stemmet had also caught the scent that the Scorpions were circling and had moved quickly to save his own skin, offering to spill all the beans for a section 204 indemnity from prosecution.

Says O'Sullivan: 'The early dominoes to fall are the ones that get off the hook and Stemmet probably knew it was time to talk, or face the music. He later had the cheek to pass a message to me that I would get people killed. Him! The one that had tossed grenades and robbed people at gun-point.'

O'Sullivan knew Stemmet was deeply corrupt and recounts a story to indicate 'just how low Stemmet could stoop'. 'A friend of mine, who was a captain in the Gold and Diamond Branch, set up a sting on a jeweller who wanted to buy diamonds. He booked the diamonds out from De Beers, who always assisted in such stings, and set up the operation. The jeweller would be buying from two warrant officers, who were unarmed and working under cover. My friend was waiting nearby with ten cops, when Stemmet rocked up with some cops in uniform from Highway Patrol and bust the undercover guys and the jeweller and took them back to Sandton police station. It happened so quickly that Paul's friend was left standing there and had to give chase.

'When he got to Sandton, Stemmet had already booked the diamonds into the SAP13 [evidence store]. My friend then asked Stemmet why he had interfered in a properly authorised sting and had arrested his men. Stemmet, who was a reservist and had not even booked on duty, and in any event did not serve at Sandton, said he was free to do these things, as he worked right out of Selebi's office. When my friend took the diamonds out of the SAP13, he immediately realised they were fake – just bits of glass. He then searched Stemmet and found the real diamonds in his pocket. He arrested him and booked Stemmet's firearm into the SAP13 along with the fake diamonds. A few months later, Selebi instructed

Bushy Engelbrecht to try and persuade my friend to consent to Stemmet getting his gun back. My friend refused, saying he was a criminal and a danger to society. Rank was pulled, and the firearm was sent back to headquarters on Selebi's instructions and handed back to Stemmet.'

The story, says O'Sullivan, illustrates perfectly how brazenly some of the corrupt characters had infiltrated the SAPS and the reserve force under Selebi's watch.

Before Stemmet washed up, all the Scorpions had were the phone records from the night Kebble was murdered, proving that Agliotti had called Selebi. They also had O'Sullivan's organogram linking various names and syndicates but still with no concrete evidence that would withstand the test of a courtroom.

Offering Stemmet indemnity was part of a long-term vision for the Scorpions. They hoped that the relatively smaller cogs in the wheel, like Stemmet, would sell out some of the bigger wheels and that there'd be a knock-on effect. This was also O'Sullivan's strategy.

Stemmet ratted on Glenn Agliotti, including his role in the Kya Sands Mandrax bust. He also implicated Selebi and came clean about the trafficking of counterfeit goods and drugs. Stemmet's confession was exactly what the Scorpions needed to register a formal investigation, ostensibly into the murder of Brett Kebble, but with the understanding that the investigation's reach could possibly stretch as far as Wachthuis.

The Scorpions met with Vusi Pikoli and presented him with the startling evidence. The Scorpions head, Leonard McCarthy, would describe the investigation as 'one of the most extensive and complex and sensitive investigations that the DSO has ever undertaken. The investigation focuses on drug-dealing, racketeering, money-laundering, corruption and murder.' In the background there is no doubt that O'Sullivan was tipping the dominoes in the direction of the Scorpions.

As it was a matter of national importance, Pikoli consulted with the then minister of justice, Brigitte Mabandla, as well as President

Thabo Mbeki, who were both fully briefed. We can only speculate as to what might have gone through Mbeki's and Pikoli's minds at the time, as the two men, both members of the ANC, had had dealings with Jackie Selebi and knew him well.

Initially, Mbeki and Pikoli would find it difficult to grasp the nature and extent of the allegations of Selebi's criminality. Much later, though, as the situation worsened for Selebi, the two men would find themselves on opposing sides, Mbeki attempting to protect his old friend, Pikoli determined to arrest him.

But in March 2006, when Operation Bad Guys was formally registered, no one could have foreseen that particular head-on collision on the bumpy road ahead.

While O'Sullivan's letter to Charin de Beer came from an 'anonymous' source, the Scorpions had been aware of his private investigations. He had tried to contact them but had met with cautious resistance and disbelief.

After Stemmet's statement, the Scorpions investigator Robyn Plitt immediately contacted O'Sullivan, clearly needing to compare notes. The two met for a lengthy coffee session in Sandton where Plitt confided that she was also investigating 'the missing Kebble millions' and that names in that case had seemed to pop up in his (O'Sullivan's) investigations.

In subsequent meetings, all at coffee shops, O'Sullivan delivered to Plitt Captain Aubrey Shlugman, to whom Agliotti had bragged that he was a good friend of the commissioner's. O'Sullivan mentioned to Plitt that he had also 'recovered information' from a reliable source that Agliotti, Paul Stemmet and police inspector .... had been involved in the smuggling of drugs, counterfeit goods and cigarettes. While he still needed proof, he was certain he would soon obtain it.

A name popped up, Anthony Dormehl, the driver who had been involved in the Kya Sands Mandrax bust. O'Sullivan recognised

Dormehl as someone he had dealt with in the past and undertook to track him down. He had, he says, also infiltrated Agliotti's organisation (as well as Selebi's office at that stage) and tapped this source for Dormehl's whereabouts.

'I met with his father, who was a pastor, told him what his son was up to and convinced him to persuade him to come to the house, which he did,' O'Sullivan recalls. The two men sat talking until after midnight. By the time O'Sullivan left, Dormehl had agreed to come clean and tell O'Sullivan everything he knew. They spent the next three days together, reconstructing Dormehl's activities over the previous few years, driving to various warehouses, taking photographs and mapping out events.

O'Sullivan was not only about to deliver, on a plate, one of the most valuable witnesses in the Scorpions' Operation Bad Guys, but threw in an added extra – a R250 million hashish bust and the kingpin at the centre of one of the biggest criminal syndicates in the country – Glenn Agliotti aka the Landlord.

Chapter 15

Operation Coffee

2006 WAS A BRILLIANT YEAR FOR the Scorpions but a rather trying one for the former deputy president Jacob Zuma. In March 2006, just as the Scorpions were beginning to make significant breakthroughs in the Operation Bad Guys investigation, Jacob Zuma found himself in the dock of the Johannesburg High Court on a rape charge that had originally been filed in late December 2005. That morning he pleaded 'not guilty' to raping the 31-year-old, HIV-positive daughter of an old friend and comrade at his home in Johannesburg in November 2005.

Charin de Beer would be tasked with cross-examining Zuma, and for several months the country was spellbound by sordid and sensational statements which the accused would make from the dock, including that he had taken a shower after having sex with the HIV-positive complainant as a form of protection. The intimate workings of Zuma's mind as a Zulu patriarch would also be laid bare as he claimed what was tantamount to a cultural duty to satisfy a woman who he believed had been aroused.

While the country's feminists were horrified by Zuma's sentiments and views on sex, the charges and the trial were to unleash the 'Zunami' of support for Zuma. The former deputy president was portrayed by supporters as a 'victim' of a purge by the ruthless Thabo Mbeki, who was determined to run for a third term as the country's president.

There were chaotic scenes outside the courtroom as supporters burned effigies of the rape victim and declared their undying support for the '100 percent Zuluboy'. (Zuma was acquitted on the charge in May 2006, removing the first obstacle to his comeback. He would soon find others along the way.)

In April 2006, Jackie Selebi, president of Interpol, travelled to Indonesia for the 19th Interpol Asian Regional Conference in Jakarta. In his opening address Selebi confidently told fellow law-enforcement colleagues, 'Interpol believes that corruption diminishes the ability of law enforcement agencies to accomplish their mission and hinders the efficient and fair functioning of society.'

Colleagues at the conference could not have known that the South African national police commissioner was addressing them in a fetching suit bought for him by a drug-trafficker, Glenn Agliotti.

'Corruption is one of the major obstacles in a successful campaign against transnational crime and terrorism,' a poker-faced Selebi told fellow police officers, adding, 'As transnational crimes, and particularly terrorism, can be facilitated by police corruption, a corrupt law enforcement officer obstructs the pursuit of justice and, as a result, renders law enforcement ineffective.'

Selebi was apparently so keen to root out police corruption that he returned to South Africa and immediately began lobbying for the disbandment of the SAPS Independent Complaints Directorate, claiming it had 'outlived its usefulness'. The commissioner had already shut down the police's Anti-Corruption Unit in 2002.

Meanwhile, the men who worked against each other in

the shadows continued to beaver away. In 2006 the Scorpions investigator Ivor Powell was in the process of compiling the controversial and 'top secret' Browse Mole report, which would later be leaked in 2007 in the run-up to the ANC's elective conference due to take place in Polokwane in December. The report exposed an alleged clandestine conspiracy involving African leaders and their possible military support for Jacob Zuma and his bid to 'topple' President Thabo Mbeki. The NPA and the Scorpions were also accused of straying from their mandate, abusing resources, spying on politicians and gaining information illegally.

The plot was not only thickening, it was soon going to bubble its way right out of the pot. And the kitchen was in Polokwane.

Away from the clamour in the streets of Johannesburg and the Zuma rape acquittal, the Scorpions and O'Sullivan were plotting the sting of the year, courtesy of Anthony Dormehl.

'I started working very closely with the Scorpions,' Paul recalls. 'In the past it had been difficult to get hold of them; now they took my calls, they listened to me a lot more, they were taking statements working out who they could trust and who they couldn't.'

Dormehl's statement is best read as is, because it provides insight not only into the *modus operandi* of the drug-traffickers but also into O'Sullivan's statement-taking techniques.

Capturing the 'peculiarities' of a witness's own voice or turn of phrase makes for a much more credible and less contestable version of events that are difficult to dispute later.

ANTHONY DORMEHL states under oath in English
I am an adult male, with details known to the investigation team. From 1997 until mid-2003, I managed a transport company known as Premium Transport, which was situated in Petit, Benoni.

2

During this period I met a person known to me as Glenn Agliotti. He was introduced to me by a woman known as Dianne. I used to transport goods for Dianne who claimed she did imports and forwarding.

3

The introduction was done telephonically. I was not informed what type of business Glenn Agliotti was involved in. I assumed that he was also involved in clearing and forwarding.

4

After the telephonic introduction, Glenn Agliotti would phone me, with instructions to go and load a consignment mostly at a 'Bond Store'. In my understanding a 'Bond Store' is a place where imported goods must remain until all duties are paid and the goods cleared by SARS.

5

During 1998 and 1999 Glenn phoned and said that some guys needed space in my warehouse and that I must co-operate with them.

6

Shortly after this phone call, I received a phone call from a person who introduced himself just as Steve. He also informed me that he is the guy that Glenn phoned me about. Steve did not say what his surname was, at that time.

7

Steve made an appointment and came to my premises, to view my store. He was accompanied by two persons. The one was introduced to me as Bob, who had an American accent. I later learned he was Canadian. The other person's name I cannot recall.

8

After this meeting a business relationship developed between us. I also learned that Steve's surname was Paparas. He gave me a business card with the name on, which I have passed on to Robyn Plitt of the Scorpions.

9

In August 2005, Glenn Agliotti phoned and asked me to move a container load of gas stoves and store it. Glenn knew that I was no longer in the transport business and I do not have storage place. I however offered to assist Glenn in moving the stoves and supervising it. No further contact with Glenn was made, but Steve called requesting labourers to help offload the truck with stoves, because they had arranged their own truck. Glenn did not say where the stoves were kept. A day or two later I took some labourers to Steve's father's plot at Endicott, near Springs. His father's name is Jimmy, whom I met when I started to transport and store goods for Steve. David Moloi and Andries Nchunu were amongst the labourers that assisted me to offload the truck. The others I cannot recall.

10

We arrived at Jimmy's plot ±10 minutes before the truck arrived. When the truck arrived, we off loaded ±100 gas stoves that were sealed in boxes with strapping around. According to Steve, who at that stage was not present, the stoves were from 'IRAN'. The name 'TEHERAN' was visible on the outside of the boxes. Only Jimmy Paparas and his gardener Johannes were present. The truck was driven by two unknown white males. The stoves were carried into the house, which was basically used as a storeroom. My worker, David, mentioned that some of the stoves were heavier than others. At that stage I thought some of the stoves had 5 plates and others 4 plates. After offloading we left. None of the stoves were opened in my presence.

11

In late August 2005, Steve informed me that the 'Landlord', this is a slang name for Glenn Agliotti, wanted me to do a delivery of 5 stoves to Pietermaritzburg. He also said that this would be a test run and 'if it works we will all be smiling'. I did not know what Steve meant, but I needed the money.

12

On Tuesday 25 August 2005, I loaded 5 stoves at the plot at Endicott, onto the Isuzu KB280 bakkie belonging to Premium Transport, where Jimmy Paparas and Johannes assisted me in the loading. I then parked the vehicle at my house and left early the next morning for Pietermaritzburg to deliver the stoves to a person whose details were given to me telephonically by Steve Paparas. Steve supplied me with a cell number and the name Lee. I was told to phone Lee when I arrived at a place called Van's Hotel, which is situated next to the N3 Highway at the Ixopo / Idube racetrack turn-off. When I arrived at the hotel, I called the number. I cannot recall the number, but it was a cell phone number.

13

I could not get hold of Lee. I phoned Steve but he was not available. I then called Glenn Agliotti on one of his cell phone numbers, ..., ... or ...., and informed him that I cannot get hold of Lee. Glenn said that I must be patient and that Steve would call me in a few minutes.

14

Shortly after, Steve phoned and informed me that he will get hold of Lee. After about half an hour, two white males arrived, also in a white 280 Isuzu bakkie. One of the guys came to me and introduced himself to me as Lee. We exchanged car keys and they left. I waited in the hotel. They arrived back just over an hour later. We again exchanged keys and they left. I did not receive any payment from Lee.

15

In the period that I had to wait for them, I opened the cubbyhole of their dirty, dusty vehicle. Inside I found plenty of receipts, one of which was for chicken feed. Lee was ±2 metres tall, well built with huge hands and very bad broken teeth.

16

I returned the same day. Shortly before I arrived home, Steve called to find out if everything was okay. I replied that I was almost in Benoni. He also informed me that I will receive my payment in a day or two. Steve paid me R4,500-00 personally in cash.

17

A week or two later Steve Paparas called and wanted to meet at JTT. This is a truck repair company in Jet Park where Steve is allegedly a share owner/partner. Steve asked me to get a quote on truck rims, brake shoes, pallets, hire of a forklift and rolls of plastic etc that would be used to export a 6m container for Bob.

18

A few days later after I worked out a quote, I showed it to Steve. He then said that I must take the quote to Bob at the 'Don' hotel in Sandton and collect the money, which I did.

19

I met Bob at the Don and gave him the quote. Bob then gave me R70,000-00 in cash, which I took home. The following day I met Steve at JTT and he told me that he only wants half of the R 70,000-00. I took the other half of the money. Steve then told me he had a plan, and instructed me to phone Bob, and say that I had been speaking to the 'Landlord' and that I had accidentally mentioned Bob's name. As previously mentioned Glenn Agliotti is known as the Landlord.

20

I was also told to say that Agliotti went mad and shouted to me, 'which Bob, which Bob, the tall bastard from Canada, is he in the country? Where is the bastard staying? He owes me money.'

21

I then phoned Bob and informed him what Steve instructed me to do. I do not recall Bob's shocked reply. The phone call was ended.

22

A few days later Steve informed me that he had told Bob that Agliotti had taken the R70,000-00 and the rest of the 'stuff' and that Bob had run away, for fear of the 'Landlord' finding his whereabouts. I did not know what Steve meant when he used the word 'stuff'.

23

Shortly after this, Steve told me that I must go to his father's plot at Endicott and collect all the boxes that were there, which I did. I loaded ±70 boxes and took them to my storeroom. The boxes were STOCK 5 double-walled and were sealed with buff tape. I could see into some of the boxes and noted there were double vacuum-sealed packages, orange in colour, marked as 250 grams coffee. There was no coffee smell from the packages. I noticed the weight of the box was heavier than described on the packages.

24

At some stage I met Steve at JTT on his request. Steve wanted to know if I knew what the contents of the boxes were. I informed him that I do not know, but it is not what was written on the package. Steve then said that it was a drug known as hashish. According to Steve the contents of the boxes originated from the ovens of the stoves, which were delivered at his father's plot.

25

In or about the end September, beginning October 2005, Steve asked me to deliver another consignment to Lee. He told me that I must load ±13 boxes containing the hashish and transport them to Lee. I did this with my Opel Corsa bakkie. I again met Lee at Van's hotel where we exchanged car keys. I waited in the pub when an unknown person approached me and asked me, 'how many did you bring down this time.' I then realized that this person was the same unknown male who accompanied Lee on our first meeting. Steve Paparas paid me cash again for this trip, I recall it was in Euro's and was a EU500 note. This money was paid to me at Modderfontein, he was driving a 330ci BMW, white in colour.

26

This person was ±1.90 metres tall, also well built in his early 30's and spoke English. I did not entertain his question and he left. Shortly after, Lee arrived back. I noticed that my spare wheel, which I used to cover the boxes, was not back on the bakkie. I confronted Lee and he undertook to return my spare wheel. I then decided to visit a friend in Durban and I departed from Van's hotel towards Durban. My bakkie's engine gave problems as I entered Durban. When I stopped I noticed a lot of oil leaking from the engine. I had to repair the vehicle and spent ±4 days in Durban. When I arrived back from Durban, Glenn informed me that my spare wheel was dropped at Avis Car Rental in Sandton. Glenn told me that Patrick, the guy Glenn asked me to arrange the wooden furniture storage pallets for, had dropped my spare there. I later collected it from Avis Sandton.

27

Subsequent to this Steve phoned me and said that he had done a deal with Bob. The deal was that Bob will get half of his hashish to sell so that he could pay off his existing debt to the Landlord. I was told to load about 30 boxes of hashish that was still in my store. A meeting was set up to meet Bob at the Wimpy, East Rand Mall, near the movie entertainment entrance. I arrived at the Wimpy and met Bob, who was accompanied by several unknown men. Bob then told me that Stan would show me the truck in which I must load the boxes. Stan is an Indian male and I think Bob introduced him to me.

28

I followed Stan to the parking area, where he pointed out a Toyota 2-ton truck with a load body. Stan then gave me the ignition keys of the truck and I left with my assistant. I cannot recall his name.

29

After we loaded about 30 boxes at my storeroom I returned to East Rand Mall. I handed the keys to Stan and left. I do not know what had happened to these boxes containing the hashish. There were still 29 boxes containing hashish stored at my storeroom.

Some months passed without contact.

30

Then early in 2006 Steve asked me to buy 12 x 210 litre steel drums and work out a way to pack the packed hashish into the drums. Steve gave me R 1000-00 to purchase the drums and also informed me of the place where I could buy the drums namely Spotless Drums in Benoni. I purchased the drums from Spotless Drums a few days later and they were delivered. I paid cash, no invoice was issued. After I spoke to a friend I informed Steve via sms that the drums could not be welded (to create a false bottom) on the 11th April 2006. Steve then mentioned plastic drums as an option via sms on the 17th April 2006 at 20h08. The above-mentioned SMS's are still on my handset.

31

The idea of plastic drums was also abandoned and Steve told me to look into jam tins. I then started phoning to try and source jam tins. I made contact with Bevcan in Vanderbijlpark, where I arranged some samples to be sent to their Roodepoort factory. I collected samples of the tins a few days later. I phoned Steve and told him that I did get hold of jam tins and Steve said that he will call me to meet up with his dad to see if his dad's machine could seal the tins.

32

On or about the 17th or 18th April 2006, I was contacted by a man who shall be known simply as 'Agent', although his full particulars are known to the Scorpions. In essence, 'Agent' advised me inter alia that:

1. He knew I was engaged in unlawful activity and that I had been so engaged for quite some time.

2. That he had certain evidence that could be used against me.

3. That my name had come up in certain intelligence reports, linking me to various individuals, all of whom he said were under investigation.

4. That he was in a position to negotiate certain indemnities from prosecution and that these indemnities would be conditional upon me making a full disclosure of all the facts, relating to my unlawful activity.

5. He said that if I did not fully co-operate he would not be able

to assist me in getting indemnity and, in all likelihood, I would face a lengthy prison term.

6. He was particularly interested in getting the names of the various people I had been involved with and he had all the names written down anyway, but needed me to confirm them, without any prompting from him. As I went through the names he confirmed that he already had knowledge of them. (Many of the names are not mentioned here, as they are the subject of ongoing investigations.)

7. He then got me to take him through all of my activities over the past few years and to show him various places I had been to in connection with such activities, which I did. This process lasted several days and I told him everything I knew and took him to many locations, where he took photographs.

8. He said he was satisfied that I had told him all there was to know and that he would now pass me over to the relevant people at the Scorpions, and advised me to cooperate with them 100%, which I agreed to do. He also asked me detailed questions about shipments of drugs and I told him everything, including the drugs still in storage.

'Agent', of course, was O'Sullivan.

✳

O'Sullivan spent months debriefing Dormehl and ensuring that the Iranian hash sting would play out without a hitch. 'What we did was we flew in my plane over the areas [Endicott Farm]. I wanted to get an idea of the relationship of these warehouses from above. It was easier to do it from the air than on the ground, as no one is looking up wondering what that aircraft is doing up there,' said O'Sullivan.

At this stage the Scorpions investigator Robyn Plitt had been paired with a more experienced and senior investigator, Andrew Leask. It was Paul who arranged the initial meeting between the DSO team and Dormehl.

It was inevitable that tensions would arise between O'Sullivan and the Scorpions investigators, particularly Leask, around issues of control. O'Sullivan had felt protective of his source while the Scorpions did not want O'Sullivan to act as an intermediary or try to lead their investigation. O'Sullivan and Leask reached an amicable agreement. After all, they had the same end-goal in sight. And so Operation Coffee, an offshoot of Operation Bad Guys, was launched.

Dormehl's statement picks up:

33

A meeting was set by 'Agent' for the 26th April 2006. We met at the McDonalds, Value Mall, Boksburg. Present as well as 'Agent' was Robyn Plitt, Andrew Leask, Slang Maangwale and others, all members of the Scorpions, to my belief.

34

Andrew Leask informed me that if I co-operate in full I would receive indemnity (Section 204 witness) in return for which I must tell them everything I know and leave nothing out. At this meeting I informed Andrew that I was in possession of ±30 boxes containing vacuum-packed hashish and I also informed him how I got into possession of the hashish. We met for ±2 to 3 hours and it was decided that I would hand over to him the rest of the boxes of hashish the following day.

35

It was also this day that Steve phoned me and told me that I must meet his dad the following day at the plot at Endicott, to look at the tins. I must also take two samples of the vacuum-packed hashish with me. It was apparent that we were going to carry out a test to see if the packages would fit in the tins. I phoned Jimmy on his cell phone no. 082 722 1843 and confirmed a meeting for 16h00 the next day, which was a public holiday. The next day a tracking device and video camera was fitted to my bakkie.

36

I then met with Slang and Trott Mphahlele, who also work for the Scorpions. They got into my bakkie and we departed to my store, where the rest of the boxes of hashish were loaded onto my private vehicle.

37

We then left towards a meeting place at Jet Park, where I met Andrew Leask and some of his people. I handed him the total of 29 boxes filled with hashish. From there Slang and I departed to Endicott to meet with Jimmy. We went into Jimmy's open garage. I called Slang by using the name Eric and requested him to bring me the box that was on my bakkie. In the box was 2 x 1 kilo hashish and the empty tins. I took out the hashish and handed it to Jimmy together with the tins. Jimmy then inserted the hashish into the tin and it protruded from the tin by ±7cm. We were looking for ways to fit the hashish into the tins, but with no luck. Jimmy also noticed that the sealing machine was too small for the tins that I brought. Jimmy then took the hashish that we used as samples and stuck it away on a shelf, behind him in the garage. We left and I dropped Slang off at the BP Garage in Benoni and departed to my house. I was also instructed by 'Agent' to note all happenings and calls between all the parties concerned and have done so.

38

What follows, are the notes I took, on the dates as indicated:-
These are important telephone numbers abbreviated

.... – Anthony Dormehl main number   (A)
.... – Anthony Dormehl Washabin   (B)
.... – Steven Paparas JTT   (C)
.... – Steven Paparas – Payasugo   (D)
.... – Anthony Dormehl home   (E)
.... – Jimmy Paparas   (F)
.... – Steven Paparas Pay-as-u-go   (G)

Tuesday 9 May 2006 at about 12:24

Jimmy called me to say that Steven told him to call me and to inform me that the jig on his machine is too small to seal the tins that I supplied. The tins are good he said because the packages could be bent to fit inside, but I must phone the place where the tins came from and find out where we could purchase a machine to seal the tins. He said I must call him back.

Friday 12ᵗʰ May 2006 at 13:17

I called Jimmy to say that I had called Bevcan in VD Bijl and got a price of R62,000 for a new and R28,000–R30,000 for a second-hand MB I A machine. He said that he would be taking his machine to an engineering factory to see if they could adapt his machine for a bigger tin and call me on Monday.

Thursday 8 June at 18h10

Steven Paparas called me for the first time in a while. I told him that he may be able to assist me with the problems with my bakkie, as I had blown my motor on the 6th June 2006. He said that his mechanic had resigned and that he would not be able to help me. He said that they finally have the machine back from engineering and they would be doing a test soon. He would let me know.

I asked him about the Landlord (Agliotti) and the newspaper article about Kebble and said that I did not understand anything they were reporting. He said that the Landlord was fine and that he had seen him this week, he looked un-perturbed. Then said he had him (Landlord) on the other line and goodbye. Steve also mentioned that it was Paul Stemmet who dropped Glenn Agliotti in the shit.

Thursday 22 June 18h45

Steven Paparas called me. Very happy, said that Bob was back in town and that he was back to set everything right with the Landlord (Agliotti) and himself (Paparas) and there's a good Christmas box for us. We would do the same as last time, and meet Bob at the Wimpy E.R.M. and that I would take the small truck, load everything and take the keys back to them. Said that they were out drinking somewhere and he would phone me on Monday or so.

Monday 26 June

15h35 Slang and Piet v der Merwe met me at Benoni Wheel & Tyre, and asked me to brief them:

I said that the previous handover of half the stuff happened long ago. They asked when? I said, before I met any of them. I said that Paparas was happy and all debts were to be settled and that I could bring the other half of the shipment. Said they could put surveillance in Mugg &

Bean etc. as well as watch the parking lot.

Paparas had called at 20h26 and cut him off short. Asked if all was well – said Wed 28th June 9h00. Andrew said, let's take one step at a time and make the recording.

Paparas called me 20h40 after I cut off call to 6673 (low battery) and asked if all was well for Wed 09h00. I said, good, asked if he would be there – maybe, if not busy.

Wednesday 28 June

Paparas called me from (D) at 08h50, asked if all is on track. I said, 'yes'. He said that the guys are going to find some boxes missing and that I must say the Landlord (Agliotti) loaded them a few months ago. He further said that he would be getting the paperwork later and would see me tomorrow.

I called Slang at 08h55 and he said he's still loading the boxes at the office.

By the time I arrived at East Rand Mall, it was much later than it should have been.

Bob and friends were not at Nando's as had been arranged but I saw Stan in the parking area.

I picked up the keys from Stan to an old truck and drove out of the mall, I was not with anyone from DSO.

I drove and found a quiet spot, making sure I wasn't followed and called Slang and told them where I was. He came there and we sat and waited for the boxes to come from Pretoria. Whilst we were waiting some Metro Police came and started looking at the truck and then told us we were under arrest for operating an unroadworthy vehicle and we could not produce the owner of the vehicle, and we were taken to Boksburg Metro offices and waited there for about two hours, until the owner came and was issued with a fine and I took the truck back to East Rand Mall after speaking to Slang, Andrew and Steve.

Obviously, the operation was not going to happen today and it was postponed until the next week.

Friday 30 June

Steven called me whilst I was in the shower and said the boys are anxious to do deal today or tomorrow. Said that he had received 'paper-work' yesterday and he has a cheque for me. Said I'm cold, he must call in ten minutes.

Steven called, I told him that I can't, I'm working, then away with the family. He said 'please'. He called again later and I repeated what I had said. He said that they were 'breaking his balls' and phoning all the time, also said the one guy with glasses was flying out on Sunday. I asked who he was and he said, 'the owner'. Told me that the Landlord 'Agliotti' was in New York, but I must say that the Landlord is controlling the whole thing if they phone and ask me about shortages, i.e. the previous PMB [Pietermaritzburg] loads.

Called again and said he has to meet them now and he was going to tell them 'Monday or nothing'. Should have happened on Wednesday but it's their fault for giving us such an old, unroadworthy truck to use. Said he might call me whilst meeting with them.

Called at 13h40, and I did not answer. Then I got a call from Bob's number (given to me earlier by Steven), SMSed to Andrew.

Steven left a message on (B) to say, 'no pressure for weekend, Tuesday 08h45.' Then gave Steven a missed call, he called me back. Said I was washing dustbins and phones were in the car. Said all good for Tuesday 08h45 and he would be there also. He said, 'please could I get all boxes ready and sealed so it would be 10 minutes to load and then we would be done with "these bastards" and he would fix me up with my cheque. He said, 'it's a good one'. Also said that I don't have to phone Bob or anyone. I must let him know when I am back in town on Monday.

Monday 3 July

06h00, message on (B) from Piet van der Merwe. Please call him about today's actions.

Slang called me at 06h30, 'Any news?', said no, Tuesday morning at 08h45.

15h10, Steven called me, asked for Wednesday!! I said, better tomorrow, but if no other way, we could do Wednesday.

Steven called again ±15h41 and said please, we must do it Wednesday. His guys cannot get a vehicle before then. Steven also said to keep back '38 pairs of shoes' (by this I knew he actually meant kg's), and bring only 700 kg to Bob. By this I understood him to mean he was going to short-change 'Bob' in the amount of 38 kg of drugs.

I called Piet and told him and he said he would call me from the office in a little while. He also said that I need to speak to the technical guys about batteries.

Piet called at 16h20 to ask how everything was, I said it has to be Wednesday, 9h00. He said fine. He would send P. Pieterse to me to organize batteries.

16h24, Steven called again to confirm for Wednesday 9h00, said fine.

Tuesday 4 July

Was called by Slang at ±08h30 and asked to come to their office – asked about 11h00 because was waiting for Leon to start my bakkie. Went to Pretoria and sat through some planning etc and had lunch. Then told to go home. Neels and Junaid arrived, diverted my cell phone to home phone and set up recorder. Made call to Steven Paparas at ±16h00. All happy. At 17h50, call from Steven Paparas missed and gave him a missed call. He called and I said if any changes (ref to recording for actual words).

19h10 Steven called – changed his mind – keep 38 behind (taped this as well). Called Andrew, busy on his line.

Wednesday 5 July

Neels and Junaid arrived at 06h00 to help record any call to or from Steven. They also listened to the first two calls recorded the night before after they had left. (Calls diverted to home line.) Had also made one call to Steven with them present the night before.

At ±07h30, we made another call to Steven and recorded. Just asked if all was well – must I keep 38 shoes etc (kg's). (Refer to recording for actual words.) Slang had arrived at ±06h20/30. We left for Nando's at ±08h30 (Slang and myself). Andrew told Slang to slow down and park, in order to arrive at 08h55–09h00. Slang said that we could go and we arrived at 08h55 to find Nando's closed and no-one there. Slang said park and call Steven. I did so, and said 'no one's here!' He said, 'they should be there in a small red car and a truck.' I said, 'Okay'. We still found no-one. Stanley the driver arrived in an old truck at 09h05 and said 'sorry'. I took the keys, and Slang got in and we left for my store where Trot etc had earlier delivered 39 boxes. These boxes were put into the truck whilst Junaid taped a tracker to the roof of the truck. We left soon afterwards to find no-one waiting. Called Steven to say we were here. He said, 'no problem, is Stanley not there?' I said 'no'. Steven said that he would be there soon, he was in the Wimpy with Bob. Said come in quickly. When Steven called again, said I have to run to do bins. Slang said, 'let's go'. I parked in disabled parking and walked to Wimpy, found no Bob, only 6–8 Scorpions. Slang and I left the Mall and I dropped him near Toys R Us, Kentucky and left for home. When I reached BP Tom Jones [Street], Slang called to say that I must come back, look for Bob etc, sit down at their table.

At 13h40 Slang and someone brought the laptop and showed me all the photos. When I saw Bob, I was unsure, he had picked up weight and the Scorpions had photographed him wearing darkened eyewear. I confirmed that it was Bob and Slang left. I returned home.

At ±18h42, Steven called from (D) to (B). I didn't answer. I tried to call back and drop to (D) from (D), diverted to home phone – recorder ready. Then he called, no number showing to (A). I answered and ran to my room and switched on the digital recorder. Meanwhile, he was saying to me that 15 Scorpions were at the plot and had called his Dad. I feigned 'shocked-surprise'. He said that it must be Bob etc because of the number of parcels short in the shipment I gave them this morning. He said that they got Jimmy's number from the old man at the plot. He told me not to worry because I was just the transporter anyway. I asked him to let me know what I could do about his 38 pieces (kg's) in my store. The first thing he said, though, was delete all his numbers off my phones. I asked him how I could reach him and he said his (C) number was good. I asked him again to let me know if he hears anything else and to call about the 38 kg in my store. He asked if I had [the lawyer] Max Houde's number, I said it should be here somewhere.

Slang called a little later and asked if Agliotti had called me. I said, 'No, but Steven had and that he knows that they were at the plot.' Robyn called asking, 'Are you sure that you did not recognize the man in the photo seen at the offices the other day?' I was irritated and said that 'I'm here to help – have been waiting for one hour to see the pictures to identify Bob or anyone else' and 'yes! I am sure!' She said they were very busy there, not forgetting me.

Then spoke to 'Agent', he said not to worry, they would look after my well-being. I expressed concern about our safety in so far as Agliotti was concerned and Steven's family (Greek). I also mentioned that I was in the phone-book.

Piet van der Merwe called me to say that they don't have Steven and have I spoken to him? I said 'no', and he said that I should ring him.

At 17h05, I called Steven from (B) to (C) and dropped and diverted it to (E). He called back and asked how I was, said 'fine' (refer to recording on cassette). He said, 'dispose of the 38 kg, I am at the attorney's.'

12h52 Call to (A) from ...., no response when answered.

Called .... Steven was at the attorney's and that he told me that his father was taken away last night.

Monday 10 July

Trott phones and says he's on his way. I told him I'm going to Edenvale and would meet him at Jones Road / Jet Park off-ramp afterwards. Met him and we left my car at the Engen and we proceeded down Kelly then Innes Roads where I showed him Unit 1 – JTT. Some surveillance guy arrived and they sent me to the Engen in Trot's car and they drove by JTT again. They came to the Engen and we parted company.

Tuesday 11 July

Trot called and asked to see me. He arrived and showed me some photos in which I positively ID [identify] Steven and a few with Jimmy. He thanked me and left.

At 14h45, Piet van der Merwe called me, asked me if I have any news, and I said no word since the last recording. He asked me if I still had devices and I confirmed. He asked me to call Steven and try for a meeting and find out where he was. I agreed and called him from (B) to (C). This was when I noticed a missed call from ...., made the day before at 17h53. I called the number – no reply. Then called (C) and dropped the call. Steven called back and I recorded it:

He asked how I was and I asked how he was. He said that he was at the attorney's and didn't know which way to turn. 'They still have my Dad,' he said. He asked me, 'did anyone follow you the other day?' I said, 'no'; he responded by saying the guys must have been followed. He asked me not to call (C) and only the new number – .... He asked me about the 38 pairs of shoes (kg's) and I said I had left them in a friend's store under some rags because I did not know how to dispose of them. He said, 'don't worry for now, just chill'.

I know and understand the contents of this affidavit.

I have no objection in taking the prescribed Oath.

I regard the Oath as binding on my conscience.

A. DORMEHL

In June 2006, a month before Operation Coffee, Jackie Selebi met with Agliotti and shared a confidential report by UK officials relating to his (Agliotti's) role in international drug-trafficking. It was not the first time Selebi had shared highly sensitive information with the Landlord. The commissioner had also shown him a 'thick' document in which allegations were made that Selebi was being paid by the Kebbles.

It was during one such meeting, Agliotti later testified, that Selebi inadvertently admitted that he had indeed been the hand behind Paul's firing from his job at ACSA. In a statement Agliotti said, 'I asked Jackie who this Paul O'Sullivan was. Jackie told me that Paul O'Sullivan had a security contract at the Johannesburg International Airport and that he, Jackie, had him removed.' Later, this admission would prove invaluable to O'Sullivan as he built his civil case against Selebi and ACSA for wrongful dismissal.

But in July that year Selebi was fully aware that evidence against him was mounting, and launched a counter-offensive. He seemed more than secure in the notion that he would be able to shrug off any allegations of impropriety by O'Sullivan. In fact he was confidently strutting about the world stage, making all the appropriate noises about corruption in law-enforcement agencies. Who on earth would believe that the president of Interpol was deeply corrupt? It was all just a nasty plan hatched by dastardly criminals to smear him because, in fact, he was just doing his job, Selebi explained to those who asked.

O'Sullivan, in turn, was aware that he was being watched and investigated. 'They were hoping they would find evidence of criminal activity. I made sure I kept my nose clean. I mean I was up against the chief of police and a 130,000-strong force that had divisions that did nothing but gather up intelligence. If I had as much as spat on the sidewalk, I would have been arrested. Every time I entered or left South Africa I was scrutinised and, if I had a suitcase, it was searched,' said Paul.

Selebi had hinted, in various interviews to sympathetic journalists, that 'a certain individual' had been behind the campaign to 'discredit' him but stopped short of naming O'Sullivan.

That month, July, Deputy Commissioner André Pruis, Selebi's great defender, contacted Paul and arranged an afternoon meeting at the luxury Michelangelo Hotel in Sandton. Paul intended to record the conversation but had been unable to switch on the device, as Pruis was 'shadowed by a man wearing grey pants and a blue shirt who positioned himself where he could watch us,' Paul later reported back to Leask.

Pruis brought with him photocopies of all the debrief notes that Paul had taken with 'CS' and told Paul that he knew Paul had prepared these. More alarmingly, Pruis also claimed he knew the identity of 'CS'. Pruis was clearly on a fishing trip as well as coming out to bat for his boss.

He quizzed Paul about various issues, the claim that Jackie Selebi had received an envelope with R50,000, that Paul had been present at a meeting with the Scorpions at McDonald's before the Alberton hash bust, and a few other matters relating to Paul Stemmet. Pruis implied that it was *he* who had had dealings with Stemmet and not Jackie Selebi. He was clearly ready to take the fall on that count.

Paul strung Pruis along, waiting for a moment to pounce. It arrived when Pruis began to discuss various 'documents' implicating Selebi, which he suggested Paul had sent to the media. Letting Paul know just how on top of things he was, Pruis admitted that he had in fact had sight of all these emails and documents even *before* they were leaked to the press. 'I told him I hoped there was a section 205 warrant lying around somewhere that confirmed my emails had been lawfully intercepted, as, if not, I would raise merry hell,' Paul told Leask later.

Pruis, realising he had been caught out, tried to change the subject, but Paul pressed on, asking for copies of his mails. It was a pointless hour-long meeting in which Pruis revealed his hand while Paul played dumb.

O'Sullivan expressed his concern to Leask that 'the CS may be badly compromised and I am not in a position to do anything other than to advise him of this fact, which I have done'.

✳

Six people were arrested in the 6 July hash swoop on the Alberton warehouse. They were Dimitrios Paparas, Robert Lottman ('Bob the American'), a notorious Canadian drug-trafficker, the drug dealers Pedro Marques and Christiaan Alblas, and the truck driver Stanley Poonin. Steve Paparas, Dimitrios's son, escaped arrest but handed himself in a week later.

The piggies soon began squealing: Lottman, Marques and Alblas all pleaded guilty and turned state witnesses. Lottman testified that Steve Paparas, acting on instruction from the Landlord, had confiscated his passport and held him hostage in a container for ten days in 2003 when a consignment of marijuana en route to Germany had been hijacked and stolen by corrupt Dutch customs officials. Alblas in turn said that while he did not know the identity of 'the Landlord', he believed the kingpin enjoyed official protection and was connected somehow to the country's police chief.

Lottman and Alblas were both sentenced to 10 years each, half of which was suspended, while Marques was handed a five-and-a-half-year jail term. O'Sullivan was delighted, as these were the first prison sentences flowing from his years of painstaking work. During the court case, prosecutor Gerrie Nel announced that the DSO would soon pounce on the mysterious 'Landlord'.

Two months after Operation Coffee, the Scorpions conducted an early-morning raid on Agliotti's Bryanston home and his offices in Midrand. While the search was billed as a follow-up swoop in the light of the Alberton drugs bust, the Scorpions were looking for leads in the Kebble murder case as well as the Selebi probe.

'Look, by this time they already had his phone records, so they searched everything. And then they took a look at his car. In the back they found a briefcase with a diary. Inside the diary Agliotti had annotated every meeting he had had with Selebi. Bingo!' said Paul. Twelve suspects were named in the Scorpions warrant, including members of Paul Stemmet's Palto.

'And what did Agliotti do after the raid? He called Selebi. It was crystal clear to Agliotti that he was going to face very serious charges and he was phoning his friend to find out how they were going to wriggle out of it. But just imagine how dumb both he and Selebi were, to continue chatting like that. They both share the same suit size, so I guess they also share the same brain,' Paul reckons.

In the meantime, there was one other suspect everyone, especially the Scorpions, was keen to interview, Clinton Nassif. But how to get him to help finally reel in Agliotti?

O'Sullivan remained in constant contact with Leask by email, filling him in on the details his sources were forwarding. Suspecting that Selebi was illegally intercepting his emails and phone calls, O'Sullivan sometimes used the alias 'Peter Jackson' and addressed Leask as 'Koos'.

A selection of the emails gives insight into O'Sullivan's working relationship with Leask, and also suggests a far less 'controlling' and 'difficult' personality than he has been made out to be.

Date: Tue, 18 Jul 2006 11:18:50 -0700 (PDT)
From: 'Peter Jackson' <satrucker@yahoo.com>
Subject: Various Matters
To: koos.burger@yahoo.com

Hi Andrew,
My contact at Wachthuis called me, this is the latest data:
  1. They (Selebi, Pruis et al.) intend shortly to arrest Paul Stemmet. He will be charged with racketeering and they intend to show

that he was at it before Selebi came into office.

2. They intend shortly to arrest Nassif. He will be charged with fraud, in that he defrauded Lloyd's of London out of an amount in respect of a damaged BMW motor car. (You will recall that, the day of the *Mail & Guardian*'s first article, back in May, Insp Ludi Schnelle, of Joburg Organised Crime, based at the old stock exchange building, advised me that, at approximately 10h00 that day, he received a call from Head Office (Commissioner de Beer) telling him to expedite the case.) The news from head office today is that the docket has been sent to the prosecutor for a decision. Apparently the strategy is that Selebi will then claim 'This is proof that I don't look after my friends'. However, of note is that there are far more serious charges he could be nailed with and these are being ignored. With a clean record, he will get a suspended sentence and a slap on the wrist!

3. They also intend to arrest Charles Bezuidenhout very soon, he will also be charged with racketeering, along with Stemmet. I could not get the details of the specific charges, but it is said that Bezuidenhout will be offered a S204 in exchange for information he will give on Stemmet, effectively making Stemmet the 'fall guy' and Bezuidenhout will get off scot-free.

4. They are tapping many phones, including mine and various parties within the Scorpions, source could not name names, but Robyn Plitt is one them and he could not remember the rest. (They thought Plitt was the head of the investigations until the bail application.) This is being done by a certain Commissioner Molango Mpega (not sure about spelling) [Mulangi Mphego, head of the police's Crime Intelligence Unit] at the direct request of Selebi.

They say if they get caught they will say they don't know who they were tapping, as they were trying to trace the source of 'destabilising documents' that are being circulated.

5. They have been and still are intercepting emails. Hence, you have got this from a different address. It is not known who is doing the intercepting, but they are paying big money for it.

6. They intend to lure me in and talk me into agreeing to sign an affidavit, in terms of which I formally withdraw my case against

Selebi. If that doesn't work, they are going to launch their own smear campaign against me and are already busy lining 'stuff' up that they can use against me.

7. André Pruis is going to 'own up' to being the main contact with Paul Stemmet and that Selebi did not really know what was going on. Since Pruis reports to Selebi and is going on pension this year, Selebi will 'reward' him handsomely for being the fall guy for Stemmet's misdeeds.

They are going to try and pull off all of the above, before the Scorpions can make any more moves and they think the Scorpions have their hands full with stuff they can't handle and by the time they (Scorpions) realise what is going on, Bezuidenhout will be a 'state witness', Nassif will be arrested and released on bail and Stemmet will be behind bars.

I must say, I'm fairly impressed with their strategy, as it shows they are not as stupid as I thought they were.

Best wishes,

Peter Jackson

✳

Clinton Nassif was a vital link at this sensitive stage of the investigation, as he had a direct association with Agliotti, who had rented his warehouses. Of course, it was also Agliotti who had introduced Nassif to the Kebbles.

In his email to Leask, Paul mentioned how Nassif had defrauded the insurer Lloyd's of London, deliberately damaging one of his luxury vehicles, a Mercedes-Benz E55 AMG, and claiming it had been written off in an accident. The swindle offered a potential opportunity, reckoned O'Sullivan.

'I tracked down the guy who had driven the forklift truck that had "dropped" the car at Nassif's scrapyard, Auto Fever, in Selby,' said O'Sullivan. O'Sullivan had learned that the driver, Mohammed Mazibuko, was facing potential drug-trafficking and assault charges and gave him a simple option. 'You can give up Clinton Nassif and tell us what happened with the forklift truck or face ten years or maybe being killed by your boss,' O'Sullivan calmly informed Mazibuko. Mazibuko opted for the former.

Nassif, in the meantime, had been warned of his impending arrest and planned to flee the country for the United States where he intended setting up new business, a call centre. O'Sullivan, in turn, realising Nassif might make a dash for it, called in some contacts and requested that all departing flights be monitored. 'I knew Nassif was planning to jump ship, and if anyone jumped ship right then, I knew it could be a big problem. I got a friend of mine at the airport to run through the ticketing system on a daily basis looking for Nassif's name.' In October 2006 it eventually showed up and O'Sullivan handed the details to the Scorpions, who at that stage were talking to the security boss's lawyers.

'They picked him up at his house early in the morning. Before they even got him back to Pretoria he started blabbing in the car. It was a major turning point because Nassif, apart from further implicating Agliotti and John Stratton, also implicated Selebi in Kebble's murder.'

Nassif also revealed that it had been Mikey Schultz, Nigel McGurk and Faizel Smith who had actually shot Kebble and that the killing had, in fact, been an 'assisted suicide'. Kebble, Nassif claimed, facing massive fraud charges, financial ruin and a jail term, had decided to make a dignified exit, staging the 'assisted suicide' to look like a hijacking. An insurance policy he had taken out before his death would ensure that his wife and children were not left destitute. Nassif gave his damning statement only after the Scorpions had guaranteed section 204 indemnity for the killers.

Roger Kebble, Brett's father, as well as Paul O'Sullivan, doubted whether Brett Kebble had really wanted to kill himself. Both suspected that John Stratton, Kebble's confidant and right-hand man, had been the puppet master pulling the strings.

Nassif's statement sets out how Stratton, as early as mid-2005, had asked him to procure some sort of tablet that would effect a heart attack and that could not be detected in the victim's bloodstream. Agliotti had also pressured him into tracking down the medication.

Later, Kebble had told him, said Nassif, that he wanted to 'go out like a hero'.

If Kebble had fessed up his fraudulent dealings, Stratton, an Australian national, would most certainly also have faced a lengthy term in jail. In the meantime, Stratton had fled to his homeland, Australia, where he no doubt monitored the events that were unfurling.

✳

In May 2006 the *Mail & Guardian* was ready to run with a piece announcing that the Scorpions were indeed investigating a case against the country's police commissioner. O'Sullivan had supplied all the details, including how the facts could be confirmed.

Under the editorship of Ferial Haffajee, and often with guidance from O'Sullivan, the newspaper had led the press pack in sniffing out the latest twists and turns in the Kebble murder, Paul Stemmet's Palto and the various other shady characters who populated the country's seemingly vast underworld.

Vusi Pikoli, the national director of public prosecutions, was anxious for the story to be held back until investigators had enough evidence and to prevent any repeat of Bulelani Ngcuka's error of judgement in the Zuma corruption matter. Haffajee complied with Pikoli's request and the paper ran a story that, while not concealing anything from readers, read so generally that it would not jeopardise any sensitive breakthrough.

O'Sullivan, on the other hand, was determined to keep up the pressure on Selebi and on 5 November the country woke to a bombshell headline in the *Sunday Times* exposing the commissioner's alleged links to organised criminals: 'Selebi and the Cop Mafia' it read.

The lead story was based on a '144-page dossier', said the *Sunday Times*, 'that allegedly reveals the inner workings of a Mafia-styled organization involving senior policemen.' Of course this was no ordinary dossier: everyone in the media knew it was part of the

'O'Sullivan Dossier' to which the paper had been referring.

'Pruis phoned me the Sunday the paper ran the story. He was very angry and started telling me that I was a foreign spy and that they had "stuff" on me,' Paul recalls. Paul recorded the conversation, in which Pruis accused him of trying to 'destabilise the South African police'. The claims were laughable and O'Sullivan can be heard goading Pruis, who becomes increasingly flustered during the conversation, repeatedly losing his cool and revealing vital information that Paul says now proves that Pruis was part of the problem.

'Pruis was an amateur. With people like that at the head of the police, it was no wonder that the criminals had a field day. I played Pruis like my ten-year-old daughter. He was so stupid he walked right into my trap,' he says with a grin.

On the evening of the report Selebi called a press conference. The apparently relaxed commissioner spoke for over an hour to the press, denying all allegations and claiming 'all these stories have absolutely no bearing on the truth'. He suggested that the entire matter was simply a 'smear campaign' and that he knew who was behind it. At the same conference, Pruis said he had challenged this man (Paul) to 'go public' and attend the conference but he had refused.

At the conference Selebi lied by claiming that O'Sullivan had himself acted in a criminal manner, purchasing a lie detector device when he was the head of ACSA security. They had nothing to go on and so conjured up an old, insignificant story as a rather lame shot at O'Sullivan. O'Sullivan had bought the machine, a voice stress analyser, whilst he was in the border police, before joining ACSA, and had it sponsored by the Jockey Club after he helped them set up an anti-corruption unit on a *pro bono* basis.

On his relationship with Agliotti, Selebi claimed ignorance, saying the only connection they had had was when they worked together on the Special Olympics promotion with Arnold Schwarzenegger. He explained away Agliotti's phone call to him the night Kebble was murdered as 'one of many'. He also denied ever receiving a R50,000 bribe. 'R50,000 is a small amount for me. I would not be so cheap.' Watching the conference, O'Sullivan thought, 'Mmm, we know it's a good deal more.'

He ended the conference with the now legendary quip, 'These hands are clean. I am not involved in criminality,' after claiming that the Scorpions did not need search warrants to see what had been paid into his bank accounts and he would gladly show them.

Selebi's comment provided a major 'sit up and listen moment' for O'Sullivan, who recorded the press conference. 'I played it back many times and kept stopping at the point where Selebi said, "They won't find anything paid into my bank accounts." I saw a tell-tale twitch in Selebi's face. As a trained interviewer, I knew right away that this twitch meant Selebi was worried.'

O'Sullivan immediately phoned Leask and told him, 'Don't look for what was paid into his accounts, look for what was not paid out.'

Shortly afterwards, Selby Bokaba, Selebi's spokesman, issued a press statement announcing that the country's nine provincial commissioners had pledged their 'unwavering support' for the national commissioner. The statement, circulated to all of the country's major newspapers, read:

Condemnation of defamatory, scurrilous and malicious allegations against the National Commissioner of the South African Police Service

The nine Provincial Commissioners (PCs) of the South African Police Service (SAPS) met last week to discuss their collective concern about the media coverage of the scurrilous, defamatory and unsubstantiated allegations levelled against the national commissioner of the SAPS Jackie Selebi.

The Provincial Commissioners resolved to request a meeting with management of the National Prosecution Authority (NPA), which request was granted and the meeting took place yesterday afternoon at the NPA Head Office in Silverton, Pretoria. The PCs who, between themselves, marshal more than 126,000 forces on the ground, sought clarity on the alleged investigation against the national commissioner as the allegations were beginning to undermine confidence in the SAPS and sought to cast aspersions on the integrity and dignity of commissioner Selebi. They further expressed their collective anger and disgust at the manner in which the alleged investigation was being carried out, which was characterised by constant leaks of affidavits and information to the media.

The meeting was prompted by boiling anger on the ground at various provinces, particularly from seasoned investigators who understand the traditional methodology of conducting investigations, who were appalled by the constant leaking of affidavits which was supposed to be in the safe keeping of an investigating agency, but mysteriously found its way to the media.

The PCs, who initiated the meeting with the head of the NPA and his deputies, without the knowledge and permission of the national commissioner, were satisfied by the outcome of the meeting after the NPA management confirmed that they dissociated themselves from the well-publicised agenda of the individual peddling the allegations, and said they can't "control" the man, as he was neither their registered source nor their employee.

The Provincial Commissioners pledged their unwavering support to and complimented the national commissioner on his inspirational and visionary leadership in his management of the organisation, more so as we approach the festive season when levels of crime tend to peak during this period. While the detractors of the national commissioner will be holidaying, he will be leading his charges – men and women in blue – from the front, as he has been doing since he assumed the reins of the SAPS.

We wish to reassure the South African public that we will not be detracted from our focus of preventing, investigating and combating crime during and beyond the festive season.

The Provincial Commissioners have mandated their colleague, the Provincial Commissioner of Western Cape, Mzwandile Petros, to speak on their behalf.'

Signed by: All the nine Provincial Commissioners of the SAPS

Earlier, O'Sullivan had publicly declared on Radio 702's John Robbie Show that 'Selebi was a crook and he would go to prison'. While some may have doubted O'Sullivan's confident prediction, Robbie remarked, 'He sounds convincing. But are these the words of a deranged man, or is there some truth to it? Only time will tell.'

❊

Behind the scenes, the ANC and its most powerful decision-making body, the National Executive Committee, had been meeting to discuss Selebi and the worrying reports that had surfaced in public. The ruling party was fraught with tension. Mbeki intended to run for a third term as president at the party's 52nd elective conference in Polokwane in December 2007 and needed as much support from party heavyweights as he could get. Mbeki's old friend Jackie Selebi was one such ally.

The political fallout, if it were to be proved that the country's police commissioner was corrupt, would be immeasurable, especially the timing of the announcement. Selebi had consistently denied in public any links to organised crime. Pikoli, after Nassif's arrest in October and his damning statement, had again met with the minister of justice and President Mbeki. The president had suggested that Pikoli meet with Selebi, face to face, and put the charges to him.

At this meeting the wily Selebi managed to convince Pikoli that everything, all the allegations, all the claims in the statements by Paul Stemmet and Clinton Nassif, were a pack of lies, that he was innocent and that he was a victim of some terrible conspiracy.

Perhaps because of their history and their difference in age and some misplaced sense of respect, Pikoli reported back to President Mbeki that he had met with Selebi and was now unsure that the commissioner was guilty. But Pikoli, wanting to hedge his bets, requested Leonard McCarthy to formally question the commissioner, just for the record.

Selebi stuck to his guns. But it was during this interview that

Selebi inadvertently admitted to McCarthy that the Khuselani boss, Noel Ngwenya, 'would have been considered my friend in that I knew he was running a company at the airport and at least he visited my house three times'.

Out of context, Selebi had let slip a valuable piece of information. It was a link O'Sullivan had been trying to prove for years and the transcripts of the McCarthy–Selebi interview finally offered verification, from the proverbial horse's mouth. Until then Selebi had publicly denied ever knowing Ngwenya.

At the time, President Mbeki was no doubt preoccupied with far more important issues – his political survival as well as other matters of state – and clearly found these conflicting reports from his national director of public prosecutions confusing, irritating and disruptive. Mbeki tried to calm public doubts and announced that he and his cabinet, 'had the greatest confidence in National Commissioner Selebi'.

A letter the Presidency penned to the Freedom Front Plus MP Pieter Groenewald reveals Mbeki's thoughts on the matter. Groenewald had written to Mbeki, asking the president to appoint a judicial commission of inquiry into the police chief. While Mbeki had been thoroughly briefed on the matter, he informed Groenewald that 'up to now nobody within the state structures has informed me that there are any investigations affecting National Commissioner Selebi that are being conducted by anybody, including the DSO (the Scorpions)'. Mbeki went on to reassure Groenewald that if such an investigation were under way, 'I would have been informed accordingly.'

He suggested that Groenewald's request had been based 'on what really amounts to nothing but rumour and speculation' and that it would be 'very wrong and absolutely absurd for the President to constitute a Judicial Commission on this basis'.

Mbeki reiterated his mantra that 'I have the greatest confidence in National Commissioner Selebi … I am certain that whatever the rumour mill is saying about him, he will continue to do his critically important work with the same diligence, dedication and selflessness he has shown ever since we appointed him as National Commissioner of the SAPS.'

It is clear that Mbeki's longstanding friendship with Jackie Selebi impaired his ability to accept or at least entertain the idea that his commissioner might be corrupt.

On 16 November, a year after Kebble's murder, two days after Pikoli briefed Mbeki and nine days after Jackie Selebi's press conference, Glenn Agliotti was arrested and charged with Kebble's murder as well as for his role in Operation Coffee. Agliotti was on his way to a morning gym session when the Scorpions pulled up at his Bryanston home and hauled him off to the Sandton charge office, where he spent a month in the holding cells.

The Scorpions had pipped the SAPS, who had struggled for a year to arrest any suspects in Kebble's killing. In an unusual display of co-operation, the SAPS declared that they would work with the Scorpions. O'Sullivan says this is because Selebi wanted to get close to the investigation to find out how much the Scorpions might have on him.

There were immediate calls, particularly from the Democratic Alliance, for Commissioner Selebi to resign or be suspended as his links to Agliotti were investigated.

The ANC's NEC met after Agliotti's arrest. Selebi was present at the meeting and afterwards, in a show of unity and solidarity, the party once again confidently reiterated its support for the struggle stalwart.

In December 2007 Agliotti pleaded guilty to a charge of dealing in drugs in relation to the Operation Coffee bust. He predictably cut a deal, testifying against his accomplices and agreeing to assist the Scorpions with the Selebi investigation. In return he was offered indemnity from prosecution on several serious charges, including corruption, racketeering, money-laundering and defeating the ends of justice.

Agliotti was handed a 10-year sentence suspended for five years and a R300,000 fine. He also had to pay an additional R200,000 to the Criminal Assets Recovery Account.

But the wheels of justice would grind painfully slowly when it came to charging and trying Agliotti for Kebble's murder. As the *Mail & Guardian*'s Adriaan Basson noted in November 2010, 'between the crime and the culmination of the trial lay four years marked by a drought of political, prosecutory and investigatory will'.

The Kebble murder case, which was concluded in 2010 with Agliotti's acquittal, was scuppered and jeopardised because it had intersected with the far more pressing investigation into the country's police chief. In acquitting Agliotti in 2010, Judge Frans Kgomo remarked that the Kebble murder case had played 'second fiddle' to the investigation and prosecution of Jackie Selebi.

But back in 2006 much of the drama was still unfolding.

Chapter 16

The One That Got Away

IT'S BEEN QUOTED IN EVERY STORY about him, but the description is apt. John Stratton, an associate once said, was the 'tungsten tip of the drill, and Kebble was the great flabby weight behind it'. Stratton, a British-born 'mining billionaire', was nicknamed 'the Turtle' and was universally disliked by almost everyone who encountered him, apart from Brett Kebble. JCI colleagues found him rude, controlling and threatening.

In *The Kebble Collusion*, Barry Sergeant describes Stratton simply as 'a repellent Anglo Australian, [who] was a director of JCI during the Kebble era'. Publicly, Stratton billed himself as a businessman and a director of various companies in the resource sector, who had managed joint ventures in the United States, Mauritius, Papua New Guinea, the Persian Gulf, India and the Solomon Islands.

Stratton met Brett Kebble in 1996 and began doing business with him around 1999 shortly after Kebble had gained control over JCI. In 2002 Stratton relocated from Perth to South Africa.

Sergeant does not mince words about the 72-year-old's influence on the then 38-year-old Kebble: 'Stratton's move to South Africa would precipitate Brett Kebble's descent from the relatively straightforward miscreant manoeuvrings that he could pull off so effortlessly, into the real dark depths of the underworld.'

Activities like the smuggling of contraband and illicit goods, wrote Sergeant, were just the beginning. Stratton, he added, 'seemed to take pleasure in anything bent and twisted'. Stratton has been credited, if that is the correct terminology, for initiating the undercover illegal operations involving Mark Wellesley-Wood and Durban Roodepoort Deep. It was Stratton who drew in the likes of Paul Stemmet's Palto and Clinton Nassif's shady CNSG and who gave the orders for the hits and the 'warnings', like the shooting of Stephen Mildenhall.

In his confession to the Scorpions, Nassif accused Stratton of disposing of vital documents and evidence after Kebble's killing. Stratton was also keenly interested in the bumbling police investigation, which must have pleased him. Shortly after he left South African in 2006, the two SAPS officers involved in the Kebble investigation, P.W. van Heerden and Corrie Maritz, flew to Perth to interview Stratton. Stratton averred that during this seven-hour interview no mention was made that 'I was regarded as a suspect by the South African Police in the death of Mr Kebble'.

Back in South Africa, of course, the Scorpions were way ahead of the SAPS team in unravelling the tangled web of lies, deceit, fraud and murder surrounding Brett Kebble and Jackie Selebi.

In 2007 Paul O'Sullivan met with Roger Kebble, who, like him, believed that John 'Turtle' Stratton should appear as a co-accused with Agliotti on charges of conspiring to murder Brett Kebble. Andrew Leask was also keen to have Stratton extradited to stand trial as Agliotti's co-accused. Stratton, he said, needed to be investigated as well for his role in the attempted murder of Stephen Mildenhall as well as for paying bribes to Selebi. Stratton, in turn, lodged an attempt to abolish the extradition treaty between South Africa and Australia, but said he was willing to be interviewed in Australia.

O'Sullivan, secure in the knowledge that he had as many 'ducks in a row' as he could have in the Selebi case, turned his attention momentarily to Stratton. If he wasn't going to stand trial, then O'Sullivan was going to make sure that his corrupt and illegal dealings were going to make headlines in Australia.

Four Corners, Australia's longest-running investigative TV series, began an in-depth investigation of Stratton's past business dealings and his involvement with Kebble and the looting of JCI. The journalists Andrew Fowler and Wayne Harley, in an episode titled 'Bad Company', screened in June 2008, tracked down and confronted the unpleasant Mr Stratton, who denied everything.

O'Sullivan, who had flown to Australia, also featured in the programme and located and pointed out all of Stratton's assets to the ABC team. Fowler and Harley did not hold back. Outlining the relationship between Stratton and Kebble and the extent of the fraud, they noted: 'While JCI was haemorrhaging, Stratton and his boss Brett Kebble were living it up, their preferred playground London. They stayed at the most expensive hotels. Brett Kebble liked the Berkeley near Hyde Park – up to $9,000 a night; Stratton an even flashier pub up the road – the Dorchester where you can pay $11,000 for a bed. For dinner, Kebble and Stratton headed to Mirabelle's restaurant, good enough to notch up a Michelin star.' The programme was a damning indictment of Stratton, his history as a 'businessman' and his role in setting up billion-dollar scams.

Earlier in 2007, O'Sullivan had contacted Ronald Dolliver, an investigator with the Australian firm In Depth Investigations, to sniff around Stratton and his Australian businesses and private life. When Stratton met with Dolliver in November 2007, he insisted that while he was aware of the charges against Agliotti, he had nothing to add. He confidently claimed that police had no incriminating evidence against him and told Dolliver that O'Sullivan was conducting the investigation because 'he has a vendetta against the Commissioner of Police'.

But Stratton was clearly rattled and tried to limit the fallout that had blown over from South Africa. In an attempt to discourage

Dolliver from investigating any further, Stratton sent a serving police officer, from another state, Tony Langdon, for an informal chat in a coffee shop.

'I attended at the arranged location at 2 p.m. on 14 November 2007 and sat down, a male person also attended the café a short time later and introduced himself to me as Tony Langdon. I thought it was strange that he was wearing an oversized shirt and slouched in the seat, it appeared that he was trying to hide something under his shirt, such as either a firearm, or recording device,' Dolliver reported back to O'Sullivan.

Langdon, said Dolliver, expressed concern at the 'publicity' Stratton had been receiving and made it clear that he was acting as Stratton's intermediary. Dolliver was not to contact Stratton directly, Langdon warned.

Dolliver told O'Sullivan that he felt that Langdon's demeanour had been threatening, especially when he intimated that 'we will take any action that is necessary to stop your investigation and we will cause a lot of problems for you and even go to the point of bankrupting you and your company'. This was classic Stratton, including Langdon's apparent veiled threat that Dolliver might come to harm.

'Langdon had succeeded in inspiring the belief in me that I may even come to physical harm myself, although there was no mention of such by him. Furthermore, since Langdon had obviously seen the very bad media coverage that Stratton had attracted, primarily as a result of our activities, it must have been clear to Langdon that our primary interest was the involvement of Stratton in the alleged murder of Brett Kebble, as well as the location of certain "missing" cash.'

Stratton never did stand trial for Kebble's murder, and today he remains a free man, living a comfortable life with his wife and business partner, Donna, in the leafy Perth suburb of Applecross.

Later, Roger Kebble lodged a R15 million claim against Stratton and Glenn Agliotti for the upkeep and support of Brett Kebble's wife and four surviving children. The Cape High Court also granted Kebble an order to attach Stratton's shares in a company called Portion 1, Erf 291, Saxonwold.

In 2008 Kebble and Stratton reached a 'confidential' out-of-court settlement 'of everything between them'. At the time Kebble claimed that he was entitled to recover these amounts 'from the persons responsible for the murder of the deceased' and that Agliotti and Stratton 'were accomplices, alternatively co-conspirators, in the wrongful and unlawful death of the deceased'.

Chapter 17

To Catch a Cop

SERVING A BODY BLOW TO JACKIE Selebi was not going to be easy. While the police chief might have found himself increasingly cornered, he was not going to go down without a fight – even if it meant tagging old friends, including President Mbeki. Between March and July 2007 a flurry of urgent meetings were convened between Vusi Pikoli, Justice Minister Brigitte Mabandla, President Mbeki, various police deputy commissioners as well as Selebi himself.

Getting the SAPS to release evidence on Selebi to Pikoli and the DSO (the Scorpions) proved challenging, to put it mildly, as Selebi continued to play the victim, insisting the Scorpions were targeting him unfairly. When Pikoli threatened to use search warrants to attach evidence, the minister of justice understood the country was on the brink of a national crisis and, together with Mbeki, begged for more time. The DSO in turn realised that time might be running out. The ANC had resolved at its pre-Polokwane policy conference meeting at Gallagher Estate in June 2007 to disband the Scorpions and place the unit under the command of the SAPS national commissioner!

It was only a matter of time before the ruling party would

neutralise one of the most effective crime-fighting bodies in the country and in late July the DSO called a special management meeting at its head office in Silverton. The DSO had several crucial investigations it was conducting, including 'the Zuma matter' (corruption charges relating to the arms deal) and Operation Bad Guys, and needed to plan a way forward. The DSO head, Leonard McCarthy, senior investigators as well as regional heads, including KwaZulu-Natal's Lawrence Mrwebi, a staunch Selebi ally, attended the meeting.

Mrwebi illegally reported back on the meeting to intelligence services, claiming discussions at the meeting proved that the DSO was driven by politically motivated concerns. Mrwebi would also later provide an affidavit that eventually turned up in a desperate attempt to thwart Jackie Selebi's arrest. According to O'Sullivan, 'Mrwebi was as dirty and dishonest as they come. He was part of a cabal of senior state employees that rejected their constitutional duty of care and impartiality and did everything and anything they could to help get Selebi off the hook. The other members of the cabal, in no order of preference, included André Pruis, Mulangi Mphego, Richard Mdluli, Nomgcobo Jiba, Ray Lalla, Manala Manzini and Arthur Fraser. On the fringes of the cabal, they had recruited Sally de Beer and Selby Bokaba, as mouth-pieces that would be prepared to lie for Selebi, in the hope of convincing the country that O'Sullivan was a "spy" who would soon be arrested.'

By 2007 it was clear there was no love lost between O'Sullivan and Selebi's cronies and supporters. He began planning, he says, a co-ordinated and devilishly mischievous plan to psychologically rattle everyone in the enemy camp. He built up a few fake email addresses, using terms such as Pink Panther, Scarlet Pimpernel, SA Trucker and Justice Seeker, and got to work on a 'terrorist-like' campaign, so they would never know where or when the next sting would come. At one point, he even managed to have them sending emails to each other, by means of his mole at Selebi's office.

O'Sullivan believes that individuals who are guilty of crimes or a cover-up of illegal activity generally respond predictably to the threat of being found out and exposed. They either deny culpability or try to deflect attention by fingering or discrediting someone else. Sometimes, of course, they do try to 'take out' their target, but Paul had already survived several shootings and was now firmly in the public eye.

While President Mbeki's and Jacob Zuma's supporters were plotting and executing complex behind-the-scenes manoeuvres in the run-up to Polokwane, O'Sullivan was drawing up his own battle plan. 'The idea was to completely wrong-foot them and have them running around like headless chickens.'

Selby Bokaba, a former journalist who had been appointed as Selebi's highly paid spin-doctor, was one such target. Bokaba, O'Sullivan learned, had approached journalists for an off-the-record meeting at which he trotted out the old Selebi story that O'Sullivan was a spy intent on destabilising the country.

Bokaba must have rued the day he crossed O'Sullivan, as it set off a series of emails which soon degenerated into open verbal warfare. O'Sullivan sometimes opened his emails with the salutation 'Hello sewer rat', or taunted him by labelling him a 'failed apartheid era Bop TV reporter', which outraged Bokaba.

The exchange started off in what are relatively polite terms in O'Sullivan's books, when he questioned Bokaba's reasons for 'spreading malicious rumours and defamatory lies about me'. 'Is this because you have something to hide yourself? Or is it that this is part of a lackey's job?' he asked. He continued: 'Either way, it is despicable and should cease forthwith. I'm a taxpayer and contribute to your salary. I note that you do not contribute to my salary, or to the country, other than blindly serving your "master". For every stone that you or any other of Selebi's cronies throw, I have a dozen lined up ready to throw back. The thing is, I don't live in a glasshouse, you do.'

The feud continued right up till October that year when Bokaba mailed O'Sullivan, telling him that, apart from the fact that 'your mother is a cheap Hillbrow whore', 'Jackie will not be convicted for any crime. I can bet my life on it. U promised the President was going to take action against him, and voila, what happened was the opposite. I can't wait for December 16 [start of the Polokwane conference] … Ur History. U'll never set foot in SA again, not even under a disguise.'

Within a year of Selebi's downfall, Bokaba was forced out of the police, after his emails were sent by O'Sullivan by way of a formal complaint and he has been job hopping ever since, having been forced to quit his job as chief director of communications at the Department of Agriculture, after making unauthorised statements to the media. Bokaba now works as a spokesman for the Tshwane City Council.

✳

In March 2007, Interpol held a three-day training symposium in Johannesburg, which proved mildly embarrassing when Selebi's minders attempted to prevent journalists from asking Ronald Noble, Interpol general secretary, uncomfortable questions about Selebi's then alleged links to the international underworld.

Until then, Interpol had offered its full support for Selebi from the time the allegations became public in 2006. In the meantime the organisation had resolved that it would discuss Selebi's position at an upcoming General Assembly due to take place in Morocco in November 2007, the same month Agliotti would be found guilty of drug-trafficking. If Selebi had managed to construct a *cordon sanitaire* around himself in South Africa, O'Sullivan was determined to ambush him outside the safety of the borders of the country.

In July 2007 Selebi was due to address Interpol's 19th Regional Conference in Arusha, Tanzania. 'I took the ads for the Tanzania conference and emailed them to him from my Scarlet Pimpernel address with the message "this will be great, see you there",' O'Sullivan says with a chuckle.

Expecting a heckler, conference organisers ramped up security, but of course O'Sullivan didn't attend. This was all intended to keep Selebi 'on his toes and looking over his shoulder'. Selebi's speech to delegates at the Arusha meeting included the usual platitudes about curbing the small arms and drugs trade in Africa as well as the devastating effect of counterfeit pharmaceuticals on Africans.

'There was another conference due to take place in Europe and I sent Selebi another mail. This time I said, "I'm going to drag your name through the mud." And of course again I didn't go.' Whether Selebi was in any way perturbed by Paul's threats to expose him, we will never know, but he seemed to believe that upping security at the events would prevent O'Sullivan from sabotaging him.

As the Interpol 76th General Assembly, which would take place in Morocco in November 2007, loomed, O'Sullivan prepared for the *coup de grâce* of his campaign. 'Firstly, I got someone I know who was close to Selebi to whisper to him that I was a bullshitter and that I wouldn't attend the conference in Marrakesh. He'd leave for that one relaxed,' Paul recounts.

The world's top policemen would be gathered at the five-star, luxury Espace Hotel Mansour Eddahbi Palais des Congrès to discuss a range of issues, including human trafficking and terrorism. Selebi was due to present his opening speech in front of some of the world's most senior law-enforcement officers and O'Sullivan was poised to use the opportunity to expose and humiliate him.

He got to work on a 12-page brochure titled 'How the Mafia Have Infiltrated Interpol'. It was headed with three photographs, one of Glenn Agliotti, captioned 'the Family', one of a smiling Jackie Selebi and a third with Interpol's logo, captioned 'the Organisation'.

O'Sullivan cut to the chase: 'This document intends to show just how transnational crime syndicates have penetrated Interpol and even have Interpol's head [Jackie Selebi] in their pocket.

'This is a chilling tale of low ethics and corruption, intimidation, human trafficking, drug trafficking, fraud and corruption, robbery, attempted murder and murder.'

O'Sullivan dealt a few more body blows and quoted extensively from Clinton Nassif's affidavit detailing Selebi's corrupt relationship with Glenn Agliotti, the Kebbles and various other suspects who had claimed to have paid him bribes. He copied and pasted several of Selebi's speeches to Interpol conferences in which he had talked the talk, highlighting that police corruption was the biggest threat to international law enforcement. O'Sullivan signed off by asking delegates whether they were prepared to deal with these grave allegations against their president or simply sweep them under the carpet.

Then he packed his bag for Marrakesh, stuffing enough copies of the 'Selebi brochure' in his briefcase. 'I flew into Morocco from London and checked into a hotel nearby. I reckoned if you're going to play in the big league, you'd better have a big bat, and my brochure was my bat.'

Dressed in his black suit and carrying his briefcase, the renegade investigator did not look out of place at the gathering of policemen. He knew how to move among the crowd as if he belonged there. After all, he had spent the best part of 30 years as a cop himself.

Selebi was due to make his address at 10:30 on the morning of 5 November. 'I waited for a tea break to make my move. Selebi was due to address the conference afterwards. I talked my way into the conference venue, telling security I'd left my ID in my hotel room. I went around the room putting a copy of my brochure on every single seat facing the top table. I was careful that no one on the top table got one.'

At the end of the conference day, O'Sullivan floated around the main hotel to pick up the vibes and feeling about the hand-out. It was clear that tongues were wagging and he was even rewarded with a beer by a couple of Australian cops who had taken to his style and wanted to know more. As he was dishing out the last of his brochures in the main hotel cocktail bar area, he was challenged by what he describes 'as a very short guy in a suit with an American accent', who approached O'Sullivan and demanded to see his passport.

O'Sullivan's response was abrupt: 'What's your jurisdiction?'

The man replied that he was on the executive of Interpol and that he was entitled to see his passport. O'Sullivan typically replied: 'Listen, mate, this is Africa, not Lyon, so get out of my face before I put you on my key-ring.' The man, whom O'Sullivan refers to as 'Shorty', left to get backup, but by the time he returned 'the Scarlet Pimpernel had vanished'.

Sensing that the brochure would cause a scandal and enrage Selebi, O'Sullivan slipped out of Morocco as soon as possible, flying to France, where he implemented phase two of the Morocco plan. 'I really wanted to rattle him, so I wrote this semi-official-looking letter that I emailed to the hotel manager in Morocco. I called about 2 a.m. local time and asked him to please pop the urgent letter under President Selebi's door.'

The manager did as he was told and delivered the letter from 'The Office for Special Investigations of Interpol, South Africa' to room 6005.

'Dear President Selebi,' it opened, followed by the headline 'Investigation regarding the Scarlet Pimpernel'. It continued: 'Further to documents dropped off at your hotel and distributed to various members of the Interpol fraternity, revealing your criminal activities, our investigations have revealed the following ...' O'Sullivan let Selebi know that this 'Pimpernel' was 'hell bent' on setting the record straight, that he had skills 'he has just started to deploy' and that 'he will leave no stone unturned getting back at you'.

O'Sullivan waited a few minutes after he had issued his email instruction before calling the hotel. 'Then I called Jackie's room myself. A woman picked up [not Selebi's wife, he noted] and I asked to speak to the commissioner. When he came on the line, I asked him what he thought of the letter and challenged him to meet me downstairs in the foyer ... He slammed down the phone,' O'Sullivan says with a hearty laugh.

O'Sullivan returned to South Africa a while later, that particular mission accomplished with flair, he reckoned. He subsequently learned that Selebi had cowered in his hotel room, while awaiting a special police escort from the Moroccan police to the conference suite.

Chapter 18

Meanwhile, Elsewhere – Jackie Spreads the Love

IN MID-2007, AS VARIOUS FORCES and factions worked to destabilise the Scorpion's case against Jackie Selebi, Paul O'Sullivan began to track other witnesses who might prove more reliable than the opportunistic Agliotti.

Back in 2004, *Noseweek*, the fearless, independent investigative magazine edited by Martin Welz, had published a story about a 'remarkable dossier' that the South African Revenue Service had been sitting on for several years. The dossier, *Noseweek* revealed, had been compiled by Knysna businessman Michael Addinall, who was serving a five-year jail term in Pretoria's Atteridgeville prison in terms of the Prevention of Organised Crime Act.

Over a period of six years ending in 2001, Addinall had illegally moved about R2 billion offshore, defrauding SARS of millions in income tax, customs duty and VAT. The 'great forex scam', as *Noseweek* termed it, had been operated by a local criminal syndicate that imported grey goods into South Africa. Foreign suppliers would under-invoice for the merchandise, which would be sold on to established retail outlets. The profits from the 'arrangement' would then be parked safely offshore. Addinall named the Johannesburg-based Imran Ismail and the Cape Town multi-millionaire Ronnie Lipman as the 'leading importers of grey goods to South Africa'.

In a series of follow-up stories in 2007, *Noseweek* exposed how several wealthy South Africans had used the scheme to send 'hot' money offshore, paying the syndicate a percentage to convert the booty into US dollars. Details of the complicated syndicate, which involved senior banking officials and a number of wealthy South Africans, had initially escaped media attention, as these had been revealed during a secret insolvency inquiry.

At a later plea bargain, Addinall had read out his statement, which contained an extraordinary nugget of information: that Jackie Selebi and another senior policeman, Gauteng Commissioner Sharma Maharaj, were both on the syndicate's payroll. Maharaj took early retirement in 2001 and died a year later at 55.

Addinall claimed that the Rosebank jeweller Steven Ferrer, who regularly discounted cheques for him, had boasted to him that the police chief Jackie Selebi was on his payroll. Ferrer, who fled South Africa in 2001, owned 'Mister Jewellery' outlets in Cape Town and Johannesburg and was implicated by Addinall as the middleman and major cheque discounter in some of the illegal forex transactions. Ferrer, Addinall claimed, 'knew everyone of consequence in Johannesburg, Pretoria and Cape Town'. Ferrer, he added, would import expensive watches and perfume and arrange to have the master waybill deleted from the system, eradicating all trace of the goods entering South Africa.

A paragraph in his statement reads: 'I knew that Steven Ferrer was the major discounter for a lot of companies doing grey imports.

He was also a personal friend of Jackie Selebi and on more than one occasion told me that he was OK, as Jackie Selebi was on his payroll.'

What *Noseweek* found puzzling was the fact that while authorities had been alerted in 2002 by another member of the syndicate that Selebi and Maharaj were on the syndicate's payroll, they seemed to simply ignore it. Even curiouser was the fact that Addinall's disclosure document had been circulated to Advocate Paul Louw (senior prosecutor at the Scorpions), the SARS investigator Johan Kloppers and Inspector Angus Rheeder from the police's Commercial Crime Unit in Pretoria, and, again, no one had seemed to pick up on the Selebi connection.

The *Noseweek* exposé set out how Ferrer claimed to have made payments to Commissioner Maharaj and Selebi on the instructions of Ismail. Ferrer remarked that he was better acquainted with Maharaj, as Selebi had only been appointed national commissioner in 2000. He explained: 'How Selebi appeared on the scene and what he was doing in order to protect Ismail, and how much he was paid, I honestly don't know.

'But there were regular payments and I know Selebi also received gifts from Ismail. They would be R10,000, R5000, R7000, those kinds of payments. That was through me. A lot of it was cash. There were occasions where Imran would say: "Listen, Selebi's driver has arrived in Rosebank. Won't you do me a favour and just go out and give him this envelope?" That's how it worked.

'I did keep certain records and on occasion I would make out a cheque so that I would have proof if it ever came to this. Jackie would often be with his driver. To this day it confounds me that the country is burning and yet he would come through in his BMW with his driver just to say hello to me.'

Paul was not going to allow the testimony of this vital witness to simply slip off the radar. Soon after the *Noseweek* stories appeared he tracked Ferrer down to Georgia, where he had fled in mid-2000 after learning that SARS was investigating him. Ferrer had subsequently opened a jewellery shop in Atlanta and was desperate to secure an indemnity from prosecution. O'Sullivan was willing to help negotiate it for him.

For several years Ferrer had tried to arrange this indemnity with little success. It was Paul's promise that he would assist him to secure this if he came clean which would later prompt Ferrer's full disclosure. 'This is a once-off opportunity to draw a line in the sand and cross that line, never to go back. This indemnity thing works and it's like a miracle. The people that received it have found a new lease on life and have been able to put their past behind them. You can too! GO FOR IT.'

O'Sullivan spent several years 'cultivating' Ferrer, who eventually returned to South Africa in 2009. 'I arranged several meetings with him with a view to obtaining a rock-solid sworn statement that could be used by the NPA against Selebi,' he recalls.

But it was not to be.

*

As O'Sullivan prepared to take Ferrer's statement, a controversial 'private detective', debt collector and former apartheid operative, Kevin Trytsman, unexpectedly stepped into the spotlight.

Trytsman had a chequered past and had received amnesty at the Truth and Reconciliation Commission for his role in the notorious and ruthless apartheid hit squads deployed by the state security apparatus. He had apparently been 'rehabilitated' and was working for the country's National Intelligence Agency.

Trytsman, Ferrer reported back to O'Sullivan, had threatened him and instructed him not to provide the NPA with any statements that had not been vetted by him first. Trytsman also mentioned to Ferrer that he was a close friend of the NIA boss, Gibson Njenje, so close in fact that Njenje was his son's godfather. Trytsman warned Ferrer that Paul O'Sullivan and the Scorpions prosecutors Gerrie Nel and Andrew Leask 'were not to be trusted'.

Trytsman's interference was a setback for O'Sullivan and delayed Ferrer's making a sworn statement, an explosive document which he eventually provided only in October 2009. O'Sullivan then turned his attention to Michael Addinall and met him several times. In the process Addinall supplied him with copious documents. A week after meeting with O'Sullivan, Addinall was arrested and taken to Richard Mdluli's office. Mdluli was then head of Crime Intelligence in Gauteng and reported directly to Mulangi Mphego. Addinall informed O'Sullivan that he had been told by Mdluli not to have anything to do with O'Sullivan, as he was a spy and would soon be arrested. Furthermore, according to Addinall, if he did not comply, his parole would be cancelled and he would be sent back to prison.

While he waited and worked on Ferrer, O'Sullivan began to conduct his own investigation into Trytsman. Trytsman, he discovered, was 'nothing more than a petty crook and a conman' who had associations with a range of known criminals and individuals involved in extortion. One of the names he was linked to was the Czech fugitive Radovan Krejcir. Krejcir had made a dramatic escape from his homeland during a police search of his villa near Prague in 2005. The billionaire 'businessman' was wanted on a number of serious charges in his own country and was linked to several murders and other crimes. Czech police had also fingered him as a major and ruthless player in the criminal underworld in that country.

A cache of illegal firearms and several billion crowns in fake Czech currency had been found during the search of Krejcir's villa, but he had managed a miraculous escape through a back door. Underworld friends and contacts then helped him procure a false passport, and he headed for Poland and the Ukraine. From there he made his way to Turkey and Dubai, finally arriving in the Seychelles on a false passport on 7 September 2005.

The fugitive Krejcir fled to South Africa in 2007 under a false name, Julius Egbert Savey, on a forged Seychellois passport and was immediately detained at the airport on an Interpol international 'red notice'. Krejcir spent his first three months in South Africa languishing in a cell at the Kempton Park police station. As criminal luck would have it, he shared a portion of this time with the Cypriot George Louka (Smith), who was closely linked to the strip-club boss, money-launderer and tax evader, Lolly Jackson. Louka, a small-time criminal hustler, had been arrested after police found around R2 million worth of parts stripped from a hijacked truck at the supermarket he ran with his *de facto* wife on the East Rand.

Louka apparently impressed Krejcir when he managed, from the cells, to source a Surf and Turf meal and caviar from the nearby Emperors Palace Casino. Krejcir could not have wished for a more fortuitous encounter, as this meeting no doubt lubricated his later entry into the top echelons of South Africa's criminal underworld.

Louka would flee South Africa in 2010 after allegedly pumping six bullets into Lolly Jackson at close range and killing him instantly during an altercation in Louka's house in Edleen, east of Johannesburg. O'Sullivan believes Louka was not the triggerman.

While Krejcir was a peripheral figure on Paul's radar at the time, he would soon find himself – as Jackie Selebi made his exit – firmly centre stage and in the investigator's relentless spotlight.

Meanwhile, Kevin Trytsman hovered on the horizon, and Paul was not going to let this valuable source escape without milking him first for information on Lolly Jackson and Radovan Krejcir.

But back in 2007 there was still only one lead player on O'Sullivan's mind, Jackie Selebi.

Chapter 19

Fallout and Endgame

WHILE HUMILIATING SELEBI IN Morocco had been another small victory for O'Sullivan, towards the end of 2007 he was a worried man.

On 24 September, the day before warrants for the arrest of Selebi and the search of his office and home were about to be executed, President Thabo Mbeki suspended Vusi Pikoli. This disturbing decision, as Pikoli was generally viewed as a man of high integrity, came after months of behind-the-scenes manoeuvrings, all seemingly designed to protect Selebi and prevent him from being charged.

The day before it was publicly announced that Pikoli had been suspended, O'Sullivan was having a champagne lunch with his aunt and uncle at a plush hotel near Ascot in the UK, prematurely celebrating Selebi's imminent arrest.

Mbeki had told Pikoli that he was particularly concerned that violent and dangerous criminals (Glenn Agliotti, Paul Stemmet, Clinton Nassif) had all been granted indemnity from prosecution in exchange for exposing Selebi. Pikoli in turn reminded the president that the NPA was perfectly within its rights to do so, especially as the suspect held an extremely powerful position as head of the SAPS and that he was a bigger threat to the country's security and well-being than the criminals who had bribed him. In O'Sullivan's words, 'supping with the devil is sometimes necessary, in the bigger scheme of things, so that the greater good can be served'.

Inexplicably, as more and more damning evidence against Selebi was made public, the president and the ANC continued to offer public support for the national commissioner. Mbeki told the citizens of the country that he had suspended Pikoli because of an apparent breakdown in relations between the national director of public prosecutions, the Scorpions, the minister of justice and the SAPS over several fraught and acrimonious months.

Perhaps in an attempt to lend credibility to his actions, Mbeki announced the establishment of a commission of inquiry, headed by the ANC heavyweight Frene Ginwala, which would evaluate Pikoli's 'fitness for office'. About a year later, the Ginwala Commission, in a three-volume report, vindicated Pikoli but rejected the allegation that Mbeki and other ANC members had conspired to protect Selebi from arrest.

O'Sullivan did not agree with the commission's findings and laid a charge of defeating the ends of justice against Mbeki, Mabandla and others.

But back in September 2007, just as the Scorpions were about to reel in the big, rotten fish, Mbeki stepped in, cut the line and allowed Selebi to swim free. For the time being.

Away from the headlines (but not for long) a full-scale turf war between the Scorpions, the SAPS and the National Intelligence Agency (NIA) was raging. For several years the Selebi ally and Crime Intelligence boss, Mulangi Mphego, had conducted an extensive covert counter-offensive operation with the decidedly paranoid moniker Operation Destroy Lucifer. The operation, launched in

2007 with Selebi's approval, included the illegal interception of communications and wiretaps on anyone and everyone deemed to be an 'enemy', including Scorpions investigators and prosecutors, Paul O'Sullivan, the DSO head Leonard McCarthy, as well as the former head of the NPA Bulelani Ngcuka.

The aims of Operation Lucifer were multifold and wide-ranging and involved determining how much the Scorpions 'had' on Selebi, turning key Selebi witnesses like Agliotti, and gathering intelligence in the ugly feud between the ANC and the DA in the Western Cape.

Suddenly, on 27 December, a new twist in the complex tale developed. Ten days after Jacob Zuma had been triumphantly installed at Polokwane as the overwhelmingly popular choice as new president of the ANC, the new acting head of the NPA, Mokotedi Mpshe, announced that charges of racketeering, corruption, money-laundering and tax evasion were to be reinstated against the ANC president. To Zuma's enemies this was proof that the charges had been politically motivated all along.

Operation Lucifer would, of course, provide a controversial lifeline for Zuma in 2008 when Mphego supplied the ANC president's lawyer, Michael Hulley, with what have now become known as the infamous 'spy tapes'. These were illicit recordings between Leonard McCarthy and Bulelani Ncguka which allegedly proved that the corruption charges were part of a larger political conspiracy orchestrated by Thabo Mbeki. According to O'Sullivan, the phones were tapped for two reasons. Firstly, to make sure that there were no rogue elements in the Scorpions who would go ahead and arrest Selebi anyway and, secondly, in the hope that they could find some dirt on Gerrie Nel, so that they could arrest and charge him, thereby throwing a spanner in the works long enough to get past the date on which the Scorpions would be disbanded.

O'Sullivan says that Selebi was delighted with the tapes, as he reckoned he could use them to ingratiate himself with the 'Zuma camp', despite using his office to help Mbeki against Zuma. Of course, Selebi did not reckon on Mdluli and the other members of his 'cabal' opting to go it alone, cementing a good relationship with Zuma's allies, and effectively hanging Selebi out to dry should Mbeki be forced to step down.

Zuma's case would bounce from the High Court in September 2008 (where Judge Chris Nicholson dismissed the charges) to the Supreme Court of Appeal (which reversed Judge Nicholson's finding in January 2009) and back to the NPA, which by then was headed by Zuma's point man, Menzi Simelane.

Zuma's legal team later lodged representations with the NPA and its new head, Simelane, arguing that the case had been politically manipulated by elements in the NPA. Simelane's announcement on 6 April 2009 that the NPA would not be prosecuting Zuma came as no surprise. A few days later, in a national election, South Africans overwhelmingly voted Jacob Zuma to the highest office of the country.

But in 2007, the new acting NPA head, Mokotedi Mpshe, a former homeland government lawyer and academic, found himself in an unenviable position, caught in powerful, swirling political undercurrents. To deal with the Selebi matter, Mpshe convened a panel of experts, including the former DSO head Frank Dutton, Advocate Mbuyiseli Madlanga, Peter Goss and Advocate Shamila Bathoi. The experts were tasked with reviewing all the evidence and reporting back to him on the viability of a prosecution.

Meanwhile, Glenn Agliotti, surveying the changing political landscape, opted, as any canny opportunist would, to hedge his bets. While he had agreed to help the Scorpions as part of his December 2007 drug-trafficking sentence, after Pikoli's suspension Agliotti began to speculate that Selebi's 'fight-back' campaign might just prove successful, in which case he would not need a plea bargain, as he would walk away from it all, a free man.

Early in the new year Agliotti changed his tune. It wasn't a difficult decision. He was no stranger to mendacity, a characteristic his legal team would try to exploit later in the Kebble trial. At two meetings arranged by Mphego and the NIA head, Manala Manzini, one of which took place at the Balalaika Hotel, Agliotti claimed (on camera) that the Scorpions had forced him to lie about his relationship with Selebi and that he had never bribed the national commissioner. Mphego, quick to extract benefit for Selebi, arranged a private viewing of the video for select, sympathetic members of the media.

A few days later Selebi used Agliotti's new improved statement to Mphego and Manzini to launch a High Court application to quash the warrant for his arrest, which was still valid. In an attempt to ward off his imminent arrest, Selebi would also deploy a statement from Lawrence Mrwebi, KwaZulu-Natal Scorpions head, revealing details of the Scorpions management meeting of July 2007.

Mrwebi later said he had been surprised to find that his affidavit, which he had given to the NIA deputy Arthur Fraser, was used by Selebi as proof that the Scorpions had been targeting him. O'Sullivan alleges that Mrwebi lied all along and always intended that the affidavit be used as and when it could, to save Selebi from the inevitable fall from grace.

In response to Selebi, the Scorpions filed their case opposing his application and setting out, in a 335-page document of damning sworn statements, the state's entire case.

Mpshe, meanwhile, announced that the NPA review panel had found that Selebi did indeed have a case to answer and that he would soon be charged. Mpshe triumphantly declared that Agliotti had done another flip-flop and subsequently renounced the statement he had made earlier in January to Mphego at the Balalaika Hotel, claiming he had been drunk at the time. Restaurant slips were obtained by O'Sullivan, of Agliotti's lunchtime soirée, showing that he and his 'partner' had consumed two bottles of wine out near Pecanwood.

South Africans attempting to follow the convoluted twists and turns in the unfolding drama at this stage no doubt felt like Alice tumbling down the rabbit hole or the character Neo in the 1999 science fiction thriller *The Matrix*, faced with the choice of taking the blue pill and remaining blissfully ignorant or taking the red pill and discovering 'how deep the rabbit hole goes'.

✳

2008 started with a bang for the Scorpions prosecutor Gerrie Nel. On 8 January, as he returned home from a year-end holiday with his family, 20 heavily armed policemen (acting on the instructions of Richard Mdluli, who reported directly to Mphego) were waiting to arrest him. Nel was cuffed in front of his family outside his home in Garsfontein, a quiet up-market suburb in Pretoria, and hauled off in his shorts to a police station, where he was held overnight. He was released the following day on R10,000 bail.

About a week later, five charges of corruption, perjury and defeating the ends of justice, relating to Nel's alleged interference in the prosecution of Cornwell Tshavhungwa, a former Gauteng Scorpions director, were withdrawn because of a lack of evidence.

But what had been behind this bizarre arrest and the show of force used to execute it? Had the SAPS declared open warfare on the Scorpions? Was this Selebi's last desperate stand? Was this the showdown at the OK Corral?

O'Sullivan watched the dramatic events unfolding from the sidelines. Would this be the moment that the man he had been trying to bring down for over seven years would finally be hoisted by his own petard or would he simply walk away from it all?

It emerged later that it was no coincidence that Nel's arrest had occurred so soon after Mphego's meeting with Agliotti at the Balalaika Hotel earlier in the year. Nel, among others, had been in Mphego's and the NIA's sights and was one of several 'suspects' who featured in Operation Destroy Lucifer. Selebi's SAPS cronies had been working with rogue elements in the NIA on securing a warrant for Nel's arrest since September the previous year, on trumped-up charges arising out of discussions discovered in the illegal phone taps.

There were three people behind the scramble for the warrant for Nel's arrest: Nomgcobo Jiba, a disgruntled Scorpions prosecutor; Lawrence Mrwebi; and their 'comrade', the controversial Gauteng head of police Crime Intelligence, Richard Mdluli.

Mdluli has served as a police officer for over 30 years, which would locate him within the discredited former apartheid police force. He joined the SAP in 1979 and rose to the rank of deputy police commissioner for crime intelligence in Gauteng. Mdluli is a man who wielded enormous power in the murky intelligence world, where he had access to confidential information on a number of powerful political players.

When Mphego later resigned after being criminally charged, Mdluli would find himself facing serious criminal charges, including murder and fraud. The charges were later mysteriously withdrawn by Mrwebi, who had been appointed in November 2011 by President Jacob Zuma as head of the NPA's Specialised Commercial Crime Unit. O'Sullivan believes the withdrawal of charges was essentially a favour by Mrwebi to Mdluli for his earlier assistance in trying to scupper the Selebi prosecution.

'Mdluli was the architect of a campaign to derail the investigation into Selebi. He created fictitious dockets, intimidated witnesses and bugged the phones of several people who would have been instrumental in bringing him to justice,' O'Sullivan told the *Mail & Guardian*.

In August 2013, Judge John Murphy ruled in the Pretoria High Court that all charges against Mdluli be reinstated. In May, Freedom Under Law (FUL), a legal watchdog founded by the former Constitutional Court judge Johann Kriegler, had launched an urgent application against the national director of public prosecutions and five other public officials, challenging the withdrawal of charges against Mdluli. In June 2012, Judge Ephraim Makgoba granted FUL an interim order blocking the commissioner of police from assigning any duties to Mdluli. While suspended, Mdluli remained the head of SAPS Crime Intelligence.

In the August judgment Judge Murphy launched a stinging attack on Nomgcobo Jiba, Mrwebi and Andrew Chauke, the director of public prosecutions who withdrew murder charges against Mdluli. Murphy criticised them for their ongoing attempts to delay proceedings and their lack of transparency. 'The attitude of the respondents signals a troubling lack of appreciation of the constitutional ethos and principles underpinning the offices they hold,' he said.

At the time of writing, the deputy judge president of the High Court, Aubrey Ledwaba, granted Mdluli leave to appeal against Judge Murphy's ruling. The matter is now set to be heard in the Supreme Court of Appeal. The door to Mdluli's reinstatement will be opened should the Appeal Court rule in favour of Mdluli, the NPA and the Specialised Commercial Crime Unit. The application by Freedom Under Law with regard to an interdict preventing Mdluli from being reinstated will continue at a later stage.

Prosecutor Glynnis Breytenbach, who had been investigating Mdluli, was unlawfully suspended in April 2012 and her battle to return to her job from which she was unfairly dismissed continued to play out in the courts at the time of writing.

But in 2008 it was Gerrie Nel's turn to feel the heat from the untouchable holy trinity of Jiba, Mrwebi and Mdluli. Jiba had blamed Nel for the 2005 conviction and jailing of her husband, Booker Nhantsi, an attorney, for the theft of R195,000 from a trust fund. At the time of the conviction Nhantsi worked as the deputy director of the Scorpions in the Eastern Cape. Later, in 2010, President Zuma 'pardoned' Nhantsi, and Jiba, despite a contentious career with the NPA, would also miraculously survive and find herself appointed by Zuma as the acting head of the authority!

In 2012 O'Sullivan, determined not to let the conspirators slip out of view, filed an over-300-page criminal docket charging that there had been a conspiracy between Mphego, Mdluli, Jiba and Mrwebi. The case has not yet proceeded. O'Sullivan has vowed to pursue it with the same vigour as the Selebi matter as 'These people are prime evil and the country simply deserves better'.

In 2008, shortly after Nel's arrest, Jiba found herself suspended, facing internal charges of bringing the NPA into disrepute. In contesting her suspension Jiba would, of course, find herself supported by Mdluli. Mdluli had also testified for Jiba in her disciplinary hearing at the NPA, following which she was fired. After the DSO was disbanded Jiba slipped back in, following a settlement with Menzi Simelane, who had to be removed after the DA brought a court application to have him declared unfit to hold office.

The night of his arrest Nel immediately procured the services of the attorney Ian Small-Smith, who had represented the Kebble hitmen, Mikey Schultz, Nigel McGurk and Faizel Smith. O'Sullivan said at the time that Nel's choice of attorney was unfortunate and would haunt him for many years to come.

Small-Smith spent the night trying to serve on police an urgent application declaring the warrant invalid, but the investigating officer in the arrest simply turned off his phone. Mokotedi Mpshe in turn told journalists that he was 'shocked and concerned' by the turn of events and that, while he had been aware that police were trying to obtain a warrant for Nel, protocol required the head of the NPA to be informed of the imminent arrest of a prosecutor in such a high-profile matter.

There were howls of protest surrounding Nel's arrest. The DA spokesperson on safety and security, Dianne Kohler Barnard, declared that Nel's arrest and Pikoli's suspension clearly amounted to a 'witch-hunt' by those seeking to protect Selebi. O'Sullivan was convinced that the entire circus was evidence of 'the dying throes of an evil conspiracy to keep Selebi out of prison'.

Meanwhile, Selebi, in a desperate last bid, filed an urgent application in the Pretoria High Court requesting a complete stay of any and all criminal charges against him. His papers were filed to coincide with Nel's arrest, to obtain maximum effect from the confusion, and the time had come, believed O'Sullivan 'to make or break it'.

The NPA hit back immediately and Mpshe released an affidavit detailing the state's case. The charges, Mpshe wrote, were in relation to Selebi's 'longstanding corrupt' relationship with Glenn Agliotti, the receipt of payments of over R1.2 million from the convicted drug-trafficker, his turning of a blind eye to Agliotti's involvement in the transporting of Mandrax (in the Kya Sands bust) as well as

Selebi's sharing of confidential UK intelligence reports with Agliotti about his transnational drug-smuggling activities.

Selebi's lawyer, Jaap Cilliers, argued that the charges were 'vague' and that prosecuting his client would tarnish his reputation. On 11 January 2008, Judge Nico Coetzee replied that Selebi's 'reputation is already tarnished' and ruled that there was no merit to Selebi's application to have charges withdrawn. The case, he ruled, would proceed.

Mpshe told journalists that the charges against the police chief were 'based on a strong *prima facie* case supported by the testimony of a range of witnesses and corroborated by real evidence'. Selebi, he said, would not be arrested but would be expected to appear in court of his own volition.

O'Sullivan was watching the proceedings that took place on 11 January with a growing sense of excitement. It was a weekend of celebration for the investigator, marking the possible end of a relentless eight-year battle that had cost him more than R5 million and almost his life. With lost income thrown into the damages, the figure was well over R15m.

On 12 January 2008, President Thabo Mbeki, who had suffered a humiliating defeat at Polokwane, announced that his police chief, a man he had appointed, supported and protected, was taking 'special leave'. Speaking from the Union Buildings, Mbeki said that it was Selebi who had suggested he take leave while the dust settled. The same day, Selebi resigned as the world's top cop in a single-page letter to Interpol. O'Sullivan was now riding out of the woods and on the downhill run.

There were immediate and unanimous calls by all the country's opposition parties for Selebi to do the right thing and resign. But the disgraced police chief was not quite ready to give up. Perhaps he had some premonition of the fact that in June 2008, three months after he shuffled into the dock of the Randburg Magistrate's Court, President Thabo Mbeki would renew his old friend's contract as the national commissioner for another 12 months!

O'Sullivan believed this proved the close bond between Mbeki and Selebi and that the friendship would cost taxpayers around R2 million in fruitless and wasteful expenditure. O'Sullivan was also convinced that Mbeki needed Selebi on his payroll, as he was still 'pulling strings' behind the scenes to prevent 'damaging evidence' from being released to the Scorpions. Selebi retained his bodyguards at a further cost of R2 million to taxpayers.

It is clear from his resignation letter to Interpol's general secretary, Ronald Noble, that Selebi was confident at the time that he would not be found guilty. He ended the note stating that he would now 'devote my energies to clearing my name'.

In September 2008 the victorious Zuma camp exacted its painful revenge on Thabo Mbeki, 'recalling' the sitting president nine months before his second term in office was due to end in April 2009. A humiliated and angry Mbeki was advised to go quietly and voluntarily tender his resignation, an instruction he duly obeyed, making the announcement on national television. Facing the nation during a prime-time Sunday night broadcast, he concluded his long goodbye, declaring that he had never interfered in the NPA's investigation into Jacob Zuma. 'I would like to say that gloom and despondency have never defeated adversity. Trying times need courage and resilience. Our strength as a people is not tested during the best of times. As we have said before, we should never become despondent because the weather is bad nor should we turn triumphalist because the sun shines,' Mbeki said.

The following month the sun would finally set on the Scorpions when an ANC majority vote in Parliament approved legislation to dissolve the unit.

In December 2008, acting President Kgalema Motlanthe finally fired Vusi Pikoli, despite the Ginwala Commission's findings that he was a 'person of unimpeachable integrity', had been 'fit and proper to hold office' and should be reinstated to his position as NPA head. Pikoli, Motlanthe suggested, had not been sensitive to 'matters of national security' and this was justification enough to sack him.

It was a tragic, shameful and worrying end of an era. In a few months Jackie Selebi's conviction and sentencing would, finally, prove to be not so much a fullstop to the 'Mbeki years' as merely a comma in a much grander narrative that is still unfolding. Clandestine allegiances, backed or thwarted by competing intelligence forces, were far from calling it a draw and the Zuma presidency, like a game of extreme *Survivor*, would provide a range of new 'immunity challenges' that continue to make headlines.

Chapter 20

The Can of Worms: Selebi on Trial – Paul's New Cleanup Begins

SELEBI CUT A PATHETIC FIGURE at the start of his trial in courtroom 4B of the Johannesburg High Court on 5 October 2009. It was an altogether different scenario from his earlier court appearances at the Randburg Magistrate's Court in February and June 2008 when he had been supported by a phalanx of police officers, many of them senior commissioners in full uniform, in an impressive show of solidarity.

O'Sullivan says he was 'deeply disgusted by this display of misplaced, blind loyalty'. Here were the country's top policemen, including André Pruis and Ray Lalla, men whose salaries were paid by South African taxpayers, supporting their boss in his final hour of disgrace. Had their priorities been so corrupted that they could no longer tell right from wrong? he wondered. But he wasn't surprised at the public show of support by law-enforcement officers.

The new chief of police, Bheki Cele, who himself would later be sacked following tender irregularities, gave strict orders that no police officer, even if taking leave, could appear at the High Court trial, unless they were there as witnesses.

One thing O'Sullivan had learned during his eight lonely years chasing Jackie Selebi was that power and money had corrupted many South Africans along the way.

There were those who – as is often the case in this country – framed the sorry saga in racial terms. The cop who was dirty was black and most of the investigators who were working on the case were white. Playing into this false paradigm would obscure the fact that the overwhelming majority of the criminals and businessmen who corrupted the national commissioner and his cronies were all white. These included Brett Kebble, John Stratton, Glenn Agliotti, Clinton Nassif, Paul Stemmet and many others, who thought nothing of helping themselves to billions that did not belong to them. The common denominator here was not race but venality and greed.

Then there were the politicians who seemed more preoccupied and concerned with protecting a comrade and their own political welfare than acting in the interests of the country's greater good. There appeared to be a general and overwhelming 'wilful blindness' when it came to accepting Selebi's culpability, the threat he posed to the country's young democracy, to the government's credibility and its ability to serve voters and the public. Selebi was being targeted by the 'CIA', 'MI5', 'MI6' and 'foreign agencies', politicians who should have known better muttered under their breath.

✻

On 7 October, two days after Selebi's trial kicked off, another of O'Sullivan's sources, code-named CS7, made contact and informed him that Kevin Trytsman had accosted and threatened him in the parking lot of a local supermarket. Trytsman told CS7 that he knew he had been working for Paul, that he (Trytsman) was working with Moe Shaik and Gibson Njenje and that they were going to 'shut down' the Selebi trial even though it had already kicked off. Trytsman also admitted that he had been behind a raid on CS7's home, that Paul was under surveillance and 'would soon be taken out' along with Andrew Leask and Gerrie Nel.

O'Sullivan immediately mobilised three additional sources to assist in gathering more intelligence on the link between Trytsman, Krejcir and Jackson, whose names were now increasingly intersecting on his radar. 'Three of my sources came back to me with very good data and it was CS7 who gave me access to a potential state witness, former banker Alekos Panayi,' said O'Sullivan.

On 30 November, O'Sullivan met with Panayi, who had worked as a general assistant with the Greek- and Cyprus-registered private bank Laiki. The meeting began around 5 p.m. and continued until the early hours of the morning as Panayi detailed how he had assisted Radovan Krejcir and Lolly Jackson to launder millions in foreign currency. The peeved Panayi wanted to get back at Jackson, who had falsely accused him of stealing money and forced him to sign a R650,000 acknowledgement of debt. Jackson had also allegedly attacked Panayi at his place of work and threatened to harm his family.

Like a shook-up soft-drink can, Panayi spewed out an omnidirectional fountain of information. 'I took the statement from Panayi in painstaking detail. He had told me he would only give evidence if he was not prosecuted, but I made it perfectly clear to him that I could not offer indemnity and that only an officer of the court could do so,' said Paul.

Paul learned that it was Panayi who had originally introduced Jackson to Krejcir, whom he had met through a fellow Cypriot, George Louka (aka George Smith) in 2007. Panayi set out how he had helped Jackson, who, along with Krejcir, had an obsession with expensive, luxury fast cars, to fraudulently import an Italian-made Pagani Zonda from Singapore. Jackson had a garage full of exotic cars worth around R90 million at the time of his death.

Krejcir shared Jackson's passion for luxury sports cars, and it was only much later that Paul discovered that there was considerably more to these vehicles than their pimped-up engines. 'Krejcir was introduced,' said Panayi, 'because his off-shore company had an account with Laiki Bank in Cyprus. Krejcir then said he was relocating to South Africa and he needed to start bringing in funds … He said he needed to bring funds in legally and illegally.'

Panayi's insider knowledge offered O'Sullivan a much clearer perspective of the links between the individuals in the new gallery of rogues that had sprung up in the space where his old organogram, with Selebi at its centre, had once been.

Four days after Paul met with Panayi, Kevin Trytsman was shot dead in the eighth-floor Bedfordview office of his attorney, George Michaelides. Michaelides later confessed to O'Sullivan that he had shot Trytsman in self-defence and that George Louka (Smith) had walked into the offices afterwards and congratulated him. As a reward, Michaelides told O'Sullivan, Louka invited him to lunch with Krejcir to 'show his appreciation'. O'Sullivan subsequently discovered that Michaelides had murdered Trytsman in cold blood, because Trytsman had threatened to go public about Michaelides's theft of millions of rands of client funds.

Trytsman's death was no loss to society at large, and O'Sullivan was relieved that he had managed to extract a considerable amount of valuable information from him on Jackson and Krejcir before he was bumped off, such as that Krejcir had been paying off Trytsman in order to try to secure permanent residence in South Africa.

'I met with him [Trytsman] in October after he had threatened my source and told him I had enough on him to have him arrested. He was very apologetic and agreed to give me what I wanted if I left him alone,' said Paul. Trytsman told Paul that Jackson had been involved in a large-scale money-laundering scam and had, of course, also led him directly to Panayi. He also admitted that his claims to fame, with Moe Shaik and Gibson Njenje, were exaggerations to buy him credence. O'Sullivan took down all the Selebi charts and started his next project, which he called 'Czechmate'.

O'Sullivan had had sight of the charge sheet that Selebi would be facing and knew it contained only the tip of the iceberg. The extent and depth of Jackie Selebi's corruption would never be revealed in court. While he hoped that the entire can of worms would be wrenched open, O'Sullivan knew it was not to be. For now he was satisfied enough that Jackie Selebi had been removed from a position of influence and power and was finally having his day in court.

As the trial got under way, Sam Sole, writing in the *Mail & Guardian*, noted that while the newspaper and journalists who had worked on their own investigation on the police chief and his links to the criminal underworld had felt vindicated, the trial would leave many unanswered questions. Sole wrote: 'the Scorpions investigation – and our own – began with a much larger canvas.

'Kebble's murder lifted a corner on what appeared to be a very extensive organised crime network – with tentacles in the police, in customs and revenue, into Joburg's bouncer gangs and the drug-distribution turf they controlled, into smuggling networks that reached back to apartheid-era covert operations, into seemingly respectable business empires with multi-million-rand turnovers.'

Paul O'Sullivan made sure he was in the gallery the morning that the man who had cost him his job shuffled into the dock and chatted to police around him. The police commissioner glared at his nemesis and O'Sullivan savoured the moment. He thought of all Selebi's cronies, including Selby Bokaba, who was also in court to support his boss, blatantly ignoring Cele's orders. Bokaba had once vowed to O'Sullivan, in one of his many vitriolic emails, that Selebi would never be charged.

The spin doctor had also remarked to Paul that so confident was he that Jackie Selebi would never see the inside of a courtroom that he (Bokaba) would jump off the Carlton Centre, a well-known Johannesburg skyscraper, if it ever happened. O'Sullivan mailed Bokaba after it became clear that Selebi would be charged and suggested that Bokaba let him know when he intended to fulfil his promise, as he (O'Sullivan) would book a ringside seat and would 'hold his coat'.

There were two central charges in *The State* versus *Jacob Sello Selebi* Midrand CAS 796/01/2008, case number R/C 45/08: corruption and defeating the ends of justice. It was a 29-page charge sheet setting out the details of each count and listing over 30 witnesses, of which only 18 would eventually take the stand. The state's 'star' witness was his nattily dressed old friend Glenn Agliotti.

The first count related to Selebi's corrupt relationship with Agliotti as well as with the Kebbles and the Zimbabwean businessman and former Hyundai boss, Billy Rautenbach (who was facing tax evasion charges in South Africa), and his involvement with Stephen Sanders and Clinton Nassif in relation to an illegal SAPS training initiative in the Sudan.

The state alleged that Selebi had received around R1.2 million in payments for various favours, including turning a blind eye to Agliotti's involvement in the Kya Sands Mandrax bust, passing on to Agliotti five intelligence reports from the UK about his (Agliotti's) international drug-dealing, sharing a top-secret National Intelligence report about information obtained from the businessman Jürgen Kögl, who claimed the Kebbles had paid off Selebi, as well as alerting Agliotti to the fact that his phone number had been picked up during the Brett Kebble murder.

On the charge of defeating the ends of justice, the state alleged

Selebi had unlawfully shared secret UK intelligence reports with Agliotti, had protected Agliotti from police investigation, had failed to pass on information that Agliotti had been involved in the Kya Sands drugs case, had attempted to influence the Billy Rautenbach case, had shared information about impending police tenders for work in the Sudan, and had helped Agliotti to obtain preferential treatment with regard to the break-in at his housing complex.

The state of course was only willing to proceed with charges that were likely to get a conviction. O'Sullivan knew that, generally, crimes of corruption are difficult to prove, as criminals seldom leave a paper trail. It was no different when it came to Selebi.

Selebi pleaded not guilty on the charges. The disgraced commissioner's plea explanation was read out to the court, in which he maintained that the entire case had arisen as a result of a conspiracy against him, led by the Scorpions and O'Sullivan. 'If it was a conspiracy, then he had bought R250 million in drugs to make it look real. Some conspiracy!' scoffs O'Sullivan.

Prosecutor Gerrie Nel had been waiting for this moment and doggedly and relentlessly unpacked the case against the commissioner.

The Selebi trial was to preoccupy the country and the international and local media for eight months. After a few technical delays the parade of witnesses, some of them more colourful than others, took to the stand. The end of each court day would see a new flurry of startling headlines and enthusiastic radio news bulletins about each twist and turn, each sensational revelation. This was, after all, the biggest and most sordid criminal trial in democratic South Africa. It was also the first time in history that the world's top cop, the head of Interpol, would go on trial for corruption, or any charge for that matter.

While O'Sullivan followed proceedings and often popped into the courtroom on days he knew key witnesses would be testifying, he already had more pressing matters on his mind: Radovan Krejcir and the growing influence of the fledgling criminal empire he was establishing inside the country.

Krejcir, O'Sullivan reckoned, made Glenn Agliotti look like a spoilt poodle and, if the Czech, who was out on bail after applying for refugee status, were to remain inside South Africa, he would present a bigger threat to national security than the corrupt Jackie Selebi. Radovan Krejcir was an unwelcome guest, and the sooner he left the country, the better.

✳

Meanwhile, over in the wood-panelled courtroom 4B, Judge Joffe presided as a gallery of witnesses began to testify.

Selebi's lawyer Jaap Cilliers's request that Judge Joffe recuse himself as he was 'biased', as well as a death threat resulting in his requiring personal protection, did not deter Joffe as the trial pushed on. O'Sullivan simply believed Cilliers was playing for time and wasting taxpayers' money in the process.

Glenn Agliotti was first up and spent several days recounting his relationship with the national commissioner, how he had gone shopping with him for a pair of shoes for President Mbeki, how he had handed over envelopes of cash, how he had introduced Selebi to the Kebbles, how the commissioner had helped the Zimbabwean businessman Billy Rautenbach escape prosecution, and how Selebi had shared three top-secret intelligence documents with him, one from the UK's Serious Organised Crime Agency.

Judge Joffe found Agliotti to be such a colourful and mendacious storyteller that he was only prepared to accept evidence from the state's key witness if other witnesses corroborated it.

Agliotti was followed by several other witnesses, including Dianne Muller, who had witnessed Selebi's receipt of a bank bag with R110,000 in cash. She mentioned other occasions on which Selebi had requested money but she had not personally witnessed this being handed over.

Several further witnesses followed, each sinking the former police commissioner deeper and deeper into a grave of ignominy.

Meanwhile, in February 2010, in another courtroom in the Johannesburg High Court, Glenn Agliotti made a brief appearance in front of Judge Frans Kgomo on charges of murdering Brett Kebble. At the time, Gerrie Nel led the prosecution against Agliotti and requested a postponement, as the case would clash with the Selebi trial. Agliotti's case was postponed to July 2010. Nel, his junior advocate, Andrea Johnson, and Andrew Leask were later removed from the Agliotti prosecution and replaced with state advocates Dan Dakana, Kholeka Gcaleka and Lethabo Mashiane. Agliotti was delighted, and the weight loss he had started suffering reversed and he quickly plumped out again.

In February 2010, far away from Johannesburg's CBD and the High Court where much of the country's media focused their attention, a plane landed at Oliver Tambo International Airport. On board was the 54-year-old German luxury car dealer, Uwe Gemballa. He had flown first-class from Frankfurt via Dubai to Johannesburg on a supposed business trip to set up a local franchise of his firm Gemballa Automobiletechni, which specialised in converting ordinary Porsches and Ferraris into 'supercars'.

Gemballa, whose business was based in Stuttgart, had been in contact with Jerome Safi, one of Radovan Krejcir's associates, about the venture. Gemballa had, by all accounts, initially met Krejcir at a hotel in Prague ten years earlier.

Gemballa sent Safi an email shortly before his departure in which he expressed his excitement at the possibility of doing business in South Africa. On 2 February, a week before his departure, Gemballa wrote: 'Dear Jerome. It was a pleasure to talk to you today and a big + nice surprise that you like so much our products that you have decided to apply being our importer in South Africa.'

Safi simply replied, 'Dear Mr Gemballa. This is my email address and I am looking forward to our future successes. Regards Jerome Saphire'. It would later transpire that the misspelling of his name was due to the fact that Safi had asked his girlfriend at the time to send the mail, and she was not sure how his last name was spelt.

Gemballa disappeared shortly after arriving in South Africa. He was met at the airport by an unknown person driving a car without a licence plate and later kidnapped outside the premises of a car repair business, Silver Star Auto in Linksfield, owned by Yiannakis Louka, George Louka's cousin, also known as 'Jannie the Mechanic'.

The day he vanished, Gemballa contacted his wife, Christina, telephonically and asked her to deposit one million euros into a bank account. His wife had suspected something was amiss, as her husband had spoken in English and not his mother tongue.

Then Gemballa simply disappeared. Paul determined that he had been driven to a house in First Avenue, Edenvale, in the East Rand, the home address of Ivan Savov, a Bulgarian national who worked for Krejcir. Gemballa was held there for three or four days while local police launched a frantic (and fruitless) search, after being alerted by the police in Germany.

Uwe Gemballa was not known in the fanatic circle of sports car aficionados in South Africa. At the time of the German's disappearance, Sam Smith, writing for the website Jalopnik.com, asked, 'Who the Hell Is Uwe Gemballa?' and remarked that there was very little information available about the man.

'Spend an hour or so Googling the phrase Uwe Gemballa and you come up with remarkably little. Old-school methods also come up short. The traditional tack of the fact-seeking journalist – pick up the phone; harass everyone you can think of; lather, rinse, repeat – has revealed details of the police investigation of his disappearance but little about the man himself.'

German authorities, it turned out, were in fact investigating Gemballa for tax evasion, and it is believed that he was part of a much larger international money-laundering syndicate that used luxury vehicles to smuggle cash internationally. The money is commonly stashed and concealed inside various cavities in the vehicle.

In February German police sent two officers to South Africa to assist the SAPS with the search. Several people were questioned, including Jerome Safi and Radovan Krejcir. Krejcir, of course, denied any connection to Gemballa.

In March 2010 the state closed its case against Selebi and Cilliers immediately applied for the accused to be discharged, claiming the state had not made a reasonable case. The application was dismissed and in April Selebi finally had his moment in the spotlight. O'Sullivan wasn't going to miss this for the world.

Selebi blew it big time and, instead of providing the court and the public with the 'shocking' revelations he had promised beforehand, his testimony collapsed in a heap of lies, contradictions and evasions as Gerrie Nel pummelled him into a corner for nine days.

In May, a month after Selebi's devastating defeat in the witness stand in court 4B, a source contacted Paul with news that the Czech-born doctor Marian Tupy had offered him a small sum of money to set up an urgent meeting with the investigator. Dr Tupy, who immigrated to South Africa in 1991, practised as a urologist and had rooms in Flora Park and Trichardt, Mpumalanga. 'My source told me that the doctor was in a spot of bother and needed some good advice,' Paul recalls.

O'Sullivan met with the distraught Tupy, who was also a keen pilot, at a Krugersdorp airfield, where the doctor informed him that he had become entangled with 'a very dangerous man'. 'I was shocked when I heard it was Radovan Krejcir,' said Paul.

Tupy told O'Sullivan that he had first met Krejcir and his wife, Katerina, in January 2008 at the home of a mutual friend in Gallo Manor. During his first consultation Krejcir complained that he was suffering from memory loss and that there had been blood in his urine. Krejcir explained that Tupy could obtain medical records from a Dr Zednicek in Prague, who also happened to be the personal physician of the Czech Republic president, Václav Klaus.

The urologist carried out a battery of tests and, while these had found nothing untoward, Krejcir kept complaining of various ailments. Tupy sent him off for more extensive tests, which also revealed no underlying medical condition.

When Tupy clearly did not pick up on the unspoken nature of Krejcir's constant visits to him, Krejcir initiated the suggestion that Tupy supply him with a false diagnosis that he was suffering from terminal cancer. Tupy, who had been curious about this new patient, had, in the meantime, embarked on his own investigation and discovered to his horror that Krejcir 'was alleged to be either first or second in command of a mafia-type organisation that was based in Eastern Europe with its headquarters in Prague'.

He had grown 'worried' about complying with Krejcir's request and had strung him along, 'hoping that sooner or later he would pack his bags and move on to his next country of adoption'. However, that was not to prove the case, as Krejcir continued to contact Tupy whenever a medical situation arose, and the fugitive eventually placed the doctor on a 'retainer'.

Tupy relented later and agreed to assist Krejcir, switching the sample from a patient who had bladder cancer with Krejcir's healthy biopsy to provide 'proof' that Krejcir was 'terminal'. Krejcir would later use this false diagnosis to defraud a medical aid of R250,000 and a life assurer of R4.5 million and persuade Czech authorities that he was not fit to be extradited to return home to stand trial.

Tupy decided to contact O'Sullivan after reading about him in relation to the Selebi case and because Krejcir was becoming increasingly demanding and threatening. 'It was clear this guy was petrified and feared for his life. I advised him to play along with Krejcir but that he should not, under any circumstances, provide the documents Krejcir needed.'

Paul suggested to Tupy that he store Krejcir's file in a safe location and that he call him if the Czech continued to threaten him.

✳

On 3 May, one of South Africa's most flamboyant strip-club owners, Lolly Jackson, was shot dead at point-blank range in George Louka's rented house in a Kempton Park suburb after an apparent drunken argument. Louka, who, as we recall, initially encountered Krejcir in the holding cells of the Kempton Park police station in 2007, was immediately suspected of being the shooter, as he had allegedly telephoned General Joey Mabasa, now the police's Crime Intelligence head for Gauteng after Mdluli's promotion to national head.

The first policeman to arrive at the scene of the murder was General Mabasa, but telephone records would later show he arrived there together with Krejcir and Cyril Beeka, an ally of Krejcir's at the time. Mabasa claimed that Louka had called him from the scene and confessed to shooting Jackson in the head and back; but the story took a not too unexpected turn when ballistics tests later linked Mabasa's police-issue firearm to Jackson's shooting. Mabasa had reported the firearm stolen during a supposed mugging a few days prior to Jackson's shooting, but the report was only made after the shooting!

George Louka, in the meantime, had been spirited out of the country to Cyprus – apparently strolling through the VIP section at Oliver Tambo Airport – by unknown accomplices, and is currently awaiting extradition to face murder charges in South Africa.

Paul had made earlier contact with General Mabasa, meeting him after Kevin Trytsman's shooting, when the general told Paul that he was personally investigating the case. O'Sullivan later handed copies of evidence he had obtained from witnesses, proving Jackson's and Krejcir's involvement in money-laundering, to an Advocate Deon Barnard at the NPA as well as General Mabasa. 'I expected to see Krejcir arrested, along with Lolly Jackson, but it didn't happen,' said O'Sullivan.

Soon afterwards Jackson was murdered, 'allegedly by an associate of Krejcir (George Louka), who coincidentally was at the office of Michaelides when Trytsman was murdered!'

O'Sullivan contacted the investigating officer in the Jackson murder, a Colonel P.W. van Heerden, to warn him to be cautious of General Mabasa and Krejcir. 'I was shocked, however, when a week later I called him to ask what had happened and when exactly he planned to arrest Krejcir and he told me Krejcir would be his "star" witness and would help put George Louka away for life! I stopped communicating with him, as he was either corrupt, gullible or incompetent,' recalls O'Sullivan. Colonel Van Heerden was the same officer who had 'failed to advance' the Kebble murder investigation against Agliotti, and O'Sullivan reckoned that 'if justice was to be done, I would have to roll up my sleeves again'.

O'Sullivan was so concerned by Mabasa's proximity to Krejcir that he called 'a longstanding friend who is also a member of the NEC of the ANC' and requested that he urgently take up the matter, which he duly did, arranging a meeting with Lieutenant-General Anwar Dramat, head of the Directorate for Priority Crime Investigation, or the Hawks. 'I gave him copies of all the statements, intelligence reports and other relevant documents I had. I also gave the documents to a Colonel Neethling and Warrant Officer Schnelle, who was investigating Gemballa's disappearance and implicating Krejcir,' said O'Sullivan.

The investigator also provided documents proving that Mabasa's wife, Dorcas, was allegedly in business with Krejcir's wife, Katerina, an arrangement, as far as O'Sullivan was concerned, that was simply a front for corrupt payments flowing from Krejcir. Mabasa was later dismissed from the unit (not without a golden handshake, conveniently 'approved' by another of O'Sullivan's targets, General Richard Mdluli).

The bodies were piling up and there was only one name that kept cropping up in relation to all of them: Radovan Krejcir.

'After Jackson's murder my source called again and told me Tupy was extremely anxious, as Krejcir had been placing him under enormous pressure to hand over the letter with the false diagnosis,' said O'Sullivan.

O'Sullivan took a detailed statement from Tupy in which he revealed that his involvement with Krejcir actually extended far beyond the usual doctor–patient relationship. Tupy was in deep, and admitted to other business dealings with Jackson, Krejcir and his 'associate', the notorious underworld figure Cyril Beeka.

Beeka, a karate expert from Kuilsriver in the Western Cape, started out as a 'bouncer' in the region and soon became the head of a vicious 'security empire'. For several years Beeka and his Pro Access Security goons controlled the Cape's nightclub scene. While Beeka had been charged for several serious offences, he was never found guilty, and rarely even went on trial.

The burly Beeka had, over the years, befriended some of the country's most dubious citizens, including the Sicilian Mafioso Vito Palazzolo (who was extradited to Italy after his arrest in Thailand in 2012) and Yuri 'the Russian' Ulianitski, who managed to wrest control of the Cape's underworld before being killed, along with his four-year-old daughter, Yulia, in an ambush in 2007.

Beeka was also reportedly closely linked to the Intelligence Services head, Moe Shaik, and had apparently acted as an undercover operative, a claim that has, of course, never been publicly denied or verified.

Dr Tupy explained to Paul that Krejcir had wanted him to fly Beeka and George Smith to Zimbabwe, 'where they are involved in the illegal smuggling of gold from different countries'.

O'Sullivan copied the statement to the NPA and persuaded Dr Tupy to hand him Krejcir's entire medical file for safekeeping. 'I copied the file, scanned it and placed an electronic copy off-shore on a computer based overseas. I knew it would come in handy.'

Tupy later mentioned that, apart from the false diagnosis, the files showed that several of Krejcir's 'girlfriends', as well as Krejcir himself, had been treated for sexually transmitted diseases.

Tupy received a suspended sentence in exchange for testifying against Krejcir but later petitioned the High Court to overturn the outcome. In an application described as 'a first in South African legal history', Tupy applied for his plea bargain and fraud conviction to be overturned in exchange for complete indemnity. Tupy was a man clearly caught in the eye of a storm. First he alleged that Krejcir had shown him the statement that he had made to O'Sullivan and had threatened to have him killed. Later Tupy claimed that O'Sullivan had 'bamboozled' him into providing the damning statement which O'Sullivan had handed to the Hawks. It is an odd accusation, as it was Tupy who had sought out O'Sullivan in the first place. In the end, Tupy's actions scuppered the state's R4.5 million fraud case against Krejcir after the doctor made a U-turn with regard to his evidence after securing his plea bargain.

On 2 July 2010 Judge Joffe convicted Jackie Selebi on a charge of corruption but acquitted him of defeating the ends of justice. He dwelt most on what Gerrie Nel referred to as the Big Five lies, but then expanded the argument to the Big Six lies, number six being Selebi's denial of showing Agliotti an intercepted email from O'Sullivan addressed to Robyn Plitt of the Scorpions, in which O'Sullivan set out the case against Agliotti in respect of the Kebble murder and international drug-trafficking. The mail was unlawfully intercepted by a shady company in Pretoria, run by Mphego and Mdluli, which was a throw-over from apartheid subterfuge.

Joffe had already provided a scathing assessment of Selebi's and Agliotti's characters during the judgment but saved his most devastating comments for the sentencing of the police chief, which took place on 3 August. If this had been an audition for an 'SAPS Idol', then Joffe would have put Simon Cowell to shame. O'Sullivan savoured every moment. He could not, he thought to himself, have put it more succinctly.

Selebi shook his head as Judge Joffe told him, 'Mr Selebi, you were an embarrassment in the witness box. Firstly, you were an embarrassment to the office you occupied. It is inconceivable that the person who occupied the office of national commissioner of police could have been such a stranger to the truth. Secondly, you must have been an embarrassment to those who appointed you.'

There was more to come, much more. Judge Joffe continued that the former national commissioner was an embarrassment to the members of the SAPS 'who you led' and that it was not possible to measure the level of embarrassment 'of police men and women who are in the front line of the fight against crime, who daily put their lives on the line for their fellow citizens and whose credibility and truthfulness is relied upon by their fellow countrymen, when confronted by the reality that their former national commissioner jettisons the truth when he thinks it will advance his case.'

The judge's comments on corruption and its devastating effects on society were particularly pointed and relevant. 'Corruption can be likened to a cancer. It operates insidiously, destroying the moral fibre of the nation. When it is discovered the damage has already been done. Whilst the particular act of corruption may be excised, just as a malignancy may be removed in a surgical intervention, society is not what it was prior to the corrupt act. The roots of justice and integrity, so vital in a fair and democratic society, have been permanently scarred by the corrupt act. The moral fibre of society has to be re-built after the excision of the corruption.'

Judge Joffe sentenced Selebi to 15 years in jail and set bail at R20,000, pending leave to appeal.

For O'Sullivan, 2010 was going to be the first year in a long while to end on a high note. The man who had 'pissed in his beer' was going to jail for 15 years. He had been vindicated, right all along.

But there was no time to sit back and savour the victory. There was more urgent work to be done. Radovan Krejcir had to be extradited from the country before he managed to cultivate even deeper roots in the expanding criminal underworld. And O'Sullivan had already taken on another big *pro bono* job, nailing rhino horn traffickers.

A month after Selebi's sentencing, Uwe Gemballa's decomposing corpse was found near Pretoria. His hands had been tied behind his back and he had been shot execution-style before being wrapped in paint-speckled plastic sheeting and buried in a shallow grave.

That same month O'Sullivan flew to Prague in the Czech Republic to meet with the country's chief of police to discuss South Africa's unwelcome visitor. A Czech journalist, Jiří Hynek, who had written extensively on Krejcir and his criminal activities in that country, set up the meeting between O'Sullivan and Czech police.

Krejcir had, for some time, embarked on a campaign to discredit O'Sullivan, claiming that the investigator was 'mad', was suffering from a mysterious psychological condition or, alternatively, that he was a 'secret agent' working for the Czech authorities. Krejcir's game plan was a classic criminal tactic – deflect attention by defaming your accuser. It was a trick that Jackie Selebi and his cronies had also deployed with no success. Krejcir would not be the last criminal to try and fail in such a last-ditch attempt to shake O'Sullivan off his tail.

'I also wanted to find out if there was any truth to the rumour that Krejcir had spread that he was a "marked man" in that country and that the charges against him had been "trumped up".'

O'Sullivan was impressed with the country. The Czech Republic was a member of the European Union and, as such, was bound fully by the European Convention on Human Rights. It was unlikely, he reckoned, that the country would risk breaking the law by 'assassinating a low-life gangster like Radovan Krejcir'.

O'Sullivan spent four hours at the Prague police headquarters where the police chief 'was able to satisfy me that they did have several *prima facie* cases against Krejcir and that he should return to the country to clear his name'.

If anyone was going to kill Krejcir, the police chief informed him, it would most likely be a fellow gangster. 'They said he'll be perfectly safe in jail,' said O'Sullivan.

The following day, as O'Sullivan stepped off a plane in Ireland, he received a phone call from Krejcir, who had been alerted to a radio news broadcast that O'Sullivan had been in the Czech Republic asking questions. 'He threatened me and told me he would make me suck his cock before he killed me.' Now that, anyone would agree, is much, much worse than simply pissing into the Irishman's pint of Guinness!

O'Sullivan was about to ramp up his offensive in ridding South Africa of Radovan Krejcir, who had become, as Sam Sole later wrote, 'a direct challenge to the authority and integrity of the state'.

Chapter 21

Bodies Pile Up

2011 ARRIVED AND, THOUGH PAUL'S reputation had been fully
restored, he was now dealing with a massive personal bill for the
years he spent self-financing the Selebi campaign. It would take
some time for him to rebuild his savings and, while work began to
trickle in, the Krejcir matter was growing increasingly urgent.

In January 2011 Paul learned that the Refugee Appeals Tribunal
in Pretoria was about to hear Krejcir's arguments against an earlier
rejection by Home Affairs of his application for refugee status.
The tribunal's proceedings are secret but in January, because of the
public interest in the Krejcir matter, his suspiciously coincidental
links to a number of murders as well as the allegations that he had
corrupted a number of public officials, several newspapers launched
a court interdict applying for access to the hearing.

While the press, including *City Press* and the *Mail & Guardian*,
attempted to storm the outside ramparts of the tribunal through
the courts, O'Sullivan managed to submit a 20-page sworn written
submission detailing Krejcir's criminal activities, backing them up
with a collection of sworn statements, running to over a hundred
pages.

*

Two months after Krejcir's appeal hearing, on Human Rights Day – 21 March 2011 – Cyril Beeka was assassinated in Cape Town. Beeka had been visiting his hometown and was driving in Modderdam Road, Bellville, with a Serbian fugitive assassin, Dobrasov Gavric, when a lone gunman on a motorcycle allegedly drove by and fired several shots at their BMW.

O'Sullivan claims Beeka had already been killed elsewhere and that this was simply a final attempt at wiping out Gavric as a witness.

A bullet slammed into Beeka's head, while Gavric, who survived the hit, was wounded in the chest. At the time, Beeka had been assisting the probe into the Crime Intelligence boss, Richard Mdluli, and had also apparently agreed to turn state witness in the Lolly Jackson and Uwe Gemballa murder cases. O'Sullivan had spent several weeks through an intermediary, persuading Beeka to come clean, and had agreed to fly up to Johannesburg on the following Monday, to start working on an application for indemnity with his lawyers.

A few days after Beeka's murder, a police special tactical unit swooped on Krejcir's palatial home in Kloof Road, Bedfordview. It was a dramatic raid, as helicopters hovered over the house and an armoured Nyala vehicle crashed through the front gates.

During the raid a few of the more than 100 task force members over-zealously battered down the door of one of Krejcir's neighbours, Simon Guidetti, whose frantic domestic worker called him as police poured into the house, yanking open doors and ripping security gates from their frames.

Krejcir's home was located behind Guidetti's house and a search of the premises yielded little apart from a 'hit list', with several names including Cyril Beeka, Paul O'Sullivan, Dr Tupy and the state prosecutor in the Gemballa case, Riegal du Toit.

Krejcir had not been at home during the raid – he later claimed to have been aware three days earlier that it was about to take place

– but his son Dennis and his bodyguard, Miloslav Potiska, were cuffed, arrested, taken to the Germiston police station and released two days later. The bodyguard has since fled South Africa.

O'Sullivan accompanied the Hawks on the raid and a further search later the same night of a house in Germiston occupied by one of Krejcir's right-hand men, Michaelis Arsiotis, and his girlfriend, Stacey Swanepoel. It was a rather dramatic FBI-style foray, as the tactical team entered the complex after cutting off the electricity supply. The heavily armed squad, dressed in flak jackets and helmets and carrying powerful torches, burst into Arsiotis's home, finding him in bed with Swanepoel.

Krejcir was a prime suspect in Beeka's murder and the Hawks were out to get him, not only for the murder but also for the R4.5 million fraud related to the cancer claim. A large-scale hunt ensued and five days later, Krejcir, accompanied by his lawyer, Eddie Classen, handed himself over to the Hawks.

Towards the end of 2011, just as everyone thought it could not get any bloodier, Lolly Jackson's laywer, Ian Jordaan, mysteriously disappeared, five hours after he sent a fax to Radovan Krejcir's lawyer, advising him that he was rejecting his claim of more than R10 million against the Jackson estate.

Jordaan was holding an estimated R1.6 million in a trust account for the strip-club owner in relation to a civil dispute between Jackson and Mark Andrews, a business partner, over the disputed ownership of one of the Teazers clubs. Jordaan was also helping to wrap up Jackson's estate when he vanished in October, only to be found the next morning, burned to death on the roof of his charred bakkie parked under a bridge in Hekpoort near Krugersdorp.

Three days later, Mark Andrews was bumped off execution-style and his body tossed next to the R59 highway. Andrews had apparently planned to hand himself over to police in connection with Jordaan's murder but was kidnapped after speaking to his lawyer.

O'Sullivan was not surprised at the mounting body count. This is a ruthless underworld where the stakes are extremely high and where the potential for huge ill-gotten wealth drives ambitious and psychopathic gangsters to test the limits of what passes for ordered and civilised life.

✳

On 25 July 2013, a week after an announcement that George Louka, Lolly Jackson's alleged killer, would be extradited to South Africa, Radovan Krejcir survived an apparent dramatic assassination attempt outside his Bedfordview pawnshop.

A row of 12 gun barrels attached to the underside of a vehicle parked opposite Krejcir's business premises were activated by remote control, showering Krejcir's bullet-proof BMW with projectiles. Remarkably, Krejcir escaped death, as he had stepped out of the car seconds earlier. The media universally referred to the 'hit' as the equivalent of a scene from a James Bond movie, the only difference being that there are usually more casualties in the Bond movies.

There are those who believe that the entire drama was set up by Krejcir to make him appear the 'victim'. O'Sullivan was on a business trip in France when the shooting occurred and was not surprised that the violence was escalating in relation to Louka's imminent return to our shores.

On 29 August 2013, Krejcir appeared in the Kempton Park Magistrate's Court for the start of the state's extradition hearing, but the matter was postponed to 12 September for a decision. Krejcir's lawyers argued that their client's appeal of his refugee status (which was rejected) and the extradition hearing should not run concurrently.

As 2013 drew to a close, the net was closing on Radovan Krejcir. A few days after a bomb had exploded in Krejcir's Money Point offices in Bedfordview, killing two people, Ronny Bvuma and Krejcir's 'enforcer', Jan 'John' Charvat, who is wanted in the Czech

Republic on charges of tax fraud. Bvuma, a South African, had been employed by Krejcir to replace his wife as director of various companies in an attempt to thwart SARS investigators.

Krejcir's business manager, Ivan Savov, was arrested at the premises after the blast in relation to another R10 million fraud case involving the controversial security company G4S. Savov is also the manager of Groep Twee Beleggings and the owner of Scara Technologies, both of which are respondents in a SARS investigation into Krejcir. Groep Twee Beleggings is registered in the name of Krejcir's wife, Katerina, and many of Krejcir's businesses, assets and properties are similarly registered in her name. Krejcir has consistently claimed he is 'unemployed'.

But on 15 November SARS finally closed in, serving Krejcir with a preservation order and placing all his assets – including his homes and luxury cars – under curatorship. Like Al Capone, it appears as if dirty money rather than bloody hands will finally see Krejcir face the law. Krejcir is said to owe over R59 million in taxes.

In 2011 Paul O'Sullivan flew to Spain, where he obtained an explosive statement from a Greek-born hit man who has lived in South Africa for over 40 years, about a 'hit' Krejcir had arranged on an 'old enemy' in Prague. The hit, the assassin alleged, was one of several Krejcir had tried to orchestrate in several countries, including the Seychelles, Germany and the Czech Republic. The hit on the 'enemy' ordered in 2009 had been scuppered by the heightened security in the Czech Republic as a result of a visit by US President Barack Obama.

On 22 November 2013, Radovan Krejcir and businessman Desai Luphondo were arrested on charges of attempted murder and kidnapping. Krejcir immediately alleged that police had 'tortured' and assaulted him and applied to be moved to a hospital because he was suffering from 'renal failure'.

A few days later two Hawks investigators, warrant officers Samuel Modise Maropeng and George Jeff Nthoroane, joined Krejcir and Luphondo in the dock. The case relates to the kidnapping and assault of one of Krejcir's associates, named

'Doctor', who worked at OR Tambo's clearance agency, because of a 'missing' consignment of R24 million worth of crystal meth, destined for Australia.

In an affidavit, the investigating officer, Captain Freddy Ramuhala, set out how Krejcir had used Luphondo and 'Doctor' as drug couriers. Krejcir had leaned on Luphondo to find 'Doctor' and he had, in turn, leaned on Maropeng and Nthoroane.

Krejcir had allegedly given orders that if Doctor could not be tracked down, a member of his family was to be kidnapped. Doctor's brother was targeted, kidnapped, held captive and tortured at Krejcir's business premises, Money Point, in Bedfordview in an attempt to 'flush out' the Doctor. The fugitive's brother was eventually released and dumped in Katlehong.

The case was continuing at the time of writing.

Krejcir, or 'Mr Banana Peel' as he likes to call himself, is about to take the fall. The man with nine lives was hoping to make our country his home. Paul O'Sullivan is determined that he will not. At the time of writing, O'Sullivan was still working closely with officials to ensure that Radovan Krejcir either serves time in a South African jail or is extradited to his home country to serve his time there.

'That will be for my next book.'

Chapter 22

After Selebi
– Saving the
Rhinos

AT THE TIME OF WRITING, ALMOST 30 months had passed since Selebi's sentencing and his subsequent release on 'early parole' in July 2012 after suffering a stroke and end-stage renal failure. Selebi had spent about six months in the Pretoria Central Prison medical wing after collapsing at his home in December 2011 upon learning that the appeal against his 15-year sentence had failed.

O'Sullivan was appalled that Selebi might not serve any time in prison, telling one journalist that 'that man has got to go to prison for the 150,000 people who were murdered in the nine years when he was chief of police, for the 500,000 women who were raped and for the million people who were robbed'.

Along with many other South Africans, O'Sullivan was sceptical of the claim that Selebi, like President Zuma's financial adviser Schabir Shaik, was at death's door. Shaik, who was released on medical parole in 2009 after serving only 28 months of his 15-year sentence, most of it in hospital, is occasionally spotted enjoying a round of golf in Durban.

The disgraced commissioner continues to 'serve out' his sentence from the comfort of his Waterkloof home and is yet to repay the R17 million he owes the state in legal fees. He continues to receive his state pension, worth almost R2 million a year, and medical benefits.

Selebi has subsequently lost his political cachet and has been largely shunned by most of his old comrades, bar one or two. After his sentencing the ruling party's spokesman Jackson Mthembu said that the sentence 'clearly indicates that South Africa as a country is governed by laws that are applied without fear or favour to anyone, regardless of their standing in society'.

And so the fullstop was placed at the end of that particular sad chapter in the country's history. But the story is far from over and unfolds daily in the endless newspaper headlines that arise from the ongoing dirty work by rogue intelligence operatives, corrupt cops and feral, seemingly untouchable criminals.

Prosecutor Glynnis Breytenbach continues to fight her unlawful suspension from the NPA. Major-General Tirhani Simon Maswanganyi, an anti-corruption crusader, was found shot dead, execution-style, with his hands tied behind his back in a field in Hammanskraal in June 2013. In June 2013 Captain Morris 'KGB' Tshabalala was arrested in connection with a R3 million cash heist which took place in Sasolburg in February. Tshabalala had allegedly supplied police-issue firearms and radios to cash-heist gangs as well as disclosing transport routes. Five months after Tshabalala's arrest, two witnesses, the Zimbabwean Phumlani Ncube and another man known only as Siphiwe, were executed. Siphiwe's body was found on a dumpsite in Soweto and Ncube, who was shot six times, was found dead in a field in Mpumalanga.

President Jacob Zuma's lawyers continue to fight a court ruling to hand over the alleged 'spy tapes' that resulted in the dropping of charges of corruption against him. Curiously, the same 'taped' conversations revealed a plot to 'deal decisively with the O'Sullivan factor', which, despite a serious complaint with the inspector general of intelligence, has not resulted in any investigation.

In August 2013, Parliament's Portfolio Committee on Police learned that several high-ranking police officers had convictions for murder and other serious crimes. It was revealed that 1 major-general, 10 brigadiers, 21 colonels, 43 lieutenant-colonels, 10 majors, 163 captains and 706 warrant officers had been found guilty of serious offences, including murder, attempted murder, culpable homicide, rape, attempted rape, drug-trafficking and robbery. Selebi's legacy? O'Sullivan thinks so.

The Transparency International Global Corruption Barometer 2013 revealed that a staggering 83 per cent of South Africans believed that the police were corrupt, and listed South Africa among 36 countries in which the police were seen as the most corrupt institution. But in spite of these worrying findings, statistics and negative perceptions of the SAPS – particularly after the Marikana massacre of 2012 – Paul O'Sullivan still believes that there are enough good policemen and -women in South Africa who do good work and daily risk their lives. 'There are a lot of very good and highly professional police in this country and we need to tip the balance back in their favour,' he said.

For someone whose entire life has been consumed with fighting crime and criminals, O'Sullivan is also remarkably sanguine about human nature. 'I believe that 90 per cent of human beings are good or want to do good.'

In the meantime, some semblance of normality has been restored to O'Sullivan's life. He has remarried and now runs a busy forensic and loss control consultancy that does a fair amount of forensic work for large companies and businesses. He employs three full-time staff members, two forensic investigators (one ex-Scorpions), an office manager and a couple of undercover sleuths.

Between paid corporate jobs, O'Sullivan continues to take on *pro bono* criminal work and has not given up on ridding South Africa of Radovan Krejcir and other dangerous fugitives of his ilk. He is aware that he is No. 1 on Krejcir's hit list and lives his life accordingly. He does not, however, allow the threat to limit his movements, but he is a man who seldom lets his guard down.

O'Sullivan doesn't read newspapers ('I already know what will be in the headlines') or books (unless they are related to his line of work) or go to the movies ('I just get irritated and can poke holes in the plot'). He finds peace of mind in open spaces and South Africa's wildlife and is a keen visitor to the country's parks and reserves. The country's 'big five' decorate his home, on scatter cushion prints and photographs, and he enjoys nothing more than a trip to those regions where he can enjoy nature. 'God's gift,' he opines.

It is this love of nature that led to Paul's significant role in the arrest in July 2011 of the Thai national Chumlong Lemtongthai, one of the kingpins in a rhino horn smuggling syndicate. In a landmark ruling, Lemtongthai was sentenced to 40 years in jail, reduced in August 2013 to 30.

O'Sullivan's involvement in the tourism industry as director of the Tourism Business Council of South Africa and the founding chairman of Johannesburg's Big 5 Tourist Destinations initiative led to his connection with the owner of the Rhino and Lion Game and Nature Reserve at Kromdraai, on the West Rand, about 10 kilometres north-west of Muldersdrift.

South Africa is, according to savetherhino.org, home to 83 per cent of rhino and 73 per cent of all wild rhino worldwide. In 2012, 668 animals were poached, almost two a day, and at the time of writing (August 2013) 553 animals had already been slaughtered for their horn.

O'Sullivan befriended Ed Hearn and his daughter Lorinda, owners of the Rhino and Lion Reserve, who had lost a considerable amount of their rhino stock to poachers and contacted Paul to ask how he could help. Ed and Lorinda founded the Rhino Rescue Project in an attempt to stop the devastation and, together with a local vet, Charles van Niekerk, developed a method of injecting red dye into the horns.

O'Sullivan met Ed Hearn to discuss ways of gathering more intelligence on the poachers and the locals who facilitate the illegal trade. At the time, the Mpumalanga Tourism and Parks Agency had engaged O'Sullivan to audit game permits and investigate poaching.

He was consulting widely and let it be known that he was on the lookout for any information on poaching. In August 2010 one of O'Sullivan's sources handed him a 'sheaf of documents totalling about 16 pages'. Studying the file, Paul realised that the rhino poaching syndicates were linked to the lucrative trade in lion bones. 'I decided to focus on the same players, as I was sure there would be an intersection of interests.'

O'Sullivan understood that it was vital to find the South African links in the international syndicate and, in May 2011, made a significant breakthrough when a source informed him that a South African, Johnny Olivier, who worked as a manager for an engineering company, was prepared to make a full sworn statement. Olivier also promised to deliver a South African shipping agent who was involved.

O'Sullivan gathered a pile of tax invoices, ATM slips, business cards, copies of passports and other evidence and spent several weeks with Olivier, taking a statement which was eventually used in the final arrest of the syndicate kingpin, Chumlong Lemtongthai, as well as five Thai hunters.

Olivier provided a detailed insight into the inner workings of the syndicate, which had traded in at least 40 rhino horns. He explained that he had chosen to blow the whistle after discovering an order from the Laos-based Xaysavang Trading Export-Import Company, indicating that Lemtongthai intended to shoot a further 50 rhino, in the coming four months. The Xaysavang Trading Company had initially dealt in the lucrative trade of lion bones, moving large quantities supplied by breeders in the Free State and North West offshore before focusing on rhino horn. 'I realised he was just hell-bent on killing as many rhinos as possible, for no other reason than harvesting the horn,' Olivier said in his statement to O'Sullivan.

Olivier revealed that the illegal hunters found a loophole in the legislation, using legal hunting permits authorised by provincial conservation authorities, having bribed the so-called wildlife protection staff to look the other way.

Lemtongthai and his partner, Punpitak Chunchom, offered millions for live rhinos, which were bought by a Brits trader, Marnus Steyl, at private local auctions and moved to a farm in the North West, where they were immediately hunted.

Lemtongthai and Chunchom would source 'hunters', usually Thai sex workers who had been illegally trafficked to South Africa, to pose as legal hunters with permits. The women would be paid R5000 per job, which simply involved hanging around the hunting lodge while professional hunters slaughtered the rhino. The women would then be asked to pose next to 'their' kill and the 'hunt' would be witnessed by an official of the North West Parks, who would measure the horn, scan a microchip and record the details of the hunt in a register. Olivier said these officials would usually receive a kickback.

The carcasses of the dead rhino would then be chopped up and delivered to a butcher in Vryburg, who would turn them into wors or hamburger patties. The rhino horns were taken to a taxidermist, who would mount them on cheap wooden bases as if they were legitimate hunting trophies. The horns would then be sent 'home' to the East, where they would end up on the black market, while the real 'owner' would have no further involvement in the matter.

Lemtongthai paid around R500,000 for each animal, R65,000 a kilo for the horns, reselling them at R380,000 a kilo. Forty rhinos had provided him with a profit of R60 million.

Chunchom was arrested in South Africa and deported for the possession of lion claws and teeth a few days before Lemtongthai's arrest. O'Sullivan determined that Lemtongthai was the second-in-command of the syndicate, which is headed by a Vietnamese citizen, Vixay Keovang aka Vixay Xaysavang.

During September and October 2011, the Hawks arrested the

hunter and 'safari operator' Dawie Groenewald and twelve others on charges of fraud, corruption, assault, defeating the ends of justice and contravening the Prevention of Organised Crime Act. While Groenewald's lawyer, Thomas Grobler, denies that he has any connection to the Thai syndicate, O'Sullivan has proof of his links. At least 20 carcasses of slain rhinos were found buried on Groenewald's farm, all of them missing their horns. Investigators have also implicated several vets in the area who have been supplying a powerful sedative, M99, used to drug the rhino.

While O'Sullivan has no qualms about gangsters becoming extinct, he is determined to stop the carnage being inflicted on the world's dwindling rhino population by corrupt wildlife vets, hunters, poachers and farmers who care only for financial reward. 'I don't want to be a part of the world where we let these things happen. If we all sit back and say that this is just the way it is, we might as well just give up,' says O'Sullivan. He lives by the famous motto from fellow Irishman Edmund Burke – 'All that is necessary for evil to triumph is for good men to do nothing.'

He's currently chasing down another syndicate of pseudo-hunters, this time street bums from the Czech Republic instead of sex workers who are used as 'hunters'. Wildlife officials have once again been implicated and are on the payroll, but not for much longer if O'Sullivan has anything to do with it.

Epilogue: The Canary in the Coal Mine

In April 2011 Sam Sole, managing partner of amaBhungane, the *Mail & Guardian* Centre for Investigative Journalism, published an opinion piece titled 'The Meaning of Radovan Krejcir'. Sole's compelling assessment of the current state of 'the country's deepening moral malaise' is a fitting end-piece to the story you have just read.

Concerning Krejcir, Sole writes:

'The Czech fugitive is a connoisseur of weak states. His choice of SA as a refuge is symptomatic of the country's deepening moral malaise.

'There's not really a single point at which a country suddenly becomes a failed state. States exist across a continuum of dysfunction. Some things still work in Zimbabwe, in Swaziland, after all. And in Italy, for instance, some things don't.

'In war the collapse of law and order happens so fast we can see it and it is usually mirrored by physical destruction, which underlines the impact.

'Organised crime and corruption are more like slow biological warfare or radiation. The infrastructure seems to remain intact – there are just bodies that accumulate haphazardly – until you realise the infrastructure (or the institution) has become so contaminated, it is no longer functional, indeed it has become a threat itself and must be abandoned or destroyed.

'And it's hard to tell how much danger you are in at any one time. The poison accumulates and the impact may be delayed. So we rely on markers – canaries in the coalmine – that tell us how bad the situation is. Has your little badge turned orange? Evacuate your country, now – or take emergency action to stop the contamination.

'The appearance on our shores of Radovan Krejcir is one such marker. Given that he was arrested on arrival in 2007 (on an international warrant issued by the Czech Republic), Mr Krejcir has done rather well.

'Out on bail, Krejcir, who is not publicity shy, said he had chosen South Africa because it had the "best Constitution in the world". What he meant is money and slick lawyers can almost always trump a weak criminal justice system – but that the rules are strong enough to restrain the authorities from resorting to extrajudicial retaliation.

'But Krejcir has tested the boundaries of that assessment. After the murder of Cyril Beeka he went on the run, his lawyers have said, partly because he feared for his life. There was some validity in that fear.

'Notwithstanding the headline in the *Sunday Times* – "Beeka exposed as SA spy" – no proof has emerged to support the claim that Beeka was an undercover agent. The strongest circumstantial evidence that Beeka might indeed have been an intelligence asset of some kind has been the reaction of the security authorities to his killing.

'Finally, belatedly, they treated Krejcir as what he has been all along: a direct challenge to the authority and integrity of the state. And we should not assume that, because the state has now acted against Krejcir in arresting him for fraud, the battle is over. His choice of South Africa as a refuge from Czech justice is a particular problem, but it is also symptomatic of a much larger malaise.

'Krejcir is a connoisseur of weak systems. It is what he grew up with in the Balkans. He can smell dirty cops and venal politicians. It's what took him to Seychelles when he fled Prague. In the capital, Mahé, Krejcir rented a house from the president's son and moved on only when the official extortion rate became too much for him – notably a demand for millions of rand to delay signing a treaty which would have exposed him to extradition.

'Even from 4000 km away Krejcir could pick out the gangrenous odour of the South African body politic. So far, he has not been proved wrong. As one foreign diplomat put it to me recently: "There are rules in this country, but no consequences."

'A short period of imprisonment at the start of his stay merely meant an introduction to the local underworld. George Smith, with whom he shared a cell, introduced him to Lolly Jackson and the Bedfordview gang. Who, Krejcir would have asked, is the slickest criminal attorney in town?

'So Ian Small-Smith was brought on to the payroll, with a host of other lawyers. And Small-Smith introduced him to Joey Mabasa, then head of crime intelligence in Gauteng.

'Somewhere along the line came Beeka, with or without a nod from the National Intelligence Agency or the South African Secret Service. That would not really have mattered to Krejcir. In the Czech Republic he was adept at managing the relationship with the security services and in South Africa he found the same biddable politicisation, factionalism and inter-agency rivalry, not to mention corruption.

'In any case, Beeka introduced him to the president's son. How convenient was that? There is even speculation that Krejcir made some political donations and that details of such benevolence disappeared with the laptop of his business manager, Ivan Savov, after it was seized as evidence in the investigation of the murder of Uwe Gemballa.

'And when, as it appears, Beeka came to contemplate cashing in some of his chips, well, there were many enemies and rivals who might have been willing to bring his life to a sudden and brutal end. Buried with Beeka, of course, will be the knowledge of his extensive access to Krejcir's affairs in South Africa.

'Appropriately, Krejcir also inherited much of the network of thugs and crooks who came to surround Brett Kebble in his last days.

'Glenn Agliotti, damaged goods but a useful guide, was extended a loan. The Elite gang – Mikey Schultz and company – were engaged around the prospect of running Jackson's Teazers empire, should Krejcir succeed in taking it over. And Krejcir fits right in here.

'I can't put it better than a perceptive commentator on the *Mail & Guardian* website.

'Following our articles on the murder of Jackson in May 2010, William Sithonga wrote: *In a society where the majority wants to be a celeb and even leaders act like shallow celebrities in terms of deportment and lifestyle, what we lack is a counter culture.*

'*Money and cool are worshipped, developing from the chaps who kill for cellphones so that they achieve cool by being feared and ability to buy lots of booze, incrementally succeeding to cool by having the flashiest cars, apparel, women and booze. Our political leaders worship at the same shrine.*

'*The society has groomed the Malemas of this world that way without a counter culture. The result is that all seek an individual profit opportunity to attain the desired goals. Politics becomes a means to get to eat, shop and live in Sandton and have power.*

'*For others, accumulation of money through crime is a means to the same ends with the exception that money buys you indirect power through purchasing a police officer, a magistrate, a prosecutor and, ultimately, a powerful politician who wants a high life but cannot afford it.*

'*Check what dominant expressions of our popular culture like kwaito and celebrity celebrate: everything that Lolly Jackson stood for.*

'*To ask a question, can a morally aware society breed corrupt leadership? Does the pursuit and worship of money start when one gets into public office or is it something that one learns before public life?*

'*In a democracy the quality of the leadership[,] be it politics, business (imagine Lolly was a businessman – a very broad, meaningless but worshipped term indeed)[,] is to a large extent a reflection on the led.*

'So, we may yet rid ourselves of Krejcir. But, unless we start to exercise discipline as a society, there is a wave of people like him coming, attracted by our sophisticated banking and legal system – and our diminishing capacity to enforce its rules.'

✳

O'Sullivan remains remarkably optimistic. He loves South Africa and believes 'it is the greatest country on earth'. Apart from that, 'the baddies are still heavily outnumbered, so it's only a matter of time before the good guys win'.

He says that after Krejcir, his next big project is 'to expose the dirty lawyers that prop up the underworld and live in big houses with electric fences and drive fancy cars paid for from the proceeds of crime'.

O'Sullivan says that some people don't seem to care that Krejcir 'can throw blood money at lawyers and that they charge double or treble their normal fees to grovel for his work and thereafter use that blood money to bring patently false and damaging actions against me in a desperate attempt at getting me off the gangster's tail'.

'That', O'Sullivan says emphatically, 'is like pissing in my Guinness, and you just don't do that!'

Afterword

On Christmas Eve 2013, a Tuesday morning, Lieutenant General Layton Mzondeki 'Sean' Tshabalala, a divisional commissioner of the inspectorate of the South African Police, was found dead in his office, located less than 50 metres from Jackie Selebi's old office in Wachthuis, Pretoria. Tshabalala had worked late the night before and staff found his door locked the following morning.

For O'Sullivan, Tshabalala's death, an apparent suicide, marked the final break in the corrupt chain of high-ranking officers who had surrounded, protected and benefited from Jackie Selebi's tenure as police commissioner.

Sean Tshabalala, a former MK operative, had joined the police in 1994. He was, at one point, President Thabo Mbeki's bodyguard but, after Selebi's appointment, Tshabalala's career skyrocketed. He went from sergeant to brigadier in a miraculous 18 months. A year later he was promoted to general. Selebi had promised Tshabalala that he would take over Border Policing and the general had been instrumental in trying to sideline O'Sullivan in November 2001 after he (Paul) had terminated the Khuselani contract at OR Tambo International Airport.

After Selebi's conviction, Tshabalala found himself increasingly sidelined and began drinking heavily. In 2008 he was convicted and fined R20,000 for driving under the influence after crashing into a police patrol van. Although Tshabalala had no qualifications or background in information technology, Selebi's successor, Bheki Cele, promoted him to head the information and system management unit of the SAPS in 2010. In December 2012 Riah Phiyega, the new national police commissioner, transferred Tshabalala to the policemen's Siberia, the police inspectorate, which is where he allegedly took his own life.

Hours after Tshabalala's death, his friend and former colleague, Selby Bokaba, was arrested at the Atterbury Road off-ramp for driving under the influence. Bokaba, once Selebi's loyal spokesman, had reportedly refused to undergo a breathalyser test at the scene and was taken instead to the Steve Biko Academic Hospital for blood tests. Bokaba is currently head of communications for the Tshwane Municipality.

A few days later Bokaba ignited a media storm when he tweeted from Tshabalala's funeral in Randburg that the former police commissioner Bheki Cele had claimed that Tshabalala was one of several police who were on a list and who were being 'badly treated' by the current police leadership. The existence of the 'list' once again unleashed an unhealthy but not unpredictable wave of paranoia in the ranks. Bokaba subsequently attacked SAPA for reporting on his 'personal' tweets and threatened to boycott and 'starve' the news agency in future. His behaviour has been labelled as 'most unprofessional' by SAPA editor Mark van der Velden.

For Paul O'Sullivan 2014 started even more dramatically.

While Radovan Krejcir languished behind bars awaiting trial throughout the 2013 festive season, he was soon back in the headlines when, on 9 January, a specialised police task team dramatically arrested three people who were en route to assassinate O'Sullivan and SAPS Colonel Nkosana 'Killer' Ximba, on Krejcir's orders.

O'Sullivan had been out doing 'counter-surveillance' in his suburb on the morning of 9 January when he noticed three people following him in a black BMW. He confronted them only to learn that they were undercover police officers preparing to arrest assassins who had been sent to kill O'Sullivan that very morning.

Working with the investigator, the task team then arrested a first suspect at a Sandton restaurant just before noon. The arrest led to two subsequent arrests, of a man and a woman, at the Road Lodge in Rivonia.

Three vehicles – a silver Toyota Fortuner, a Nissan panel van and a BMW X6 – were recovered. A police-issue R5 assault rifle (believed to have been used in the assassination of Krejcir 'associate' Bassam Issa in October 2013), two 9mm pistols, blue police lights, five balaclavas, gloves, several cell phones and number plates were confiscated at the scene. At the time of writing the names of the four suspects (one more suspect was subsequently arrested) had not been released, as they had not yet pleaded in court.

In an email to Eddie Classen, Krejcir's lawyer, and copied to select, trusted journalists, O'Sullivan suggested that Classen tell his client 'that I will do all that I can lawfully do, to strip him of everything he or his crooked family members have acquired through his criminal conduct, and see that he rots in jail FOREVER'.

O'Sullivan believes Krejcir issued the instruction for the assassination to take place at noon on the Thursday so that he could claim that he had had nothing to do with it, as he would have been 'behind bars in C-Max'.

'They walked straight into a trap and Krejcir's attempt was thwarted. Again!' O'Sullivan informed Classen.

O'Sullivan suggested that if Classen appealed the court's decision not to grant Krejcir bail, 'I shall legally intervene ... as it is not in the interests of justice to have that gangster on the streets. However, after the chaos of his failed hit on me and the colonel that was behind his arrest late last year, you may wish to reconsider your futile attempts at trying to get him out of jail.' The investigator ended the mail with a cheerful 'Thinking of suing me for defamation? Go ahead, bring it on, I will wipe the floor with you and bring a counter-claim that will make your claim pale into insignificance.'

O'Sullivan is determined to ensure that Krejcir is punished for his crimes and that he serve a suitably long sentence in South Africa.